*Family
Connections*

SUNY Series in American Social History
Elizabeth Pleck and Charles Stephenson, Editors

Family Connections

A HISTORY OF ITALIAN AND JEWISH
IMMIGRANT LIVES IN PROVIDENCE, RHODE ISLAND
1900–1940

Judith E. Smith

STATE UNIVERSITY OF NEW YORK PRESS · *Albany*

For my family

PUBLISHED BY
STATE UNIVERSITY OF NEW YORK PRESS, ALBANY
© 1985 STATE UNIVERSITY OF NEW YORK
ALL RIGHTS RESERVED
PRINTED IN THE UNITED STATES OF AMERICA

FOR INFORMATION, ADDRESS STATE UNIVERSITY OF NEW YORK PRESS,
STATE UNIVERSITY PLAZA, ALBANY, N.Y., 12246

LIBRARY OF CONGRESS CATALOGING IN PUBLICATION DATA
Smith, Judith E., 1948-
Family connections.
(SUNY series in American social history)
Bibliography: p. Includes index.
1. Italian American families--Rhode Island--Providence--History--20th century.
2. Jewish families--Rhode Island--Providence--History--20th century.
3. Italian Americans--Rhode Island--Providence--Social life and customs.
4. Jews--Rhode Island--Providence--Social life and customs. 5. Providence (R.I.)
--Social life and customs. I. Title. II. Series.

10 9 8 7 6 5 4 3 2 1

Contents

Illustrations

FIGURES

MAPS

TABLES

Acknowledgements

I AM VERY pleased to acknowledge my indebtedness to my parents.
Edward A. Smith and Beth Kulakofsky Smith, and other family,
friends, and colleagues for their assistance to me in the process of
writing this book. My initial interest in immigrant families has grown
from and been sustained by my own personal history. As the
granddaughter and great granddaughter of Jewish immigrants from
eastern Europe to Worcester, Massachusetts, Des Moines, Iowa, and
Omaha, Nebraska, I grew up experiencing firsthand the value of a
primary commitment to family relationships, the critical importance
of mutual support, and the complexity of the negotiations between
family priorities and individual decisions. I have been fortunate to
live for the last twelve years in a newly created extended household,
which has placed these issues at the center of my own adult life.

The staffs of the Rhode Island Historical Society Library, the
Rhode Island State Records Center, the Rhode Island Jewish
Historical Society Library, the Providence Public Library, and the
Slater Mill Historic Site were most helpful in locating the materials
used in this study. The reference staff at the Rhode Island Historical
Society Library was particularly agreeable about responding to long-
distance queries. Maureen Taylor, the graphics curator at the Rhode
Island Historical Society Library, and Tom Leary, curator of the
Slater Mill Historic Site, gave special assistance in locating the

photographs used in this study. It is a particular pleasure to be able to use the photographs taken in Providence by Lewis W. Hine which are part of a collection given to the Slater Mill Historic Site by Mrs. C. Raymond Munson in memory of Alice Hunt and Edith Woodhead Marshall. Daniel Horowitz and Susan Porter Benson directed me to relevant unpublished Providence materials in the National Archives. Sharon Strom gave me access to the Rhode Island Women's Biography Project before it was catalogued. Laura Schwartz referred me to the WPA life history sources in the Peoples of Connecticut Ethnic Heritage Collection at the University of Connecticut. Daniel Wood did most of the record linkage with the 1935 Rhode Island state census, Robert Macieski and Cynthia Butler painstakingly checked citations, and Lane Riker and Robert Macieski did the preliminary photography research. Sonya Michel and Jessann DeCredico provided transcripts of interviews they recorded. I especially appreciate the willingness of the families whom I interviewed to share their memories with me, They were open and generous, giving me the benefit of their time and insights as well as wine, cake, Italian cookies. I particularly want to thank Joe Conforti, Arthur Ferri, Jonathan Malino, Larry Blum, and Joseph Pleck for helping to arrange these interviews.

The research for this book was guided in its initial stages by the enthusiasm and sharp and astute critical insights of Howard Chudacoff, Louise Lamphere, and Mari Jo Buhle. Papers based on this research benefited from critical readings by Donald Bell, Mary Ann Clawson, Miriam Cohen, Maurine Greenwald, Louise Lamphere, Elaine May, Barbara Melosh, Sonya Michel, David Montgomery, Christina Simmons, Sharon Strom, and Rudolph Vecoli. Janet James, Sandra Joshel, and Paul Spagnoli, my colleagues in the history department at Boston College, gave extremely helpful comments on portions of the manuscript. Succeeding drafts of the entire manuscript were immeasurably improved by the very thoughtful and insightful comments of Harold Benenson, Susan Porter Benson, Jeremy Brecher, Howard Chudacoff, Bruce Laurie, Barbara Melosh, John Modell, Jim O'Brien, Elizabeth Pleck, Ellen Rothman, Christina Simmons, Jim Smith, and Louise Tilly. Alan Zaslavsky checked the tables for statistical significance and the book has benefited from his and Lew Ferleger's expertise in numbers and statistics. I also want to thank my father, Edward A. Smith, for translating the signs in Yiddish and Hebrew which dimly appear in the photograph of Charles Street in Providence on p. 15.

Sections of this book draw upon earlier published articles and permission to reprint portions is gratefully acknowledged. Some of the ideas in this book appear in "Our Own Kind: Family and Community Networks in Providence," *Radical History Review* 17 (Spring, 1978), pp. 99–120, used by permission of *Radical History Review*; "Italian Mothers, American Daughters; Changes in Work and Family Roles," in *The Italian Immigrant Woman in North America* edited by Betty B. Caroli, Robert F. Harney, and Lydio F. Tomasi (Toronto: The Multicultural History Society of Ontario, 1978), pp. 206–221, used by permission of The Multicultural History Society of Ontario.

The maps that appear in the book were drawn with careful attention to detail by Eliza McClennon, Staff Cartographer, Geography Department, Boston University. Funds for typing portions of the manuscript were provided by the Dean of the Graduate School of Arts and Sciences at Boston College. One chapter was particularly attentively typed by Anne Bluethenthal.

Colleagues in the history department at the University of Rhode Island, the women's studies department at the University of Massachusetts at Boston, and the history department and American Studies committee at Boston College have provided rich intellectual comradeship during the years in which this book has been in the making. My students in urban history and labor history probably heard more than they ever thought they wanted to about Rhode Island immigrants; their active interest in and engagement with this subject was an ongoing source of stimulation for me.

I want finally to thank Larry Blum, Jim Smith, Sarah Malino, Barbara Melosh, Elizabeth Pleck, Christina Simmons, and Susan Porter Benson for their commitment to this project and for the insights they cheerfully contributed in response to repeated and last-minute consultations. My housemates Noel Jetté and Alan Zaslavsky cooked me meals and asked me questions about my work that helped me to keep its social relevance central to my thinking. My husband Larry Blum took on extra child care responsibility to give me time to finish this book, lent his own sharp analytic skills to questions of interpretation, and most importantly, shared his life with me. I am grateful that my children Ben and Sarah and Clara Jetté Zaslavsky each learned to live with the piles of papers generated by this project without giving in to the temptation to throw them in the air or color on them. In the most heartfelt way I thank Ben and Sarah for keeping me rooted in the daily realities of family life and in touch with my own hopes for the future.

I-1.   Behind a Federal Hill tenement, 1912. Photograph by Lewis W. Hine, courtesy of the Slater Mill Historic Site.

Introduction

F AMILIAR IMAGES from American documentary photographers have shaped our concepts of immigrant life in American cities early in this century. This photograph by Lewis Hine takes us behind a Providence tenement in Federal Hill, the Italian neighborhood, on a fall day in November 1912. Its images—laundry on the clothesline, trash on the ground, people in the narrow space between buildings—makes this photograph similar to countless others that Hine and other photographers took to capture the immigrant presence in American cities. As a reformer, Hine probably intended the picture to convey overcrowded housing conditions, too many people, not enough room.[1] But before our eyes, the certainty and assurance of the photographic record fade and we are left wondering how those depicted here would have described themselves. Who were these people, and how were they related to each other? Were they grouped coincidentally in the photographer's frozen moment, or were they family, neighbors, friends? What were the actual boundaries between household and tenement, inside and outside, family and friendship, individual and community?

For the most part, immigrants have described themselves as members of families. Whether they travelled alone or in groups, their uprooting was given meaning by their identities as family members.

Listening to them describe daily life in the old country and the new, one is struck by the resonance and repetition of references to family. Observing the actual process of migration, one discovers that family ties directed immigrants from communities in Europe to particular cities and neighborhoods in the United States. As they struggled to shape new lives for themselves in the new country, family networks mediated the experience of work and neighborhood.[2]

Families thus form an obvious part of the immigrant experience. Less visible are the actual meaning, content, and boundaries of these family relationships, taken for granted by immigrants and rarely articulated. The family is a social as well as a biological construction, and we should not be surprised to find that expectations about relationships and interpretations of family interest differ widely. Women and men, parents and children may not share an identical vision; their experiences within the family circle may be quite diverse. For example, the value of cooperation may be accepted by all members and indeed may make possible the family's survival under difficult economic circumstances, but the burden of support and access to resources may fall unequally and influence each one's stake in resolving disagreements regarding family property. Relationships within a given household are also shaped by those external to it: the quality and quantity of contacts with kin, neighbors, and friends outside the household affect the interactions of those who live together on a daily basis. Finally, the exterior worlds of work and politics, each an arena for social life and historical change as well as for individual experience, impinge on family life.[3]

Immigrant families were almost by definition immersed in the process of historical change. Transformation of the customary community, which was itself the cause of their emigration, and resettlement in an environment with radically different economic, political, social, and ideological structures meant that in their lifetimes, immigrants experienced change that elsewhere spread over generations. Given also the continual alteration of family forms by the complex and shifting interaction of inherited cultural traditions, by the social relations of production, and by the legal structures of the state, immigrant history provides an unusually rich case study of family development.

Family Connections examines the changing context of life in Europe and America for two groups—southern Italians and eastern European Jews—who came to Providence, Rhode Island, in the late nineteenth and early twentieth centuries. Following the ebb and flow over two generations brings critical questions into sharper focus. What were the distinctive qualities of families in Europe on the eve of migration, of migrating families, of families of the first American-born generation? How did each confront its changing social and economic world? In the same local urban economy, how did Providence's Italians and Jews sustain or modify ethnic differences? In what distinct ways did men and women participate in family life? What particular combination of generational and historical change explains the emergence and disappearance of characteristic family forms, and what do these forms tell us about the societies in which they appeared?

This narrative begins in southern Italian villages and eastern European Jewish communities. There, in response to diminishing control over their economic destinies, Italian smallholders, day laborers, and artisans, and Jewish artisans and tradespeople turned inward to their families and outward to communal institutions, expanding familial economic cooperation and reciprocal assistance. Within a family, all who would eat had to work, and mothers and daughters, sons and grandfathers ingeniously found ways to add lire and rubles to precarious family incomes. By complicated exchanges of gifts and aid, families enlarged the network of kin who were indebted to them and whose assistance would be a kind of insurance for needy times to come. Men joined together in mutual benefit associations which commonly provided sick and death payments to supplement family resources with communal ones as a hedge against disaster. Ultimately, the families in this study took their fates in their own hands and left Europe. Arriving in Providence, they transferred this culture of economic cooperation and reciprocity to a city caught up in its own urban and industrial transformation. They found ways to use Providence factories and neighborhood shops to accommodate European family work traditions; men, women, and children continued to pool all resources generated by income-producing work. The expansion of kin networks would continue as immigrants arranged housing and employment for later arrivals. Mutual benefit associations would flourish, building on European ties and articulating reciprocal values.

The immigrant experience was thus conditioned and partly shaped by the European cultural context, and then, in the United States, by the local constraints of a modern commercial-industrial city. In turn, the next generation would confront a world made by their parents and revised by larger economic forces. Facing continuing social and economic change in the 1920s and 1930s, the first American-born generation would alter patterns of family economic cooperation, reshape kin configurations, revise associational life. Both the shifting outside world and the reordering of individual and

family priorities would create a new context for family life, diminishing the influence of patriarchal authority and loosening the closely
woven networks of kin and community. Familial values that had
resounded through ethnic neighborhoods, at work and in community life would be redefined as the boundaries of family life
became less fluid. All these changes would have significant and
different ramifications for individual family members—women and
men, parents and children.

American historians have previously approached the study of
change in family life from several perspectives, none of which seems
entirely adequate to explain the particular dynamics of the immigrant family. Some scholars have argued that industrialization
caused the family to lose its role in economic production, women
and children to become less economically significant, and kinship to
decline as a basis of work organization. While this approach placed
an important emphasis on the impact of economic structures, its
assessment of industrialization as the key factor in changing the
shape of the family has not been supported by recent scholarship.
Long before industrialization, enclosure movements had deprived
peasant families of customary rights to land, forcing landless
peasants to leave their homes to work as wage laborers. In some
circumstances, industrialization consolidated rather than destroyed
families as work groups. Certain stages of technological development
accompanying industrialization stimulated the growth of cottage
industries where whole families together produced commodities, and
in other instances, families moved as groups into the factories.
Rather than breaking the bonds of kinship, industrialization may
have actually increased economic exchange among family and kin in
some cases.[4] Immigrants may have moved from less to more
industrialized settings, but this factor in itself did not necessarily
change the family.

Another group of historians has interpreted change in family life
as part of a transition from traditional to modern cultural values,
arguing that immigrant families were disrupted and dissolved in the
process of adjusting to American life. While this approach implied
important criticisms of the undermining of traditional cultural
values by Americanization and assimilation, it leaves no room for
understanding the ways in which persisting ethnic cultures may have
actually helped immigrants confront new circumstances. More
recently, historians have made a persuasive case for the stability and
continuity of immigrant family values. But enthusiasm for the
evidence of persistent ethnic and family values sometimes obscures
the dynamics of cultural and familial conflict in a changing economic

and social setting.[5] The focus on the continuity of ethnic and family culture has sharpened the historical awareness of ethnic variation within working-class culture and of the resiliency of cultural patterns outside the dominant culture, but the distinction between *traditional* and *modern* assumes a linear change that oversimplifies the complexity and diversity of immigrant experience.

This book about Italian and Jewish immigrant families joins other recent works that reject a sharp dichotomy between pre-industrial and industrial socieities, traditional and modern cultures, arguing that *preindustrial* and *traditional* are terms too static to describe Europe on the eve of migration and *industrial* and *modern* terms too unitary to describe the world immigrants found in American cities. Both the old country and the new world were societies in flux, and the focus of these recent studies has shifted to the immigrants themselves as actors in the transformation process. Cultural norms, economic resources, and the particular structures of local urban economies led them to order their households and shape their families in distinctive ways. Within the urban, industrial environment, they created new values, work patterns, and family relationships, conforming to the promise and constraints of life in an American city but also maintaining a measure of continuity.[6]

Family Connections addresses the question of how the interaction of the local economy, customary family expectations, and community resources shaped family consciousness and behavior in southern Italy and eastern Europe, in the Providence of immigrant arrival, and in the Providence of settled and mature ethnic communities. Locating a comparative analysis of two groups in a specific city allows a systematic inquiry into the family experiences of immigrants who, coming from different backgrounds, confronted the same environment. What happened to these families? How did generational dynamics interact with economic, social, and cultural change for Italian and Jewish families in Providence between 1900 and 1940?

These family experiences have been explored through local records and oral history. The process of life over two generations emerges from the reconstruction of work and residential histories of 162 Italian families and 72 Jewish families who lived in central areas of the Italian neighborhood of Federal Hill and the Jewish neighborhood of Smith Hill and were enumerated in the state census of 1915. Using annual city directories, the 1925 and 1935 censuses, and available birth, marriage, and death records, each member of a household headed by immigrants from southern Italy or eastern Europe was traced from 1880 to 1940. The entire population of a limited neighborhood area was studied in order to situate immigrants in the context of broader kinship networks. These were identified by tracing maternal and paternal kin and married sons and daughters (see Appendix for selection, linkage, and tracing procedures). The population selected is representative of immigrant families whose circumstances led them to settle near the center of an ethnically identified area. Boarders were traced as members of census households, but most of the evidence concerns immigrants who lived as parents, children, or relatives in households in 1915. A few of the families returned to Europe, but the overwhelming majority of them became permanent residents of the United States and most of them permanent residents of Providence. To the quantitative facts gleaned from the public record, oral histories of Providence immigrants and their children added a critical interior and emotional dimension. Their memories were sometimes supplemented with relevant material from life histories and autobiographies of southern Italian and eastern European Jewish immigrants in other northeastern commercial and industrial cities.[7]

A strength of both these sources is their ability to portray actual immigrant families over time, in the process of defining their relationship to one another. Balancing the systematic contribution of quantitative records against the particularistic memories contained in oral history brings us closer to comprehension of immigrant lives as immigrants themselves understood and evaluated them. Situating the study in Providence, a city with varied work opportunities, broadens the historical study of immigrant family accommodation; other studies have been set in cities where a single industry such as textiles or steel was dominant. Analyzing two ethnic groups who came from very different economic and social circumstances in Europe, but who arrived in the same years and confronted the same economic environment in Providence, throws the similarities of their experience as well as their more obvious differences into sharper focus.

The experience of Providence immigrants illuminates the nature of daily survival strategies for newcomers in an uncertain urban environment. It also reveals the links between familial and ethnic culture and broader allegiances of solidarity, and suggests some of the differences between male and female experience within families. Beyond the scope of this study are other areas where the impact of changing immigrant family forms might also be observed; institutional religion, political participation and activism, and a wider range of voluntary associations, including labor and community organizations. And further comparative study of a variety of immigrant groups in different cities will test the representativeness of these findings.

The first chapter of *Family Connections* outlines the historical circumstances immigrants faced in European communities and in Providence from the late nineteenth century through the depression and recovery years of the 1930s. Chapters 2, 3, and 4 chart the course of familial change in the settings of work, kinship, and voluntary associations. Chapter 2 analyzes the relationship between family and work in terms of the values of family economic cooperation. Heightened for immigrants in the uncertain economies of their villages, these values were reshaped in Providence by the imperatives of technological and economic change and the shifting choices of the next generation. Chapter 3 traces the relationship between family and kinship networks in terms of household expansion, propinquity of related households, and neighborhood sharing. Expanded networks of kin and neighbors were a new phenomenon created in response to special vulnerability in late nineteenth-century Europe and the disruptions of migration and settlement. In Providence, the networks were realigned by the changing developmental cycle of immigrant families and by the changing neighborhood setting. Chapter 4 assesses the spread of fraternal associations on the eve of migration and in Providence as an extension of kin-like relationships in community life and as a public expression of the values of family solidarity and reciprocity. The decline of mutual benefit associations in the 1930s paralleled the redefinition of the family economy and the contraction of family and kin networks. The specific contours of Italian and Jewish family lives were often different, but in these particular areas the overall direction of change was strikingly similar. In the end, extended households and broadened conceptions of obligation and assistance did not disappear. Neither individualistic values nor isolated families resulted from the process of change. As the years passed, family solidarity and ethnic loyalties took on new shades of meaning, within which could be seen the residue of immigrant culture and the reconstruction of a younger generation.

Chapter One

The Historical Setting

THE HISTORY of these immigrant families begins in the late nineteenth century in southern Italian villages and in eastern European Jewish communities where men and women were conscious of being caught in the crosscurrent between a repetitive past and an unknown future. Willingly or not, their lives were touched by tumultuous forces connected with the transitional phase of European development between the breakdown of traditional society and the onset of advanced industrialization. All over Europe, the introduction of a commercial economy transformed the customary community, and in the process, provided the impetus and the means for transoceanic migration. Immigration was directly connected with the development of communications, markets, commerce, and capital—themselves the signposts of economic change. Roads and railways, canals and steamships, post offices and telegraphs, banks and agencies were the products of those forces that were transforming the self-contained existence of rural Europe as well as the means that immigrants used in beginning their personal journeys from the old world to the new.[1]

Italian small landholders, day laborers, and artisans, and Jewish artisans and tradespeople shared the experience of being drawn into a market economy. In southern Italian villages the meaning of this experience was that prices for agricultural products were increasingly affected by the development of national markets, that manufactured goods were sold into the countryside and competed with the handiwork of artisans, and that more land was being bought and sold and hence turned into a commodity, particularly as communal forests and pastures were accumulated by a new rural bourgeoisie. In eastern Europe, the emancipation of the serfs and the gradual economic development of the countryside that accompanied railroad construction undermined Jewish employment that was dependent on Russian and Polish landlords. Jews, forced by residence laws, crowded into the cities and towns of the Pale of Settlement, where too many craftsmen saturated whatever market existed. Factory goods from industrial centers competed with the products of Jewish craftsmen and peddlers, and master artisans became far less independent, producing for stores rather than individual orders. Everywhere daily life was governed less by internal and communal rhythms, and more by the demands of impersonal wage labor.[2]

The currents of change swirled in many directions. Altered access to property affected dowries and provisions for marriage. Movement of villagers in search of work brought them into contact with the unfamiliar and widened the boundaries of village life. New commitments to voluntary associations competed with the claims of religious traditionalism. This transformation of property relations, of social life, and of the foundations of the customary community was an essential precondition of immigration and a common part of the preimmigration experience of southern Italians and eastern European Jews. Though other circumstances were sometimes influential, often it was the glimpse of widening horizons abroad amidst the awareness of the unalterable course of change at home that prompted large numbers of Europeans to travel in search of the means to survive and prosper.[3]

The quickening pace of economic and social transformation that stimulated immigration continued to touch the lives of the particular immigrants who settled in Providence, Rhode Island, in the last decades of the nineteenth century and the first years of the twentieth century. A colonial port and mercantile center, Providence's importance had increased as the state had industrialized. Its own industries of woolen and worsted, jewelry, and machinery manufacture had contributed to the state's economic productivity, and as the structures of manufacture and marketing had grown more complex, the city had developed the banking and commercial resources to service them. Not coincidentally, the immigrants' arrival years marked the decades of Providence's greatest expansion. Between 1870 and 1910, manufacturing employment in Rhode Island increased by 245 percent, population grew by 250 percent, and the total labor force expanded by 284 percent. Providence prospered with the state and proudly claimed a place as "the metropolis of southern New England." The city boasted of the largest tool, file, steam engine, screw, and silverware factories in the world; Nicholson files, Corliss steam engines, Rumford baking powder, Gorham silver flatware, Davol rubber, Brown and Sharpe tools, and Fruit of the Loom textiles were among the nationally known products manufactured in Providence. First in the nation in the manufacture of woolen textiles and jewelry, third in the production of machinery and machine tools, the city offered plentiful employment.[4]

Providence cotton and worsted mills, machine shops, and jewelry factories had long drawn immigrants from the surrounding countryside, including substantial numbers of women who worked in the textile and jewelry factories. Married as well as single women came to Providence for the wages exchanged for work in the mills. By 1910, over one-third of the females in the city who were sixteen years of age and older were gainfully employed, and one-third of the female textile workers in the state who were over sixteen years old were married, widowed, divorced, or separated. Migration doubled the population of the city between 1880 and 1910, and bustling crowds of strangers bumped elbows with longtime residents as they filled the streets on their way to and from work. Like other American cities whose population increased with late-nineteenth-century industrial growth, Providence was busily adding to its physical plant. Signs of construction were everywhere as new streets, bridges, gas mains and water pipelines, electric-streetcar tracks, schools, police and fire stations, and city buildings attested to Providence's expansion. The cityscape varied; downtown buildings and the fashionable and spacious residences on the east side marked two distinct areas, but the industrial development of the city had taken place over too long a period for manufacturing to be centralized in one district. Some of the larger factories were situated along the rivers and the railroad lines, but large numbers of machine shops, textile mills, iron foundries, rubber works, soap factories, and jewelry establishments were erected throughout the city, usually surrounded by haphazard blocks of small shops and modest workers' housing, shading sometimes after a distance into open spaces.[5] Ablaze at night with electric lights, housing a full-time movie house as early as 1906, displaying an opulent abundance of mass-produced consumer goods in the plate glass windows of Callender, McAuslan and Troup's Boston Store, built in 1866, and Shepard's Department Store, built in 1880, Providence was a testament to the wonders of fast-paced modern industrial life.

As they settled in the city, Providence's immigrants redesigned its residential character. Italian and Jewish immigrants to Providence followed other earlier waves of migration, from Ireland, England, French Canada, Germany, Sweden, and the Azores and Cape Verde Islands. In turn they were joined by Poles, Lithuanians, Armenians, and Syrians. Soon the Yankee WASP residents of Rhode Island were a minority in the state—albeit a powerful minority that maintained economic control and continued to dominate political life through the first third of the twentieth century. In 1910, seven out of ten inhabitants of the state were immigrants and their children. In 1915, about a third of Providence's population were foreign-born, and another third were the children of immigrants. Immigration accounted for nearly three-fourths of Providence's population growth between 1900 and 1910. The antagonism of previous groups of residents to the new arrivals and the preference of immigrants for familiar neighbors worked together to produce distinct ethnic neighborhoods in Providence. The structure of migration—the tendency of family members and fellow villagers to follow earlier migrants and depend on them for initial housing—also contributed to the development of immigrant settlements. The expansion of electric trolleys, operating in Providence since 1892, opened up new residential areas to those who could afford to live further away from the factories; the older areas closer to downtown became available as centers of settlement for the new immigrant groups.[6]

Federal Hill, the neighborhood selected by Italian immigrants in this study, was a formerly Irish district west of downtown which was settled by Italians soon after they began to arrive in large numbers in Providence after 1888. Their original settlement was informally restricted to a few blocks, and residents recalled frequent fights between the remaining Irish children and the newcomers as the number of Italian immigrants increased. The settlement expanded to fill the surrounding blocks with Italian families, with Italian bakeries, grocery shops, tailor and barber shops, and (after 1889) with Italian Roman Catholic parishes that proclaimed the neighborhood's ethnicity to outsiders. The Fabre Line, which picked up passengers in Naples and Palermo, brought southern Italians directly to Providence after 1911. By 1915, more than 20,000 Italians, mostly from southern Italy, had settled in Providence. Italian immigrants contributed more than 8 percent of the city's 1915 population of nearly 250,000, and their children comprised an additional 6 percent of the city's residents. The Federal Hill neighborhood soon became solidly Italian and densely populated. The rapid influx of immigrants had strained the city's already-short housing supply, and

1-1. A girl playing with a goat in a back yard, Spruce Street, Federal Hill, 1912. Photograph by Lewis W. Hine, courtesy of the Slater Mill Historic Site.

1-2. A woman and children in front of a midwife's house, Spruce Street, Federal Hill, 1912. Photography by Lewis W. Hine, courtesy of the Slater Mill Historic Site.

1-3. Delivering bread on Spruce Street, Federal Hill, 1912. Photography by Lewis W. Hine, courtesy of the Slater Mill Historic Site.

1-4. Two elderly men are stopped in the doorway of one of the buildings on Charles Street, Smith Hill, 1899. The sign in Yiddish and Hebrew reads in part: Seller of books, phylacteries, mezzuzot, prayer shawls . . . and fine New Year's cards. Photograph courtesy of the Rhode Island Historical Society (RHi X3 979).

contractors had responded by filling all undeveloped lots with multi-unit tenements, many of these the type known as triple-deckers. The neighborhood took on its characteristic look, with a mix of older workers' cottages built for single families and new tenement dwellings. No matter how many families the housing was originally intended for, immigrant families and friends filled the apartments according to their own needs, and a 1916 housing survey found that in two sections of Federal Hill, nearly 40 percent of the houses were occupied by more than three families. A contemporary observer described how much the neighborhood seemed to reinforce the preservation of the shared European culture, with "Italian shops, Italian banks, Italian tenement houses, and Italian dialects on every hand."[7]

The eastern European immigrants in this study lived in the eastern part of a neighborhood north of downtown known as Smith Hill. As eastern European Jews began to arrive in Providence in the 1880s and 1890s, and in large numbers after 1900, they settled amidst the Irish in this working-class district behind the State Capitol. By 1915, one contemporary estimated that more than 8,000 eastern European Jewish immigrants lived in Providence, comprising more than 3 percent of the city's population, and that their children were an additional 3 percent of the city's residents. The eastern European Jews who lived on Smith Hill dominated an older, poorer section of the neighborhood near the railroad tracks and the Mahassuck River industry which the Irish were already beginning to vacate. Along the main streets, Yiddish signs went up to mark the bakeries, the butcher shops, the tailor and secondhand shops that occupied the ground floors of the shabby pre–Civil War workers' housing which the Jewish immigrants had inherited from the Irish. The first buildings constructed as synagogues appeared in 1893 and 1906. Outsiders experienced the Smith Hill neighborhood, nearly as ethnically distinct as Federal Hill, as a separate world where "the foreign-born generation mostly keeps to itself."[8]

The neighborhoods were a vital arena for immigrant life, but they were not immune from the effects of the continuing process of residential movement by which they had, themselves, been created. Metropolitanization would move employment further away from the neighborhoods in the years after 1920, and the streetcar lines expanded the possible range of commutes from home to work. Newer areas offered wider streets, more stately triple-deckers, and the possibility of small yards. Between 1910 and 1920, Providence grew at less than one-third the rate of other parts of the surrounding metropolitan area, and by 1940 the city began to lose population to

1-5. Jewish shops along Charles Street, Smith Hill, 1899. New and secondhand clothing hang outside. Photograph courtesy of the Rhode Island Historical Society (RHi X3 4006).

1-6.　In front of a corner store on Chalkstone Avenue, Smith Hill, 1903. A man walks by with a stove pipe in his hand and a pack on his back; a woman holds her child; a baby carriage and an older child are nearby. Photograph courtesy of the Rhode Island Historical Society (RHi X3 4808).

1-7. Backyards of buildings along Charles Street, Smith Hill, 1899. Two young children are in the yard. Photograph courtesy of the Rhode Island Historical Society (RHi X3 880).

the suburbs. In the 1950s, Providence would lose more inhabitants to the suburbs than any other major city in the nation. Commercial amusements also competed with self-generated immigrant neighborhood social life, especially for the loyalties of the young.[9] After having successfully conquered the ordeals of transoceanic migration and resettlement, Providence immigrants and their children would still find profound challenges ahead in coming to terms with a constantly changing residential and cultural environment.

During the years in which immigrants who settled in Providence after the turn of the century were busily constructing lives for themselves and their famlies, the industrial dream betrayed its promise and the apparent prosperity turned to decay as the textile industry in Rhode Island collapsed. Work in textiles, as well as in jewelry and machine shops, had always been seasonal and unstable, and the 1905 and 1915 state censuses showed that Providence textile workers, jewelry workers, laborers, and machinists consistently had the highest proportion of unemployment. In addition to periodic recessions, the general economic position of Rhode Island was weakening in relation to increased industrial production in other parts of the country, facilitated by cheaper access to raw materials and fuel in the West, and lower taxes and a nonunionized labor force in the South. Unlike industries such as iron and steel, meat packing, and oil in which a few big companies were consolidating their control over raw material sand markets, Rhode Island's textile industry was threatened by increasing competition, constant crises of overproduction, and a failure to control the prices on finished goods. Southern competition particularly diminished Rhode Island's share of the national market in textiles. Manufacturers tried sporadically to use new machinery to cut labor costs and speed up productivity quotients for workers, expanding the number of machines tended. Like the manufacturers of machine tools and jewelry, textile manufacturers formed associations to attempt to maintain wage advantages through uniform structures and open-shop policies. The most devastating strategy for Rhode Island industrial workers was common by the 1920s: Rhode Island textile-mill owners began to close the mills, cut back production, and move their capital and major operations to the South.[10]

The collapse of the textile industry had a ripple effect through the rest of the state's economy. Textile-machine firms, makers and distributors of mill supplies, and related iron works were forced to convert their production or seek new markets, and many of them collapsed. Providence's economy fluctuated substantially with the decline of the textile industry. Although machine shops, costume jewelry factories, rubber plants, and electrical-parts industries continued to employ industrial workers, the decline of textile production in the 1920s followed by the local effects of the national depression in the 1930s meant a permanent loss of employment in manufacturing and construction. Between 1919 and 1939, Rhode Island industrial statistics revealed a 20 percent decrease in manufacturing employment, a loss much more profound in its effects than the average national decrease of 3 percent. Service jobs, employment in state and federal agencies, and positions in education would provide most of the new employment in the state after 1932. The Rhode Island work force looked very different in 1940 than it had in 1920; the percentage of all gainfully employed workers engaged in sales and service occupations increased from 38 to 46.3 percent; the percentage of workers employed in manufacturing and construction fell from nearly 60 to 51.5 percent. Providence's transformation was even more dramatic. Between 1920 and 1935, the number of industrial workers dropped from nearly 60 to 44 percent of the labor force. The white-collar sector expanded accordingly; the number of clerical workers increased from 8.1 to 11.5 percent, the number of service workers rose from 7 to nearly 12 percent, and the number employed in trade and retail increased from 9.6 to 14 percent. The shift toward white-collar employment did not necessarily imply economic advancement; the census categories encompassed a variety of kinds of work from secure and well-compensated positions to poorly paid and seasonal service employment.[11] Still, the shrinking of industrial work opportunities and the expansion of the white-collar sector presented a major structural change during the lives of immigrants and their children. The children would survey an occupational landscape vastly altered from the one that had greeted their parents' arrival from Europe. The options that faced the generations were fundamentally different.

"Changing, all is changing," might well have been the immigrants' constant refrain in response to most of the circumstances of their adult years. The unraveling of their customary communities in Europe, the explosive growth of their arrival port of Providence, the consolidation and then the diffusion of the ethnic neighborhoods they created, the crash of Rhode Island's industrial economy—these formed the context of the immigrants' dreams and promises, compromises and accommodations. These seemingly impersonal changes struck at the very heart of the immigrants' daily and personal lives; in response, immigrants transformed family economic cooperation, familial patterns of exchange, neighborhood networks of association—and even the family itself. The ways in which southern Italian and eastern European Jewish immigrants faced these circumstances and shaped them are the substance of the pages that follow.

Chapter Two

A Family Culture of Work

A SICILIAN immigrant once described America: "Here one eats, but not for free." Italian and Jewish immigrants came to Providence in order to work. Most immigrants did not see their work in terms of individual choice or personal advancement, but as a struggle to make a family living that dominated the hours apart from sleep. The experience of scarcity in Europe had oriented people to assume that each family member must work, so men, women, and children came prepared to labor in order to sustain the family. Although the household was the primary unit of economic organization in southern Italy and eastern Europe, in neither country was the household economically self-sufficient. Southern Italians and Jews had grown extremely resourceful in seeking out a wide variety of income-generating activities to combine for a family living. The tradition of family work shared by southern Italian and eastern European Jewish immigrants had two main components. First, the head of the household determined each member's responsibilities for generating income and decided how precious resources might be spent. Second, all those who lived and ate together under one roof pooled their economic resources, labor, and any wages each might earn. The formulation of a "family economy" thus combined an assumption of patriarchal authority with a commitment to economic collectivity and cooperation.[1]

The norms of a family economy guided the work patterns of Italian and Jewish immigrants in Providence. Immigrants adapted the expectations of men's, women's, and children's work roles which had evolved in the particular agrarian economy of the Italian south and the artisan-commercial economy of the Jewish Pale to fit the opportunities they found in new workplaces and neighborhoods in Providence. Newly arrived artisans and shopkeepers met the demands of fellow townspeople for familiar goods and services, laborers moved with brothers and cousins into the factories, and women and children worked both in their own kitchens, cooking and cleaning for boarders, and behind the counter in family shops. However, during their working years in this country, immigrants experienced the degradation of their skills through new management policies and technological change; they faced, moreover, a sudden and seemingly irreversible contraction of the economy in the 1930s. Male and female artisans found that painstakingly crafted goods were unable to compete in price with mass-produced items. Husband-and-wife storekeeping teams saw personal customer relations on which they based their neighborhood shops undermined by new kinds of retailing in department stores and chain supermarkets. Factory workers found their workplaces disappearing—often with a chilling suddenness. The immigrants' sons and daughters would find employment in a very different economic context than that which they had known. Economic and social change would lead children to challenge certain aspects of family authority and would encourage mothers to adjust the nature and timing of their economic contribution. Italian and Jewish families would have to renegotiate the terms of economic cooperation, but at least until 1940, family collectivity rather than individual aspiration remained the central purpose of work.

Family Economic Collectivity in Europe

Southern Italian immigrants to Providence came from towns in Abruzzi, Campania, Basilicata, Calabria, and Sicily (see map 2-1). With some regional variation, the household was the primary form of economic organization. Property arrangements and demographic factors in the south tended to encourage the formation of small work groups, in contrast with the extended-family households, laboring

Map 2-1. Local Origins of Southern Italian Immigrants to Federal Hill
Neighborhood, Providence
Source: Birthplaces as recorded on marriage and death certificates,
neighborhood data.

gangs, and courtyard groups more commonly found in central Italy and Apulia. Most of the land in the south was divided into small parcels which were cultivated independently. Except in Sicily, there were few large estates still intact by the end of the nineteenth century. The division of the large estates did not lead to equal land distribution, but it did increase the number of peasants who owned land. Generally, small, medium, and large holdings ranged side by side. Land changed hands frequently, and the short duration of contracts and the instability of ownership discouraged improvements to the soil, thus limiting productivity.[2]

In the peculiar economy of the Italian south, divisions among small farmers, sharecroppers, and day laborers were sometimes blurred. The yearly income of the day laborer was seldom surpassed by that of the average small landholder or tenant farmer. Land-owners had to pay heavy taxes on all kinds of property. Partible inheritance traditions and use of the land as dowry produced increasing subdivision and fragmentation of the land. Many small owner-operators and their children eventually became landless. Even when families owned land, plots were often too small and unproductive to sustain them fully. Sometimes a family owned one small plot of land and rented or sharecropped several others. Generally some family members spent part of their time in pursuits other than tilling the family's land—hiring out for wages on a day-labor basis or working at nonagricultural tasks.[3]

The small size and uncertain productivity of the land holdings, operating in combination with demographic factors, limited the agricultural work group to an individual family, usually parents and unmarried children, although households sometimes included aging parents who could no longer work.[4] Southern Italian families maintained themselves by combining income from a variety of different sources. One Sicilian immigrant to Providence described how her family combined work in their own fields, agricultural day labor, and craft production for the market. Although they owned their house and the land around it, their annual income was just enough to sustain them. They raised crops and produce to eat, and on slack days the children picked fruits and vegetables on neighboring farms for a minimal wage while the mother wove extra lengths of cloth to sell.[5] Survival of the family demanded the work of all family members: mothers as well as fathers, children as well as parents. During harvest, frequently all family members worked in the fields. As well, women cooked, cleaned, cared for children, washed and patched clothes, and marketed extra produce. Ordinarily these tasks were done only for the benefit of a woman's own family, but they also gave poor women an opportunity to work for hire.[6]

Parents trained their children at an early age to work for their families. According to one Sicilian immigrant, "What the boy learns is what the father and mother think best for him."[7] Sons of peasants accompanied their fathers to the fields to learn to cultivate the land, to sow, harvest, and thresh grain, to care for flocks of sheep or pigs. Daughters learned from their mothers to cook, clean, care for younger children, gather an adequate wood and water supply, bargain at the market. They also learned to sew, to knit stockings, to do a share of the household weaving, and sometimes to embroider.[8] Learning to work was a central part of childhood.

Family economic control could extend over considerable space and time. The operation of the family economy did not require unity of skill or a single workplace. Rarely did all members of a family work in the same physical space, since families frequently farmed several plots at some distance from each other. In some parts of western Sicily, for example, women worked nearby garden plots while men worked fields at a greater distance from their towns. Family members did not necessarily do the same kind of work; mother, sons, and daughters might each take a turn doing a different kind of wage labor if the family required additional income. Central to the family economy was the assumption that any money earned by individuals doing outside work belonged without question to the family. An anthropologist doing fieldwork in Sicily in 1928–29 found that even after emigration, sons were still expected to send money home.[9]

The same economic pressures affecting peasants in these regions limited the market for artisans' work. As one Sicilian immigrant explained, "City with small population never have use for much trades because the people never have chance to have money or dress up."[10] By the late-nineteenth century, the crafts were in a state of decline, but an apprenticeship was still required to become a tailor, barber, shoemaker, mason, or carpenter. A hierarchy of skill produced distinctions among craftsmen. The most skilled artisans travelled from village to village; these included leather and metal workers and clockmakers, who made rather than repaired goods. Tailors and dressmakers usually worked in only one village. Less skilled cobblers who mended shoes and tinkers who mended pots usually peddled their trade from house to house in only one village. By this period, a division of labor was also common in clothes-making and weaving. Instead of producing an entire product, tailors performed the task of cutting the cloth and weavers set up patterns on the loom. The actual sewing and weaving could then be finished by untrained hands.[11]

Artisans commonly worked in family groups, and artisan skills were passed from generation to generation. One immigrant explained that he was, of course, a shoemaker, because his father and grandfather had been shoemakers in the old country. As a Sicilian immigrant recalled, he had begun to learn the trade of cabinetmaker at the age of eight because his father and grandfather were both cabinetmakers and they wanted him to learn their trade. The children of artisans were thus in the best position to be able themselves to become skilled craftsmen. But the marketing of goods manufactured in other parts of Italy further curtailed the opportunity for independent craft production.[12] Artisans confronted increasing competition for a diminishing market.

Jewish immigrants to Providence came from the western provinces of Russia and Poland, the area known as the Pale of Settlement, from Galicia in Austria-Hungary, and from Roumania (see map 2-2). All during the nineteenth century, periodic settlement decrees, meant to remove Jews from rural areas and thus from competition with peasants, combined with declining economic opportunities for Jews in the villages to consolidate Jewish residence in the crowded cities of the Pale. By 1897, Jews represented 58 percent of the urban population of the northwest provinces of the Pale; about three-quarters of the population of Pinsk, almost two-thirds of the population of Bialystok. Jews were particularly the dominant urban group among the many nationalities in the Pale, and the cities were particularly Jewish territory.[13]

The settlement laws placed Jews in a highly precarious economic position. Regulations explicitly prohibited Jews from working on the land, and the settlement laws had the effect of keeping them out of the larger industrial establishments—sugar mills, mines, smelting and iron works, glass works—since these were mostly situated outside the towns. So Jews worked in trades, artisan crafts, and small manufacturing, disproportionate to their numbers. Jews made up only 11.5 percent of the population of the provinces that composed the Pale, but by 1898 they comprised four-fifths of its commercial class, two-fifths of its artisan class, and one-third of its industrial class.[14] Within the Pale, they were restricted to a few hundred larger and smaller towns that were not particularly well suited to either commerce or industry. Kiev, the most important commercial and industrial center, was closed to Jews.[15] Without freedom to compete regionally, Jews were forced to undersell each other locally. As one

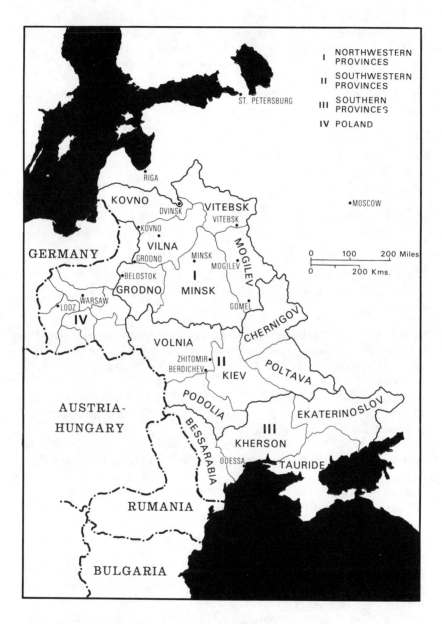

Map 2-2. The Pale of Settlement in 1905

Source: Henry J. Tobias, *The Jewish Band in Russia from JB Origins to 1905* (Stanford, Calif.: Stanford University Press, 1972), opposite p. 1, used with permission of the publishers, Stanford University Press. © 1972 by the Board of Trustees of Leland Stanford Junior University.

immigrant explained, "There were ten times as many stores as there should have been—tailors, cobblers, barbers, tinsmiths." Of course a Gentile could simply move on to another town to avoid the competition, but "a Jew was limited to the circle of the Pale."[16] Seasonal unemployment and frequent periods of poverty resulted. By the 1890s, about 20 percent of the Jewish population in the Pale required charity to buy the matzoth with which to celebrate Passover; in Vilna, nearly 38 percent of the Jewish community received charity for the holiday.[17] Artisan characters in the folk songs of Jewish workingmen vied with each other to claim the most bitter struggle for a living:

> *A cobbler*: No one lends me money, no one gives me credit, I am a cobbler and go barefoot.
> *A tinsmith*: I sit mending the roofs of strangers, but my house leaks from all sides.
> *A tailor*: A tailor sits and sews and sews and has the misery but no bread:
> A tailor sits and plies his needle and doesn't earn a single *groshn*[18]

These economic pressures sometimes forced people to carry on several occupations simultaneously or successively. As a Yiddish expression wryly explained: "The best cobbler of all tailors is Yankl the baker."[19]

The severe economic constraints within which they were forced to live prompted Jews to limit the size of a work group to an individual family. The individual family work group was particularly suited to the small-scale trade and manufacture in which Jews most commonly took part, frequently in small shops located near (or even in) their homes. According to a contemporary observer, "the artisan's home is the artisan's shop. Here women cooked food, children cried, and an artisan worked at his craft in a corner. Sometimes a skilled workman would rent part of such a room from another artisan if his own living space was too small."[20] The limits on economic opportunity made Jewish households extremely dependent on the labor of all family members. The lack of division between home and work gave women and children many opportunities to contribute to a family economy.

As in Italy, women cooked, cleaned, and cared for children, and they also took an active part in producing and marketing home-manufactured items. Accounts of the shtetl acknowledged the prominence of women in the crowds at the marketplace, both as sellers and as buyers.[21] Yiddish folk songs gave testimony to the involvement of wives in the craft or trade of their husbands, drawing attention to the precariousness of earning a living from the crafts and also to the economic unity of the artisan's family: "Coachmens' wives must tar the axles. . . . Butchers' wives must carry the meat. . . . Weavers' wives must throw the spindle. . . . Carpenters' wives must saw the boards."[22] In the northwest provinces especially, daughters, widows, and sometimes wives worked in small shops and factories as seamstresses, milliners, and knit-goods and cigarette makers.[23] In these circumstances, it was poverty that led to the necessity of working wives. The immigrant daughter of a blacksmith described her father's periodic bouts of unemployment:

> My father didn't make much. . . . Sometimes he was busy for a couple of months, like all the workingmen . . . the workingmen had a season. If they was working four months, and they saved the money, really they was very stingy, and they saved some money for the slack times, and come the slack time, then they ate up the money, and then they didn't have enough.

In these "slack times" her mother went to work as a bagel peddler:

> My mother started to take all the bread, bagels, rolls. She used to pick up in the morning, she used to get up at 4, 3:30 in the morning . . . she carried two big baskets, one basket had the bagels and the rolls, one the bread. She had her customers, she used to deliver to every customer what they ordered.

Walking the streets with heavy baskets added an exhausting burden to her mother's already long day of child care and housework, and the compensation she earned was meager, but the family had no resources to devote to arranging any other kind of work:

> She didn't make much. By the baker she paid a penny a roll, so how much could she make? She didn't make much, but . . . she made a few pennies, you know, for a bite to eat. . . . Some women had businesses, sell meat, sell bread. My mother used to take it to the customers because we didn't have the money for a place.[24]

As in Italy, parents taught their children to work at an early age. One Jewish woman remembered working at an inn her family managed, pouring out drinks and collecting money when she was still too small to reach the counter. In addition to male outdoor tasks and female household work, children learned their parents' particular skills. The daughter of a tailor from a small town near Minsk in Lithuania recalled that "as soon as we were able to hold a needle, we were taught to sew."[25] Children learned to be extremely resourceful in exploiting any potential wage-generating activity in their overcrowded village economies. In the tailor's family, when the father was forced to leave home in order to avoid conscription into the czar's army, mother, grandparents, and children joined their efforts to replace his income. The daughters learned to spin and to mend any lost stitches in the stockings their blind grandmother made to sell. The mother sewed for women in the village and the grandfather mended pots. The daughter of a Hebrew teacher in a small town in Lithuania remembered how she and her brothers and sisters "helped out" by plucking chickens, rolling cigarettes, and washing clothes for people. The daughter of a Jewish blacksmith in Orlov, Pobelov, shared responsibility with her brothers and sisters for guarding the family's rented apple orchard, growing vegetables in a rented garden for the winter, and gathering berries in the woods. Her mother assisted in the blacksmith shop in addition to caring for her nine children. As in Italy, any income generated by individuals belonged to the family.[26] Family survival was dependent on the pooled labor resources of its members.

Wealthier families included their children in family enterprises, not out of economic necessity as much as to teach them to value family unity. The son of a merchant from a town in Grodno, Russia, who owned three barges which carried goods up and down the river, remembered that he and his brothers were working as men at age sixteen, poling the barges to and from the market. The daughter of a wealthy merchant in Polotzk learned to keep her father's books and to deal smoothly with his Polish and Russian customers.[27] In these instances, family economic cooperation did not involve the pooling of wages since usually no money changed hands. Still, sharing in family work expressed an important sense of familial economic collectivity. The merchant's son recalled that poling the barge down the river was hard and the hours were long, but "nevertheless we enjoyed the work and did not mind the work because we felt that we were doing this for our father and therefore for ourselves."[28] Children were taught to see individual economic interests as indistinguishable from family well-being.

Social and economic change in southern Italy and eastern Europe unsettled ordinary family strategies by undermining the local basis of the family economy, thus creating the conditions that prompted emigration of family groups. In southern Italy, population increases expanded the number of young men and women entering the local labor market. Commercialization of agriculture in other parts of Italy made traditional agricultural methods of the south less competitive and heightened families' needs for extra nonagricultural income. But industrialization in other parts of Italy diminished the availability of artisan work on which sons and daughters had depended to supplement the family budget. As emigration began to depopulate the countryside, artisans had to face half-empty shops or join the exodus themselves. Although the increased availability of land to rent or to buy offered the hope that families might be able to accumulate land to supplement their resources, the actual means of adding to the family income were diminishing.[29] One peasant from Abruzzi described both the raised hopes and the economic constraints that prompted his father's emigration to the United States:

> The year before, my father had been trying to better our conditions. He had hired two large pieces of arable ground on which he had toiled almost every minute of daylight during that whole season. Having no money to make the first payment on the land, he had to borrow some at a very high rate of interest. At the end of that season, after selling the crops, he found that he had just barely enough money to pay back the rest of the rent and to pay back the loan with the enormous interest.... That season of excessive toil made my father much older. His tall strong body was beginning to bend. He had become a little clumsy and slower. And the result of his futile attempt made him moody and silent. He would sit on our doorstep in the evening and gaze out.

Not surprisingly, the father came to redefine economic opportunity in terms of migration.[30]

Jewish families also experienced new uncertainty and instability in their attempts to sustain themselves economically. The abolition of serfdom in 1861 dissolved the traditional relationship between nobles and peasants, and with it, the role of Jewish agents and middlemen. The waves of pogroms—violent attacks on Jewish communities—in the 1880s and 1890s were brutal evidence of the new, more uncertain relationship between Jew and peasant. The introduction of modern industrial tools depressed, but did not displace, artisan crafts, while increased machine production for markets forced artisans to produce for stores rather than for individual customers. All through the last part of the nineteenth century, the economic position of Jews deteriorated even as their numbers increased; from 1847 to 1897, the population of Jews in the Pale tripled.[31]

Emigration was itself a familial strategy to relieve these economic problems, a strategy with particular appeal in areas dominated by household production. In areas of central Italy, for example, a higher concentration of property ownership meant that the dream of owning one's land was beyond the reach of most people, and the large groups of laborers who worked together on the vast estates turned to political and trade-union organization, rather than to migration, to better their conditions. The broader distribution of land in the south, which once would have tied sons to native villages through inheritances, now provided an impetus to seek work across the ocean. Many Italian families initially conceived of emigration as a way of reaching out to longer-distance job opportunities in order to supplement the family income and to accumulate land.[32] Although some Jews fled Russia in the wake of the pogroms, for most Jewish families (as for Italian families) emigration was an attempt to take advantage of less-circumscribed economic opportunities.[33] Social and economic conditions directed family strategizing toward migration.

The Italian and Jewish immigrants who came to communities such as Providence expected to work as part of a family toward common family goals. Some had particular skills and experience. Depending on the region of origin and on the year of emigration, from 10 to 25 percent of male Italian immigrants, roughly 15 percent of female Italian immigrants, and about 60 percent of Jewish immigrants had worked as artisans or in manufacturing in Europe.[34] Nearly all the immigrants, whether peasants or day laborers, artisans or small traders, were accustomed to making decisions about work according to family rather than individual priorities, even if they did not work at the same place at the same time. They expected each member of the family to contribute labor to the task of making a family living, as he or she had done in Europe. Both Italian and Jewish immigrants were used to taking initiative for searching out and engaging in various kinds of income-generating work. Because most either hired out their own labor or hired labor themselves, sold farm produce or produced crafts, they were of necessity accustomed to exchange in the marketplace. Both peasants and artisans placed a premium on skill in manipulating money and commerce. Some may have already undertaken short-term migration. This wide range of experience proved to be a crucial resource in confronting the circumstances that lay ahead.

IMMIGRANT FAMILY WORK EXPERIENCE IN PROVIDENCE

How did the immigrants who found their way to Providence situate themselves there?[35] Half of the Italian immigrants, who were probably unskilled laborers and agricultural workers in Italy, found jobs as laborers and factory workers when they arrived in Providence (see table 2-1). They came to a growing city, echoing with the sounds of construction. Major municipal building projects, like the State House constructed between 1896 and 1901 and a streetcar tunnel completed by 1914, provided some immigrants with jobs as unskilled construction workers, excavators, and hod carriers. Other unskilled laborers and former agricultural workers found work in the jewelry shops, foundries, machine shops, and textile mills that skirted the neighborhood (see map 2-3). While many Italian immigrants were familiar with the pick and shovel, tools of the laborer, the factories were new workplaces. Italian laborers looked for work with stable conditions and familiar faces. Many gravitated to the more secure jobs, working for the city or for the railroad, jobs that they kept for thirty and forty years. Factory operatives tended to cluster in certain companies and rooms that others before them had marked as good for Italians. One immigrant machinist, working at one of the largest machine tool companies in Providence, found himself so frequently in the company of other Italians that he never needed to learn English during his forty years of working there.[36]

Smaller numbers of Jewish immigrants worked as laborers or in factories. Instead, 46 percent of the Jewish immigrants in the neighborhood began their work lives in Providence as peddlers and shop assistants. The daughter of one Jewish immigrant to the Providence area described the transformation of her father from a Hebrew teacher in Russia to a peddler in this country. He had assumed that he would be a Hebrew teacher here since he knew no English. But his friends who had preceded him to the area had a grocery store and a dry goods store.

> Papa says, he could never do anything like that, so his friends sent him to Rabbi Bachrach, a well-known, wise rabbi then, who asked him what he wanted to do. He said he wanted to be a teacher and the rabbi asked him, do you

2-1. An Italian laborer helps dig gas mains for the Providence Gas Company, ca. 1900. Photograph courtesy of the *Providence Journal-Bulletin*.

TABLE 2-1. Occupations of Italian and Jewish Male Immigrant Household Heads Over Time

Occupation	First Recorded Job				Job in 1915				Last Recorded Job			
	Italian		Jewish		Italian		Jewish		Italian		Jewish	
Laborer	27%	(42)	7%	(5)	11%	(17)	—	(0)	19%	(30)	—	(0)
Factory operative	20%	(31)	10%	(7)	22%	(33)	8%	(5)	17%	(27)	4%	(3)
Skilled	7%	(11)	—	(0)	6%	(9)	—	(0)	6%	(9)	—	(0)
Craft, artisan employee	19%	(30)	8%	(6)	16.5%	(25)	5%	(3)	14%	(22)	10%	(7)
Retail employee	6%	(10)	46%	(32)	16.5%	(25)	40%	(25)[a]	11.5%	(18)	30%	(21)
Craft, artisan self-employed	17%	(27)	6%	(4)	19%	(29)	6%	(4)	19%	(30)	6%	(4)
Retail self-employed	1%	(2)	17%	(12)	6%	(9)	30%	(19)	11.5%	(18)	41%	(29)
Professional	3%	(4)	6%	(4)	3%	(5)	11%	(7)	2%	(3)	9%	(6)
TOTAL	100%	(157)[b]	100%	(70)[b]	100%	(152)	100%	(63)	100%	(157)	100%	(70)

Source: Neighborhood data.

a. Includes 23 peddlars (37%).

b. 1915 job data were derived from the 1915 state census. First and last recorded jobs were derived from the city directories. The *N* in "First Recorded Job" and "Last Recorded Job" includes 5 Italian and 7 Jewish male heads of household who had died by 1915.

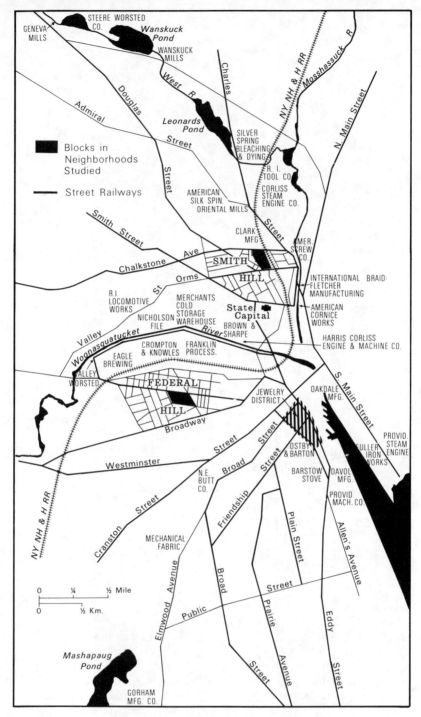

Map 2-3. Providence Factories, 1918

Source: Sanborn Insurance Atlas, 1899, Corrected to 1918 (Providence: Sanborn and Perris, 1899), vol. 1–2; *Providence Street Directory*, 1915 (Providence: Sampson and Murdock, 1914); Gary Kulik and Julia Bonham, *An Inventory of Historic Engineering and Industrial Sites* (Washington, D.C.: Government Printing Office, 1978), pp. 168–219.

2-2.   A man with a pushcart in front of Hyman Yaffee's Bakery Shop at 175 Chalkstone Avenue, Smith Hill, 1903–5. Photograph courtesy of the Rhode Island Historical Society (RHi X3 1164).

want to make money or do you just want to keep on
teaching—in those days Hebrew teachers made nothing,
practically.

When her father replied to the rabbi that he had a wife and daughter
he wanted to bring over, the rabbi advised him definitely to become a
"businessman," so the former Hebrew teacher took up his new
occupation, peddling from house to house.[37] Although peddling
required no more skill or capital than factory work, it involved credit
transactions which placed the peddler potentially in the position of
an entrepreneur. One Jewish immigrant expressed the personal
hopes and ambitions that were kindled by becoming a peddler:

> [The partner] took me to the factory where the tinware was
> made. There was an English man there who gave me a
> basket filled with a variety of tinware. The bill came to $6.40
> and was written in English which I could not understand.
> But I felt happy that I had become a businessman. I went
> back to my lodging feeling that I might become a big
> businessman—perhaps even a tinware manufacturer.[38]

Some Jewish manufacturers continued to sell door to door until they
grew too old to work, while others managed to set up small shops
and let the customers come to them. The fact that relatively few from
the Russian Jewish commercial class immigrated to the United States
meant that there was opportunity for immigrants without prior
commercial experience to compete for markets in the newly forming
local Jewish economies, such as Providence.[39] Forty-one percent of
the Jewish immigrants in the neighborhood became self-employed
grocers, butchers, fish dealers, or dry goods shopkeepers.

Only 6 percent of the Italians in the neighborhood worked as
teamsters or peddlers. Perhaps the explanation of one Italian who
immigrated to Bridgeport, Connecticut, also described the situation
in Providence. According to this woman, employment as a laborer or
factory worker was preferable to working on one's own as a
peddler.

> Sometimes when the Italian men could not get the jobs in
> the pick and shovel they used to try to work in the foundry
> and if they could get no job in that place they start to sell the
> rags. Maybe sometimes they get a horse and the wagon and
> they go to sell fruit. . . . In Italy you never hear this. In Italy
> we have no people that go with the wagon to get rags.

Coming from rural origins in southern Italy, she had no previous experience with peddling; street vendors were more common in Italian cities.[40]

Relatively few of the recent Italian arrivals tried to start their own retail businesses. They seem to have been inhibited by lack of access to capital and credit resources and by lack of direct experience with retailing. One Sicilian shopkeeper in Bridgeport described these obstacles, remembering that in the early days of immigration, "the people that come here they afraid to get in business because they don't know how the business goes." Working on the farm or "in the trade," rural southern Italians may not have had experience with small businesses.[41] But by 1915, a few more Italians had situated themselves with corner grocery shops and liquor stores, having accumulated the necessary savings and having learned the merchandising skills. The needs of other immigrants in the crowded ethnic neighborhoods guaranteed customers. Grocers stocked imported olive oils and pasta, butchers made special spicy sausages to meet the taste of their neighbors and customers. As one Italian storekeeper explained, "I specialize in Italian grocery because Italians always eat the Italian style."[42] Many kept accounts for credit, and shoppers could bargain in their own dialect.[43] Almost 12 percent of the Italian immigrants in the neighborhood eventually became retail proprietors.

Nearly half of all the Italian immigrants to the neighborhood in Providence worked as skilled craftsmen and artisans. Many of the Italian tailors and stonecutters, watchmakers and bakers were able to transfer their skills, and they found a steady clientele for their goods and services in the Italian neighborhood. Tailors depended on their countrymen's loyalty when buying a wedding suit. Barbers learned the new American hairstyles, and Italian men were comfortable having their hair cut and hearing the news in a place where the dialect from their region was spoken. The camaraderie of the neighborhood was not an unmixed blessing. One daughter whose father was a barber in the Italian neighborhood in Providence and whose husband was a barber in a downtown shop explained that in the Italian neighborhood, "You had to be content with talk but no tips, but if a man got a haircut downtown, he felt obliged to leave a tip."[44] Perhaps this differential explains why some artisans worked outside the neighborhood: several tailors fitted suits in downtown department stores by the 1930s, and one barber was hired by the shop of a large downtown hotel.[45]

The neighborhood market enabled some craftsmen to establish themselves as self-employed proprietors. By 1915, many had their own shops, or at least a front room in their tenements, and they continued in business for themselves until they retired. Nearly one-fifth of Italian immigrants in the neighborhood became self-employed craftsmen. Of course some craftsmen, shoemakers in particular, faced considerable downgrading of their skills in this country. They found themselves relegated to shoe-repair work, as this Bridgeport shoemaker reported:

> The real shoemaker trade, like I learn it on the other side, is hard because you have to make the shoe yourself. That's why you have to be better than the mechanic. In this country it is only shoe repair. This is nothing.[46]

Consequently, shoemakers found it difficult to make a living at their trade. Nearly half of the shoemakers who came to the neighborhood eventually took up other work. One Italian immigrant to Providence, who had followed his father and brother into shoemaking in Italy, came to America to establish himself as a shoemaker. He left after several months, discouraged by factory competition. When he returned, eight years later, he took up the trade of tailor.[47] Another shoemaker found himself working in a textile mill in Providence. He married a co-worker and had a child in Providence, but then decided to return to shoemaking as he had known it in Italy. He took his wife and small child back to southern Italy and lived for five years in his wife's native village, working in a cobbler shop next door to his house. In 1911, he decided that he preferred factory work in American to shoemaking in Italy, so the family returned to Providence to stay.[48]

Some immigrants may have used a combination of factory employment and artisan skills to tide them over the unstable cycles of industrial work that they found in Providence. One immigrant to Providence who was trained as a shoemaker by his father-in-law used his craft as a resource during periods of unemployment. Whenever he faced a layoff at the big hardware and machinery manufacturing company where he worked, he would open a repair shop and conduct business as a shoemaker. When the company was hiring again, he would sell the shop and work again as a machinist, his trade from Italy.[49] Other immigrant craftsmen used their skills to escape from what they considered to be the intolerable grind of the factory and the arbitrary authority of the foreman. One Bridgeport shoemaker who had also worked as a nickle plater and as a brass polisher explained his preference for his craft:

I go back to the trade because that's my life. Nobody tells me when I have to work, nobody could tell me how I have to work, and I'm the boss, myself. When I want to read the papers I sit down and I take my time. If you work in the shops you have to be like machine. . . . Why, I feel just like a king, because I have to do only my work, and that's all. When I feel like to quit, I quit; when I feel like to work, I work . . . the man that got the trade never be's sorry because he have the trade and keep it and always have half-a-dollar in the pockets.[50]

Some craftsmen defended their trade specifically in terms of its potential service to the family, hoping that their skills could be transmitted to their children to provide for the next generation. This Italian tailor in Bridgeport described his choice of a trade in these terms:

I want that my oldest boy learn my trade because I tell him that you could always make at least enough for the family. This way when I get older I could give him the business, and I could work too, and when I get tired he could take care of the business for his own.[51]

Artisan and retail shops also served as social centers for the Italian community. Neighbors used grocery stores as banks, corner stores were common meeting places, and restaurants and saloons were the focal point of male sociability.[52]

Fewer Jewish immigrants worked as artisans in this country. Some found that their craft skills were made obsolete by machines. This was the experience of one Jewish immigrant to New Haven:

I was a tailor in Russia, and a good one, too. I liked my work. I liked it like a painter likes his work. When I used to finish making a coat it was good and I would get much pleasure from it. I would look at it and feel good all over like I made a beautiful sculpture. . . . In America, when I went to work in a factory, I felt like a machine. Here is a bigger speed-up, hurry-up.[53]

The stirrings of industrialization in the Pale already may have begun to erode Jewish artisan skills, making their craft less compelling. This was the case with one Jewish shoemaker, already discontented with his craft in Russia, who worked as an unskilled operative in a machine shop in this country.[54] Perhaps this explains the work experience of a Jewish immigrant to the neighborhood in Providence who worked as a woolen weaver in Russia and as a bakery peddler here.[55] Artisans in the crowded shtetls had to market aggressively to sell their wares,[56] and immigrants may have fallen back on their commercial rather than craft skills when they arrived in Providence. Roughly 10 percent of the Jewish immigrant men in the neighborhood worked as artisan employees in Providence, and 6 percent worked as self-employed craftsmen. Like those Italian artisans who stayed in their trades, Jewish craftsmen valued the autonomy possible for a proprietor. One Jewish immigrant, apprenticed to a tailor in Russia, reminisced about how he felt when he was able to open his own shop in New Haven. It was a "grand feeling" for him to come and go as he liked "without being told by a boss."

In these ways, Italian and Jewish men transformed themselves into an indispensable part of Providence's economic life. Some Italian laborers and Italian and Jewish artisans found new workplaces but familiar occupations in Providence. Some Italians came to know new working conditions in the factories. Many Jews took advantage of new commercial opportunities engendered by the growth of the immigrant neighborhoods and the bustling marketplace of the city. But as in the old country, economic burdens did not rest only on men's shoulders. The differing ways in which immigrant men situated themselves had great importance for the opportunities women and children found in Providence to help put together a family living.

Many Italian and Jewish wives found ways to contribute to a family economy as they had done in southern Italy and in Russia, although childbearing and childrearing placed very real constraints on the ability of mothers to work outside the home.[58] Many of the work opportunities which mothers had found in Italy had grown out of an agricultural economy—working as day laborers in neighboring fields, for example, or raising and peddling chickens and eggs. It would be harder to take a baby to a factory than to place her under the nearest shade tree in the fields. In the shtetl, Jewish mothers had similarly depended on the overlap of home and work to care for children at the same time as serving customers at an inn, sewing for soldiers, or selling dry goods in a front room. But in Providence, immigrant women found themselves in a city in which working women had been a part of the factory landscape since Rhode Island's industrial transformation in the nineteenth century.[59] Some of women's old-country artisan skills lost their cash value in Providence; delicately crafted lace and fine hand weaving could not

2-3. Wood scavenged from the dump helped women to stretch scarce family income. This immigrant mother and child were photographed at the refuse dump on West Exchange, Federal Hill, 1903. Photograph courtesy of the Rhode Island Historical Society (RHi X3 18).

2-4. Male teamsters appear to have unloaded the refuse that the women and children are picking through at the dump on West Exchange Street, Federal Hill, 1903. Photograph courtesy of the Rhode Island Historical Society (RHi X3 486).

compete with the products of Rhode Island's textile mills. But immigrant women brought with them a profound confidence in their abilities and great resourcefulness in exploiting unfamiliar kinds of opportunities for work. One Italian immigrant to Providence, who had lived on a farm and in a small city in Italy, exuded this confidence in her words: "I never have a lot of money, but I have my hands. . . . The money you have, that no mean nothing, only I know." She was proud of her skills: "I know how to do, I know everything." And she was sure that at least people from a similar background would be able to recognize her strengths, because "that's the way they look, in the old country."[60] Immigrant wives would find an economic place in Providence.

In Providence, immigrant women's household work had an increased economic value because of the community's greater dependence on a market economy. Without gardens, the cost of feeding a family depended on women's skill at bargaining with grocers, fishmongers, butchers. With little home ownership in the early years and no communal norms of long-term leases as had been the case in many Italian towns and Russian villages, the extent of pressure to pay rent would depend on women's skill at dealing with the landlords.[61]

In addition, many immigrant wives were frequently able to find ways to generate income in conjunction with their household responsibilities. At least 41 percent of Italian immigrant wives and 31 percent of Jewish immigrant wives in the neighborhoods were engaged in some work that made extra money for their families (see table 2-2).[62] Most of this work took place in their homes.

Sometimes women had artisan skills that they could exploit successfully in this country, such as dressmaking. The wives of neighborhood craftsmen and artisans whose shops were in front of or below their rooms could and frequently did work alongside their husbands in the shop. Women could make and sell goods without neglecting home duties. Some women ran neighborhood shops on their own. When one Providence Jewish immigrant's husband died, she moved her children to a tenement with a shop on the first floor and ran a neighborhood market and variety store for fourteen years. Another Jewish immigrant woman, whose husband was a peddler, kept boarders. When one of her tenants was deserted by her husband, the tenant asked to convert the front room of the tenement into a grocery store. The tenant moved away after a few months, but the landlady couldn't see letting the store go to waste, so she took it over and ran it profitably enough to pay off the mortgage on the tenement as well as mortgages on some other property her husband owned.[63]

TABLE 2-2. Recorded Income-generating Work of Immigrant Wives, 1915–35

Occupation	Italian		Jewish	
Keeping boarders and wage-earning relatives	29%	(47)	17%	(12)
Shopkeepers	4%	(6)	11%	(8)
Dressmakers	3%	(5)	1.3%	(1)
Factory operatives	3%	(5)	—	(0)
Industrial homeworkers	1%	(2)	—	(0)
Service workers (housekeeper, laundress)	1%	(2)	1.3%	(1)
No reported work	59%	(95)	69.4%	(50)
TOTAL	100%	(162)	100%	(72)
Total recorded working wives	41%	(67)	31%	(22)

Sources: Neighborhood data; N family interview, Providence, Rhode Island, 2 September 1977; school lists of families doing homework collected in preparation of U.S. Department of Labor Children's Bureau Bulletin No. 100, *Industrial Homework of Children* (1922), National Archives, Record Group 102, box 978-9; school lists of families doing homework and interview schedules of homeworkers collected in preparation of U.S. Department of Labor Women's Bureau Bulletin No. 131, *Industrial Homework in Rhode Island* (1935), National Archives, Record Group 86, box 297-8.

Wives often earned money at home by cooking and cleaning for boarders and lodgers, who were likely to be families who had just arrived or new immigrants working for the passage money to bring other members of their own families to this country. The needs of the newer migrants for room and board meant that women could be economically productive by extending the services they were already providing for their own families. In cities of eastern Europe, Jewish women had earned money by keeping boarders,[64] but Italian women were first introduced to this strategy in American cities. One Italian immigrant wife in Bridgeport explained how she came to take care of her house and cook for four boarders. When she first arrived, she "didn't want to do this because everyone wants to have their own house." But she changed her mind about taking in boarders because "everyone was doing this thing." Boarders were a way of life in immigrant neighborhoods, as she recalled:

> That time some of the people that came from the other side didn't have no place to stay and we took some of the people in the house that we knew. . . . This is the way that everybody used to do it that time. . . . The Italian people were not the only ones that used to have the boarders, all the other nationalities used to do the same thing. After a long time

2-5. Women populate an open-air market on Federal Hill as buyers and sellers, 1925. Photograph courtesy of the *Providence Journal Bulletin.*

these people that used to have the board they had their families here and they start to have their own place.[65]

Industrial homework offered another way for women to work at home. Various Providence industries divided and subdivided the process of manufacture, resulting in the proliferation of small tasks which could be done outside the shops. Homeworkers provided manufacturers with a cheap reserve labor force for the busy seasons. Snaps to card, chains to link, military buttons to stamp on a foot press, rosary beads to string, artificial flowers to stem, lace threads to pull: all were widely available in Providence on a seasonal basis. Often the work was subcontracted through neighborhood networks, with one woman acting as a distributor for families within several blocks.[66] Clearly, for women who had children at home, homework was an important alternative to going out to work: "I have two children and would rather be home to get them something to eat at mealtimes." As little money as homework generated, it provided a way for women to be economically productive. One woman remarked that she liked to have her own money: "I like to work and would rather have $50 earned myself than $100 saved out of my husband's pay."[67]

Most of the newly arrived wives did not go to work in the factories in Providence. Frequently they had neither mothers nor aunts in Providence to care for their children during factory hours. They had no contacts in the factories to allow them to quit and resume work in response to cycles of childrearing, or to be given a "mother's shift" which would match school hours. But oral history evidence suggests that some immigrant wives did work outside the home. They were able to do so if they had worked in Providence before marriage and had work experience and connections to employment. As a general rule, married women moved in and out of the work force depending on their husband's income and employment, the number of children to care for, the number of children who could work, the kinds of work open to women, and the availability of child care resources.[68] The Jewish woman who had peddled bagels in Bialystok when her husband had a slack season picked up her baskets again in this country when her husband was unemployed.

My father was a presser by pants. There was no work. My mother started to work with the rolls and the bread. So at least we had bread.

2-6.   A family shop on Federal Hill; the cigar factory of R. Delloiacone, 205 Atwells Avenue, 1912. Photograph taken by Lewis W. Hine, courtesy of the Slater Mill Historic Site. Hine's own description of the photo reads: "Eight year old boy and ten year old girl are stripping. This room is the living-sleeping-and working room and adjoins the store. Very dirty and ill-kept." Descendents of the family who owned the shop viewed this photograph in 1982 at an exhibit of Hine photographs at Slater Mill Historic Site and told the director of the museum that the only eating that went on in the work room was a lunch, prepared collectively, and that the only sleeping that went on there was by children who napped while their mothers worked on cigars. This information was provided by Patrick Malone, director of the Slater Mill Historic Site.

An Italian immigrant wife in Bridgeport explained the process by which she made the decision to work outside her home. After she got married to her husband, she "stay [home] a little bit" but her husband did not make enough money so she "go to work in the laundry because I want to help." She knew that her husband did not like her working, but as she put it, "I go just the same," adding that "in Italy when the husband doesn't make enough money the wife she have to work, too." When she had a baby, she stayed out of work for three years, but then she felt that she had to go back to her job when her husband lost his. When her husband found work again, he wanted her to stay home, but she was unconvinced by his argument.

> When my husband was lay off I go to look for job myself, nobody tells me. . . . Now my husband wants that I stop work because he have job now. I tell him "no" because I want to help a little bit. Maybe after we pay bills I stop.[69]

Immigrant wives who did work outside of their homes had to solve the problem of what to do with their children during working hours. One Providence Italian woman depended on the proximity of her husband's barbershop to their tenement for him to watch their two daughters while she went to work. As her daughter remembered the arrangements, there was just a small yard between the back door of the barbershop and the house, and she and her sister ran in and out of the shop all day long. Another Italian immigrant wife arranged for her oldest daughter to look after her younger children while she and her husband worked as farm laborers on the outskirts of Providence. Working in the neighborhood was a compromise that allowed women to have some access to their children while also holding regular employment. One Italian immigrant woman raising a family on her own in Providence had worked at home illegally making wine, anisette, and liquor. After she was caught by a government agent, she found a job at a bakery in the neighborhood. Here she could "keep an eye on" her five children, and when she finished her regular day's work, she used the ovens to bake pies and cookies which she sold on order to three or four neighborhood stores. Her children did the delivering.[70]

Children in Providence were very important contributors to a family economy, as the incident above suggests. Children younger than fifteen often worked with their mothers on whatever tasks the mothers took on. They helped at home by doing domestic chores for boarders. One Italian daughter helped her mother take care of their

2-7.   Children's family labor. A child carrying home a big bag on Spruce Street, Federal Hill, 1912. Photograph by Lewis W. Hine, courtesy of the Slater Mill Historic Site.

2-8.   A child engaged in industrial homework. Elvira Christofano, making chain bags in a room that appears to be a tailor shop, 110 Spruce Street, Federal Hill, 1912. Photograph by Lewis W. Hine, courtesy of the Slater Mill Historic Site.

three boarders by washing and ironing their clothes. Children also gave up their living space to provide extra income. A Jewish salesman's daughter remembered that her family had met hard times by renting the room that her invalid grandmother had been sharing with her aunt; now her grandmother and mother took her room and she and her aunt shared the sofa in the living room. Young children also routinely helped their mothers work on industrial homework. In 1918, Children's Bureau investigators reporting on child labor in Providence found that homework was so common in the Italian neighborhood that children brought chains with them to school to link at recess on fine spring days. The investigators were horrified to discover that teachers in the neighborhood schools had actually encouraged their students to do homework during class so that the pupils might earn money to contribute to Liberty Bonds or the Red Cross.[71]

As exploitative of workers as homework may have been, it was one of the ways in which immigrant families inculcated the values of family economic cooperation. A Jewish son remembered the whole family sitting around the kitchen table bending wire or setting stones, together doing the work his father brought home from the jewelry shop where he worked during the busy season before Christmas. One Italian daughter whose father owned a bakery remembered home-work as part of a family orientation towards constant work:

> We were raised to work every minute. When a child was five or six and could hold a plier, my mother would sit us around the table and we would link jewelry. We'd link chains and rosary beads, or mesh purses. Even the boys did this.

For another Italian daughter, whose father was a self-employed barber and whose mother worked in a textile mill, working on mesh bags was her earliest economic contribution: "I was a little kid, I used to help and make that extra little money."[72]

The oral history evidence suggests that families did their best to minimize the pressures on their children even though they depended on their financial contribution. Parents tried to take advantage of their home workplaces to humanize the environment in which the homework was done. The Jewish son quoted above remembered homework as "play for me." In the Italian bakery owner's family,

> It was like a game. Visiting kids would sit down and link in our house. Whoever did the most would get some extra

2-9 and 2-10. Children's labor in the home workplace. Ernest and Thomas Lonardo, eleven and fourteen years old, setting stones in cheap jewelry, 6 Hewitt Street, Federal Hill, 1912. Girls, six and nine, working on chain bags in the home of Mrs. Antonio Caruso, 132 Knight Street, Federal Hill, 1912. Photographs by Lewis W. Hine, courtesy of the Slater Hill Historic Site.

2-11.   Children's labor as news sellers. Italian newsboys, Federal Hill, 1903;
photograph courtesy of the Rhode Island Historical Society (RHi X3 121).

snack or candy or fruit. My mother would make between $2
and $4 dollars a week this way.

In another Italian family, 1920s Hollywood movies and fresh-baked
pastries were part of the setting for doing jewelry homework:

[I] was about . . . thirteen years old. And then my mother
would send me to the Uptown Theatre, in the afternoon,
after school, and I would watch the movie. And then, at
night, when we would sit down and do the work, I would tell
my brothers and sisters about the movie I saw. . . . I used to
tell them the whole movie. And that kept us busy doing the
work. We used to stop and have our milk and cocoa, some
pastry; my mother would bake during the day.[73]

2-12. Irene Cohen, ten-year-old newsgirl, 1912.

2-13. Dominic M. Giouchino, eight-year-old newsie, 1912. Photographs by Lewis W. Hine, courtesy of the Slater Mill Historic Site.

For these children, homework seemed no different from other domestic chores that their parents expected them to perform to help the family.

Family businesses absorbed child labor as easily as they did female labor. Particularly when family businesses were located near living quarters, domestic chores naturally extended into work in the shop. Both sons and daughters lent a hand, and in many cases keeping a family enterprise going consumed a large share of the family's life together. One Italian daughter remembered how much of her young adolescence was spent in her family's Providence bakery. When she was still in school, she rose at five o'clock in the morning to make the bread and clean the trays before going to classes. When she graduated from the eighth grade, she went to work in the bakery full-time, using her math education to manage the bakery's books. Both of her brothers also worked in the bakery. None of the children faced an explicit demand for their full-time labor in the bakery, but it seemed natural to them to join their parents there.[74]

Sons and daughters usually began to work outside the home at age fifteen or sixteen. Families trying to find legal employment for their underage children often had a hard time of it. One immigrant daughter remembered that her parents "put me in a long dress. They made me look old." Still, when her father asked for working papers, the official in charge laughed at him: "Kids like this should ask for working papers?" The official asserted that the daughter was too young and too small; she did not have the age or the height. So she went back to the only kind of work she could do in her neighborhood: "I have to watch children. Be a sitter. You make five cents a day, that's all." Legal employment seemed a great advantage over this underpaid casual work. In Rhode Island in 1902 the age of legal employment was thirteen; it was fourteen by 1907 and fifteen by the mid-1920s.[75]

In 1915, 95 percent of Italian sons fifteen and older who were living at home were recorded as working. Seventy-eight percent of Italian daughters fifteen and older were recorded as working. Fewer Jewish children but still sizable majorities were at work—67 percent of the sons and 58 percent of the daughters (see table 2-3). Children not at work were presumably in school or working in the home. The 1915 census did not record school attendance but other studies of the same period suggest that the differences between work-force participation of Italian and Jewish children probably reflect differing rates of school attendance as well. Jewish immigrants may have had

TABLE 2-3. Wage-earning Children at Home, 15+, 1915

	Italian		Jewish	
Sons Employed	95%	(56)	67%	(28)
Unemployed	5%	(3)	33%	(14)
TOTAL	100%	(59)	100%	(42)
Daughters Employed	78%	(40)	58%	(18)
Unemployed	22%	(11)	42%	(13)
TOTAL	100%	(51)	100%	(31)

Source: Neighborhood data.

greater opportunities for achieving literacy in the old country than Italian immigrants had and so may have come to America more prepared to take advantage of public schooling here. The commerical work that Jews were more likely to undertake may have given their families more resources to devote to education and more inclination towards education than the kinds of work into which Italians settled.[76]

When children did go to work outside the home, they often followed family connections.[77] In 1915, 20 percent of Italian children and 17 percent of Jewish children in the neighborhoods were in the same occupations as their fathers. Sisters and brothers also paved the way for each other at work: 34 percent of Italian sons and 60 percent of Italian daughters worked in the same occupation as a brother or sister did, most frequently in tailor shops, dressmaking establishments, and barbershops, but also in jewelry shops, textile mills, and neighborhood markets. Forty-seven percent of Jewish sons and 25 percent of Jewish daughters worked in the same occupation as a brother or sister, most frequently in retail shops, but also in factories and craft shops. Fathers, brothers, and sisters in the same workplace might be able to fill openings with family, train the newly hired in their jobs, try to protect less experienced employees from arbitrary authority or sexual harassment, and generally operate as a familiar group in an impersonal setting. One Italian immigrant daughter recalled the sense of security and safety she felt going to work at the age of fourteen at a woolen mill in North Providence where her brothers and sisters worked.[78] Family members who shared an occupation rather than a workplace obviously could not have the same impact on each other's daily work lives, but they could share valuable information about job openings, wages, hours, and working conditions.

For children, one of the most important differences between working at home and going out to work was the payment of an individual wage. When children helped with homework, cared for boarders, or worked behind the counter in family shops, the income produced was clearly generated by family effort and obviously belonged to the family. But children working outside the home were paid what were unmistakably their own wages. The values of familial economic cooperation dictated that children contribute their wages to the support of the family. Immigrants themselves had been expected to send wages home to parents left behind in Europe, although the distance across the ocean made this norm impossible to enforce. One Italian immigrant remembered that he had come with the blessings of his father and the directive not to "forget the family": as soon as the immigrant son could send money home, he was to do so "right away." A Jewish immigrant had left a blind father and a stepmother in Russia, and again, the father had asked his son not to forget him, which the son knew meant that he should send home the first money that he earned in America. Applying the expectation of support to his own children, one Italian immigrant assumed that when his children grew up, "They take care of themselves and help the family too." When his children were old enough to work, he expected them to find employment and to make money so "the family could go ahead."[79]

Immigrant sons and daughters commonly recalled passing their unopened pay envelopes to their parents. But sometimes their wage work made them feel entitled to a bit of its compensation, as this Jewish immigrant daughter recalled. She had come to the United States, joining her father in the garment shops to work for the passage money to bring the rest of the family to this country, so her wages were claimed even more clearly "for the family." But one day she heard a girl boast to a friend about the penny she had with which she intended to buy candy. The immigrant daughter felt that she would like to have a cent "with which to do as I pleased." She asked her father for a penny and he gave it to her with a frown, saying, "see that this never happens again." As she wrote, "I felt as if the coin were burning my fingers. I handed it back quickly." But she was deeply hurt by her father's remonstrance, feeling that she worked from morning till night like a grown person yet was not readily entitled to a single cent. When the daughter passively protested her father's disapproval by refusing to eat supper, he beat her with a twisted towel.

Finally he threw it down and said, panting for breath, "Girl
I'll break you if you don't change." And I said in my heart,
my father, we shall see.[80]

Clearly the disposition of family money was a cornerstone of parental
authority in the family, and a child's attempt to make a claim on
those wages was a serious challenge to that authority.

Most of the time children turned their wages over to the family
without question, and unmarried children's labor could then
substitute for married women's paid labor. When their children were
very young, mothers had no alternative to their own labor to
supplement the family income. In 1915, nearly half of the young
married Italian women and one-fourth of the young Jewish women
in the neighborhoods were recorded as taking in boarders and
housing wage-earning relatives. Countless others probably did
homework or helped their husbands run grocery and tailor shops.
When the children began to reach the age of fifteen, working age in
Rhode Island, mothers were more likely to depend on the children's
wages to add to the family resources than to work themselves (see
table 2-4).[81]

In one important respect, familial economic cooperation extended beyond the boundaries of individual family groups of parents
and children. Separate households probably did not pool incomes,
but kin outside the household were very crucial in the process of
finding work. The economic constraints that Italians and Jews had
faced in Europe had made family cooperation a critical strategy for
survival, but at the same time the small size of fields in southern Italy
and the competitiveness of the overcrowded labor market in the Pale
had discouraged the formation of work groups larger than one
household. Working conditions in Providence, together with the
exigencies of migration, stimulated the forging of new connections
between households.

The recruitment structures of the factories and the entrepreneurial opportunities in the immigrant neighborhoods were
amenable to extended family networks on the job. The factory
foreman's control over hiring made it relatively easy for immigrants
to get jobs for one another. Men offered to speak to their foremen for
newly arrived brothers, and if there was work, the brother usually got
it. Sisters did the same for younger sisters. As immigrants themselves
moved into positions with responsibility for hiring, the possibilities
were expanded for working with other family members. As one
Italian immigrant who worked in a rubber plant recalled:

A little later on, I was more in a position, you know what I mean, to help some of my relatives to get a job. See? And so, I think I must have gotten at least seven or eight of them, I got Angelo the job over there, and my brother Michele the job, and my brother Tony, one time, and I think there were a couple of others on the outside too.[82]

Over half of the Italian factory workers in the neighborhood who had brothers in Providence worked with them in textile mills and jewelry shops (see table 2-5). In other cities, various ethnic groups were similarly able to establish contacts that enabled them to work with kin. Recent research has uncovered networks of kinship among Italian hosiery workers in Norristown, Pennsylvania, Italian cannery workers outside of Buffalo, New York, French Canadian textile workers in Manchester, New Hampshire, Slavic steelworkers in Steelton and Pittsburgh, and Italian steelworkers, railroad workers, and gas company laborers in Pittsburgh.[83]

The artisan tradition in Italy and eastern Europe, where fathers taught sons their craft and passed down to them the tools of their trade, meant that artisans arriving in Providence with their brothers were likely to share the same kind of work. Half of the Italian tailors, barbers, and shoemakers in the neighborhood who had brothers in Providence worked at the same trade. This was true for three-fourths of the bakers, watchmakers, and stonecutters. Commercial experience accumulated by families meant that small retail proprietors might take up the same line of business as their brothers. Junk dealers, wine sellers, poultry dealers, and butchers in the Jewish neighborhood had brothers in the same occupation (see table 2-5). Kin ties in Providence probably facilitated credit arrangements that enabled the new migrants to open up shop.

In Providence, then, as in other cities, immigrants were able to settle initially into occupations consonant with premigration work and family expectations. They worked in jobs for which they were prepared by work experience in the old country or jobs that seemed to fit with familiar patterns of life. Men, women, and children found opportunities within a commercial-industrial economy to make their labor yield a family living. The neighborhood market provided a stimulus to small-scale artisan production and commerce, and for many artisans and shopkeepers, home and workplace overlapped. Women and children used this setting and others to join their husbands and fathers in generating a family income, and kin networks spread through factory workrooms and local shops. But during the years in which these immigrants neared the end of their working lives and their sons and daughters established themselves in

TABLE 2-4. Income Sources in Addition to Head-of-Household Income, 1915: Contribution of Women and Children

	Wife 18–35				Wife 36+			
	Italian		Jewish		Italian		Jewish	
Keeping boarders and/or relatives	39.2%	(33)	23%	(5)	13%	(8)	5%	(2)
Recorded paid employment of wife	2.4%	(2)	—	(0)	3%	(2)	5%	(2)
Recorded paid employment of children	2.4%	(2)	—	(0)	65%	(40)	63%	(24)
Some combination of above	—	(0)	—	(0)	8%	(5)	3%	(1)
Income from head of household alone	56%	(47)	77%	(17)	11%	(7)	24%	(9)
TOTAL	100%	(84)	100%	(22)	100%	(62)	100%	(38)

Source: Neighborhood data.

TABLE 2-5. Male Kin Connections at Work, 1915–35

Occupational Classification	Men in Neighborhood in This Occupation		Men in Same Occupation as Brother[a]		Men with One Son in Same Occupation[b]	
	Italian	Jewish	Italian	Jewish	Italian	Jewish
Laborer	19% (30)	— (0)	4% (1)	— (0)	— (0)	— (0)
Factory operative	17% (27)	4% (3)	55% (6)	— (0)	63% (5)	— (0)
Skilled	6% (9)	— (0)	33% (2)	— (0)	— (0)	— (0)
Craft, artisan employee	14% (22)	10% (7)	63% (7)	— (0)	17% (4)	60% (3)
Retail employee	11.5% (18)	30% (21)	50% (2)	33% (3)	— (0)	27% (4)
Craft, artisan self-employed	19% (30)	6% (4)	56% (9)	— (0)	46% (12)	66% (2)
Retail self-employed	11.5% (18)	41% (29)	50% (8)	80% (8)	100% (16)	38% (10)
Professional	2% (3)	9% (6)	— (0)	— (0)	50% (2)	25% (1)
TOTAL	100% (157)	100% (70)				

Source: Neighborhood data.

a. Percentage of men who have brothers in Providence.
b. Percentage of men who have sons of working age 15+.

occupations, Providence and its local economy were in flux. Artificial wartime prosperity yielded in the 1920s to the decline of the cotton textile industry; then came the depression of the 1930s, which accentuated the shift in the kinds of employment available in the city. Aging immigrants and their sons and daughters faced a new set of economic possibilities, and they adjusted the norms of familial economic cooperation accordingly.

CHANGING DYNAMICS OF FAMILY WORK

Immigrants interviewed in Connecticut in the late 1930s were themselves conscious that work was changing. Large-scale economic and technological shifts in the organization of production had an impact on their own lives which they could describe. An Italian mason blamed machines for the hard times: "Man puts something in one machine and comes out all finished; pretty soon the machine do all the work and the people have nothing to work." An Italian cabinetmaker analyzed the effect of the specialization of labor on his loss of a market: "Now the shops have one man do all one kind of work with the machine and the other man do the other part. . . . This way they could sell so cheap that the people don't want to buy the work that I make." For an Italian grocer, the economies of scale which national supermarket chains could use to lower their prices meant that his neighborhood market could no longer attract customers:

> All the people like to buy in the chain stores they have uptown. One time the people from one nationality used to buy from people their own kind; now they are buying where they could get for cheaper money.

Competition from mass-produced goods sold by retail stores drove a Jewish tailor to give up his trade. Especially during the Great Depression, "most men cannot afford to have custom-made clothes . . . [now] I sell new and misfit clothes in my shop . . . where I must also do repairing, cleaning, and pressing to eke out a living."[84] The small artisan and retail shops that were so numerous in the immigrant community were beginning to disappear. The large structural shifts in the economy observed by these artisans included innovations in marketing and retailing, expansion of government and corporate bureaucracy, and increasingly technological and management-oriented directions of production. Taken together, they meant that children of immigrants would almost inevitably pursue long-term employment in jobs different from those their parents had found.[85]

Not surprisingly then, in Providence, many fewer sons worked as laborers and as small craft and retail proprietors. Instead, they worked as factory operatives, as clerks and salesmen in large retail establishments, and as professionals. Daughters were more likely to work in factories than their fathers or mothers had been, and were probably the first in their families to have the fluency in English and the familiarity with American culture to enable them to get jobs in offices and department stores (see tables 2-6, 2-7, 2-8, 2-9). Many of the children's generation moved into workplaces outside their parents' experience. Sons and daughters of self-employed tailors, dressmakers, and shoemakers became salespeople and clerks handling merchandise that competed with their parents' handicraft. Sons of junk peddlers sold automobiles, while sons of neighborhood shopkeepers sold insurance. Daughters worked as telephone operators and as secretaries. Sons and daughters of factory workers who themselves worked in jewelry shops and in the dwindling number of textile mills worked at high speeds on new machines that made the mechanical skills of their parents obsolete.[86] The decline of unskilled laborers and self-employed craftsmen and the rising proportion of semiskilled factory operatives and retail and clerical employees in Providence paralleled national economic trends.[87]

Inside families, these changes in occupation signified a break in work traditions. No longer were most children assuming occupations arranged for them by their parents. The aspect of the parent-child relationship that was based on the teaching and learning of specific work skills was frequently lost. Some sons of artisans did continue to work as tailors and barbers, a watchmaker taught his sons to repair watches, and a stonecutter trained one of his sons to work with stone. But generally, only self-employed craftsmen had the opportunity to train their children, and the opportunities for their sons and daughters to be self-employed were becoming increasingly rare. One Jewish cooper's son became a barrel dealer, but a Jewish baker's son worked for other people. One son of a self-employed Italian tailor tried to enter business as a tailor himself, but by 1935 he had been unemployed for several years and his household was supported by his wife's and two sisters' wages as factory workers. Only in the retail sector were fathers who managed their own businesses very likely to have sons and daughters follow them in their occupations (see table 2-6, 2-7, 2-8, 2-9). For example, an Italian florist-undertaker had three sons working in his business by 1940. Four of the five sons of a

TABLE 2-6. Italian Fathers and Sons: Occupations, 1940[a]

	FATHER'S OCCUPATION								
SON'S OCCUPATION	Laborer	Operative	Skilled	Craft Employee	Retail Employee	Craft Self-employed	Retail Self-employed	Professional	TOTAL
Laborer	5% (3)	7% (2)	17% (2)	12% (3)	7% (2)	4% (2)	— (0)	— (0)	6% (14)
Operative	42% (23)	36% (11)	41% (5)	16% (4)	14% (4)	12% (6)	— (0)	— (0)	23% (53)
Skilled	13% (7)	7% (2)	— (0)	12% (3)	7% (2)	6% (3)	4% (1)	— (0)	8% (18)
Craft employee	13% (7)	7% (2)	17% (2)	28% (7)	14% (4)	24.5% (13)	— (0)	— (0)	15% (35)
Retail employee	20% (11)	40% (12)	17% (2)	28% (7)	45% (13)	23.5% (12)	60% (15)	25% (1)	32% (73)
Craft self-employed	— (0)	— (0)	— (0)	— (0)	— (0)	16% (8)	— (0)	— (0)	3% (8)
Retail self-employed	2% (1)	— (0)	— (0)	— (0)	3% (1)	4% (2)	8% (2)	— (0)	3% (6)
City appointment	2% (1)	3% (1)	— (0)	— (0)	3% (1)	2% (1)	16% (4)	50% (2)	4% (10)
Professional	3% (2)	— (0)	8% (1)	4% (1)	7% (2)	8% (4)	12% (3)	25% (1)	6% (14)
TOTAL	100% (55)	100% (30)	100% (12)	100% (25)	100% (29)	100% (51)	100% (25)	100% (4)	100% (231)

Source: Neighborhood data.

a. Occupation listed is latest recorded occupation for both fathers and sons; for fathers, occupation in 1940, or last occupation listed in Providence, or last occupation listed prior to death; for sons, occupation in 1940 or last occupation listed in Providence.

TABLE 2-7. Jewish Fathers and Sons: Occupations, 1940[a]

SON'S OCCUPATION	FATHER'S OCCUPATION								
	Laborer	Operative	Skilled	Craft Employee	Retail Employee	Craft Self-employed	Retail Self-employed	Professional	TOTAL
Laborer	0	0	0	— (0)	3% (1)	— (0)	2% (1)	— (0)	1.5% (2)
Operative	0	0	0	9.5% (1)	16% (5)	12.5% (1)	3% (2)	— (0)	8% (9)
Skilled	0	0	0	— (0)	10% (3)	— (0)	7% (4)	40% (2)	8% (9)
Craft employee	0	0	0	36% (4)	3% (1)	37.5% (3)	5% (3)	— (0)	10% (11)
Retail employee	0	0	0	18% (2)	62% (19)	25% (2)	49% (29)	20% (1)	46% (53)
Craft self-employed	0	0	0	9.5% (1)	— (0)	12.5% (1)	3% (2)	— (0)	3.5% (4)
Retail self-employed	0	0	0	27% (3)	6% (2)	12.5% (1)	19% (11)	— (0)	15% (17)
Professional	0	0	0	— (0)	— (0)	— (0)	12% (7)	40% (2)	8% (9)
TOTAL				100% (11)	100% (31)	100% (8)	100% (59)	100% (5)	100% (114)

Source: Neighborhood data.

a. Occupation listed is latest recorded occupation for both fathers and sons; for fathers, occupation in 1940, last occupation listed in Providence, or occupation listed prior to death; for sons, occupation in 1940, or latest occupation listed in Providence.

TABLE 2-8. Italian Fathers and Daughters: Occupations, 1940[a]

DAUGHTER'S OCCUPATION	FATHER'S OCCUPATION								
	Laborer	Operative	Skilled	Craft Employee	Retail Employee	Craft self-employed	Retail self-employed	Professional	TOTAL
Service worker	— (0)	3% (1)	— (0)	— (0)	— (0)	— (0)	— (0)	— (0)	.5% (1)
Operative	59% (30)	58% (19)	60% (6)	27% (7)	20% (4)	34% (17)	13% (2)	— (0)	40.5% (85)
Skilled	— (0)	6% (2)	— (0)	— (0)	— (0)	— (0)	— (0)	— (0)	1% (2)
Craft employee	11.5% (6)	9% (3)	10% (1)	8% (2)	5% (1)	22% (11)	6% (1)	25% (1)	12% (26)
Retail employee	18% (9)	21% (7)	30% (3)	38% (10)	30% (6)	32% (16)	50% (8)	25% (1)	29% (60)
Clerical employee	11.5% (6)	3% (1)	— (0)	27% (7)	35% (7)	12% (6)	25% (4)	25% (1)	15% (32)
Retail self-employed	— (0)	— (0)	— (0)	— (0)	— (0)	— (0)	— (0)	— (0)	— (0)
Professional	— (0)	— (0)	— (0)	— (0)	10% (2)	— (0)	6% (1)	25% (1)	2% (4)
TOTAL	100% (51)	100% (33)	100% (10)	100% (26)	100% (20)	100% (50)	100% (16)	100% (4)	100% (210)

Source: Neighborhood data.

a. Occupation listed is latest recorded occupation; for fathers, occupation in 1940, last occupation listed prior to death; for daughters, occupation in 1940, last occupation listed in Providence, or last occupation listed prior to marriage.

TABLE 2-9. Jewish Fathers and Daughters: Occupations, 1940[a]

DAUGHTER'S OCCUPATION	FATHER'S OCCUPATION								
	Laborer	Operative	Skilled	Craft Employee	Retail Employee	Craft Self-employed	Retail Self-employed	Professional	TOTAL
Operative	0	0	0	12.5% (1)	10% (3)	— (0)	2% (1)	17% (1)	6% (6)
Skilled	0	0	0	— (0)	— (0)	— (0)	— (0)	— (0)	— (0)
Craft employee	0	0	0	25% (2)	— (0)	— (0)	— (0)	— (0)	2% (2)
Retail employee	0	0	0	50% (4)	63% (19)	83% (5)	48% (23)	— (0)	52% (51)
Clerical employee	0	0	0	12.5% (1)	27% (8)	17% (1)	44% (21)	33% (2)	34% (33)
Retail self-employed	0	0	0	— (0)	— (0)	— (0)	2% (1)	— (0)	1% (1)
Professional	0	0	0	— (0)	— (0)	— (0)	4% (2)	50% (3)	5% (5)
TOTAL				100% (8)	100% (30)	100% (6)	100% (48)	100% (6)	100% (98)

Source: Neighborhood data.

a. Occupation listed is latest recorded occupation; for fathers, occupation in 1940, last occupation listed in Providence, or last occupation listed prior to death; for daughters, occupation in 1940, last occupation listed in Providence, or last occupation listed prior to marriage.

Jewish junk dealer ran related businesses ranging from selling used automobiles to reprocessing mill waste.[88] In 1935, 27 percent of employed Italian sons and daughters in the neighborhood and 14 percent of employed Jewish sons and daughters worked at the same occupation as their fathers, most of these in stores.

Looking at the occupations of children in relation to the occupations of their fathers, one can observe a process of class reproduction, lending an important continuity to the options, if not the actual workplaces, of the children. The sons and daughters of retail proprietors, self-employed craftsmen, and craft employees generally moved into white-collar work, while the sons and daughters of laborers and factory workers generally became factory workers. Training acquired in a craft shop was useful in developing retail skills, while the content of work in a factory led most naturally to other factories. The propensity of Jewish immigrants for retail rather than craft work, and the high proportion of Jewish immigrants who became self-employed, might explain the high proportion of their children who worked in selling and management rather than in production.[89]

Profound changes in personal orientation toward work underlay these changes in employment. Despite the increasing instability of their employment during these years, immigrant artisans and shopkeepers felt that the autonomy of self-employment and the possession of a skill gave their work its meaning. But parents found it difficult to transmit their work skills and, even more important, their values about work to their children. Perhaps when several Connecticut artisans and shopkeepers took stock of their work in the late 1930s, they spoke for their counterparts in Providence as well. An Italian grocer valued his ability to control his work time. Even though business was slow, he felt better with his own shop "because I have the time for myself." An Italian shoemaker prized his right to keep on working until he himself made the decision to retire. In the factory, "when you are forty-five, they chase you out." As a shoemaker, he could work until he was ninety-five: "Just so long that your hands don't shake you could do this work." Artisans took advantage of the uneven pacing of craft work to play music, to discuss "world events and current news" with friends who stopped by. The immigrants had prided themselves on the respect they commanded in their community from the exercise of their skills as well as on the broad range of their interests.[90]

However, immigrant artisans and shopkeepers were less and less sure that they could command this respect from their own children, less and less sure that their children would be willing to learn a trade or take over a small neighborhood shop. They understood that public education was supposed to substitute in part for the apprenticeship through which they themselves had been trained. "Now when the kids want to learn the barber trade they go to barber school; if they want to be mechanics they go to trade school." But immigrant craftsmen felt that this school training was shoddy; "they learn the trade too fast and they don't learn it good because everything is too mechanical." They resented their own loss of authority in the transfer to institutional training. "In this country you can't force them to do something, in Italy they have to learn if they want or no." Parents felt that their influence with their children was undermined by the children's involvement in a peer culture. On "the other side," children had to "follow the word of the father and the mother," but in this country they had their own ideas about what they wanted to do. An immigrant tailor watched his sons playing with children of various ethnicities, and heard them agree that "when they get big they learn something in the shops." He attempted to persuade his thirteen-year-old son that factory work was not "steady," and that learning skilled work was more dependable because "he always have the trade." The tailor wanted his son to begin to work with him in his shop, to "stick with me." But his son wanted an American childhood, free from the trade and he was willing to place his hopes for the future on the factory rather than go through an apprenticeship. "He doesn't want to learn now; he says he got lots of time." Other parents agreed that their children also did not "think about the time to come, but they want to make money for now." They were unwilling to spend earning years learning a trade: "What's the use to learn trade now because every thing is machine." From the immigrant craftsman's point of view, having no skill meant that even after working in the factory for a long time, "still you have nothing." But the children seemed to see things differently, at least according to their parents. They looked for work's reward in its compensation, not in its activity. "The kids today, if they get the nickel in the pockets, they don't want to learn nothing . . . you give them the [moving] pictures and the girls and they don't care for nothing."[91] Parents watched their children absorb attitudes toward work which grew out of their exposure to modern industrial culture—attitudes that questioned the very foundation of their parents' world view.

In Providence, the precariousness of neighborhood craft and retail shops and the shrinking opportunities for self-employment partially explain why immigrant sons and daughters found long-term employment in large industrial and commercial operations.

Assessing their own experience of unemployment from seasonal factory layoffs, and that of parents and neighbors who were in and out of work as unskilled laborers and as craft and artisan employees, many saw the retail sector as promising the most secure jobs. Others took part in the grass-roots agitation to demand more job security in industrial work which in the 1930s provided the reason most often articulated by the rank and file for joining unions.[92] Immigrant parents had hoped that the trades and small shops that their children might inherit would save them from dependence on the factory. But the search for a secure job was replacing the inheritance of the trades as the dominant motif in the lives of their children. The combination of large-scale structural changes in the job market and a new definition of security characterized the context of work for the American-born generation.

Even though in 1940 most sons and daughters were working in jobs their parents did not arrange for them, parents continued to exercise authority in service of familial economic goals and familial work values by their control of financial resources for extra schooling. As a high school diploma became a prerequisite for an enlarging share of available employment, the expenditure of resources on education took on increasing importance in families. Sometimes families' need for supplementary income continued to require the sacrifice of education, especially in the depression years. In 1935, between 70 and 80 percent of all Italian and Jewish sons and daughters in the neighborhood fifteen years of age and older who lived at home were at work (see table 2-10). One Italian daughter whose father was a frequently unemployed carpenter had to leave high school in order to go to work in a jewelry factory and so could not finish the course for a career in commercial art. Another Italian daughter of a garment worker hoped to become a hairdresser with her own shop, but "financially this was not possible, and if it were, her father would not permit her" to go to hairdressing school. Instead she went to work in a textile mill where other members of her family worked. In other families, long-term economic planning included a high school education for some children to enable them to help the family with the wages from more stable white-collar employment.[93]

Parents also exercised more direct control over children's employment. Sometimes parents insisted that their children remain within a family business, despite opportunities elsewhere. One Jewish daughter trained as a bookkeeper was offered a job working for the New York, New Haven and Hartford Railroad with a ten dollar raise, but "her mother did not approve since it would be working in an

TABLE 2-10. Wage-earning Children at Home, 15+, 1935

	Italian		Jewish	
Sons				
Employed	80%	(80)	73%	(27)
Unemployed	20%	(20)	27%	(10)
TOTAL	100%	(100)	100%	(37)
Unemployed and in school	85%	(17)	90%	(9)
Daughters				
Employed	72%	(66)	70%	(19)
Unemployed	28%	(26)	30%	(8)
TOTAL	100%	(92)	100%	(27)
Unemployed and in school	54%	(14)	63%	(5)

Source: Neighborhood data.

office with men," so she continued to work for her brothers' clothing store in Providence. Another Jewish daughter hoped to become a teacher, but her father directed her toward bookkeeping, arguing that she was too small to take control of a classroom. She remembered his words:

> Frankly, Anna, you're a little girl, and some of the kids are tough in school, and all that, and I don't think it will be good for you.

He also argued that teaching was too unrewarding financially. As an alternative, he suggested employment for her in his own big clothing store: "look, you'll come work for me."[94] In these instances, parents marshalled family authority to prohibit work choices that seemed to take children too far from the family circle.

Even though modern managerial innovation required the introduction of personnel offices, family networks in the workplace continued to be dense because the retail sector proved as susceptible to family-hiring influence as blue-collar employment.[95] For example, in one Italian family, three children whose father had been a barber found jobs working for a chain of drugstores that employed their uncle. Pairs of sisters worked as saleswomen at Shepards or the Outlet Company, downtown Providence department stores, while their brothers worked as stock clerks for the same employers.[96] In 1935, 39 percent of employed Italian sons and 56 percent of employed Italian daughters worked in the same occupations as their brothers and sisters, most frequently in retail establishments. Forty-one percent of employed Jewish sons and 25 percent of employed

Jewish daughters worked in the same occupation as a brother or sister. Sometimes children were able to gain positions that enabled them to arrange employment for their parents. This seemed to have been the situation in one Italian family where the father had been frequently unemployed as a tinsmith and blacksmith. In 1929, his oldest son had gotten a job as a superintendent at an Italian-owned knife factory, and by 1935 his father and two brothers also worked there as cutters.[97] Helping each other find jobs continued to be an important service family members could perform long after the initial years of settlement.

Increasing exposure to American cultural values of economic individualism in the context of the sporadic prosperity of the 1920s led some sons and daughters to strike deep at the values of familial economic cooperation by questioning their contribution to the family economy. These sons and daughters began to experience a stronger sense of their own needs, peer pressure towards certain kinds of consumption, and a feeling of entitlement to their own earnings. The daughters in one Italian family came to resent "turning over every cent they worked for and having a small allowance handed out to them to buy needed clothing, personal items, and for leisure activities." They became adept at sewing, knitting, crocheting, and "making do," and they also arranged for a larger share of their wages indirectly, by "borrowing from mother." Other children simply withheld a part of their paychecks. While an older sister dipped into her wages only to treat herself to carfare on payday, her younger sister felt much more entitled to personal expenditure; she remembered that she was "different from the way she [her older sister] is altogether." What it meant to her to get her first pay from her first job was to spend at least some of it on herself. As she recalled:

I'll never forget the time I got my first pay . . . I went downtown, first, and I spent a lot, more than half of my money . . . I just went hog wild, I guess.

The custom in the family was that the children "used to have to hand our pays in." When she came home, she knew she would have to face a confrontation with her father. She gave him what money she had left, and without words, her father let her know that her behavior was unacceptable. He threw her pay back at her. Her father perceived her challenge to the family economy as a challenge to his authority. The daughter won the round: she just picked up the pay envelope and took the rest of it. In reality, there was little the father could do to enforce the norms of economic cooperation and he knew it. The next week, her father did not throw her again-depleted pay envelope back at her but "just kept what I gave him."[98] The confrontation between father and daughter over entitlement to her wage was resolved with his relinquishing of authority; she successfully claimed personal power within the family by separating herself from its collective demands. Economic individualism in this instance meant both the decline of patriarchal authority and the expansion of possibilities for women.

No longer able to take the economic contribution of children for granted, mothers would increasingly share with fathers the burden of family support. In the years after 1940, mothers with young children became the fastest growing sector of the labor force. In the 1920s and 1930s, conflicting sets of pressures defined women's contribution to the family economy. Income-generating work that could be combined with household tasks became less available. Immigration restriction laws passed in the 1920s shrank the supply of boarders; industrial regulations enacted in the 1930s attempted to prohibit homework.[99] Dressmaking, like other independent craft production, suffered from competition with mass-produced goods. More and more, work for wives meant work outside the home (see table 2-11).

But several circumstances made it easier for immigrant daughters to find work outside the home. For one thing, immigrant daughters were likely to have mothers living in Providence who might be available for help with child care. This had been less frequently the case for their mothers, who had often left parents in the old country. (Of course, residential dispersion of the ethnic settlements and the scattering of some immigrant children in the 1920s and 1930s in new neighborhoods further from downtown could place mothers and daughters at quite a distance.) Second, immigrant daughters were likely to have worked outside the home for a good many years prior to marriage, and they often had work experience and connections with supervisors which made it easier for them to return to work after absences due to marriage and children. One Italian daughter who had watched her younger brothers and sisters while her parents worked asked her mother and mother-in-law for help when she returned to work in the textile mill where she had worked before she was married. After the birth of each child, she would stay home for a while, and "then my mother would take care of the babies, or his mother, and then I'd go back to work." She

TABLE 2-11.   Changing Work Location of Employed Wives, 1915–40

Occupation	Italian				Jewish			
	Mothers		Daughters		Mothers		Daughters	
Housekeeper for boarders and relatives	29%	(47)	unrecorded		17%	(12)	unrecorded	
Storekeeper	4%	(6)	3%	(4)	11%	(8)	3%	(2)
Dressmaker	3%	(5)	3%	(4)	1.5%	(1)	—	(0)
Housekeeper, laundress	1%	(2)	—	(0)	1.5%	(1)	—	(0)
Homeworker	1%	(2)	3%	(4)	—	(0)	—	(0)
Factory operative	3%	(5)	11%	(15)	—	(0)	2%	(1)
Saleswoman	—	(0)	2%	(3)	—	(0)	14%	(9)
Clerical worker	—	(0)	4%	(5)	—	(0)	3%	(2)
Hairdresser	—	(0)	1.5%	(2)	—	(0)	—	(0)
Manager	—	(0)	.5%	(1)	—	(0)	3%	(2)
No reported work	59%	(95)	72%	(96)	69%	(50)	75%	(50)
TOTAL	100%	(162)	100%	(134)	100%	(72)	100%	(66)
Total recorded working wives	41%	(66)	28%	(38)	31%	(22)	25%	(16)

Source: Neighborhood data.

never worked steadily until her children were grown, but she worked most of the years while her children were growing up. She knew the foreman, and she remembered that "I always got my job back." Another Italian daughter worked continuously as a spooler in a textile mill from age fourteen on; she changed to the night shift after she had children so that her husband could watch their babies while she was at work.[100] In these cases, working daughters turned almost automatically into working mothers.

Of course the responsibility for children placed an extra burden on mothers working outside the home. One Italian daughter who had worked for eight years in a box factory before she got married felt that she had to return to work when her husband's steady wages as a sign painter no longer seemed to stretch far enough to cover their expenses for food, gas, rent, and furniture payments. Interviewed by the Women's Bureau, she described how worn she was by the combination of managing her home and struggling with her employer for the restoration of her previous wage rate, so that she could pay her mother to look after her baby. She knew that her employer took every possible advantage of his female employees, but

2-14 Immigrant daughters in factory workplaces. Women working in 1939 at California Artificial Flower Company, started by an Italian immigrant in a shop on Spruce Street on Federal Hill in 1922. This photograph taken in the new factory building on Resevoir Avenue. Photograph courtesy of Providence Public Library.

she, like many of the other women and girls, stayed because the work was steadier than elsewhere. As the interviewer recorded:

> Mrs. DeRocco gets up at 5 o'clock in order to get her husband's breakfast and some of her work done before going to work. After she gets home she gets the supper and has her work to finish and the baby to put to bed. She cried during the interview and was obviously unstrung from her week's effort.[101]

A Jewish wife returned to a candy factory where she had worked before marriage, leaving her children with a neighbor whom she paid to care for them. After five years of this arrangement, she came home on a wintry day to find her children playing outside in the street. Feeling powerless to demand better supervision from her neighbor, she left her job, sacrificing the needed income to make sure that her children were safe.[102] Wives worked under tremendous strain, balancing the structure of outside employment with domestic demands in the face of family economic need.

Because they had to leave their homes for work, and in response to their children's demands for greater access to their own wages, the timing of mothers' work shifted. Immigrant mothers worked until their children reached working ages, and then they depended on their children's wages to provide needed extra income. Daughters of immigrants often stayed home with small children and went to work when their children were older, in school, and able to look after themselves. Often they devoted their own wages to keeping their children in school longer, hoping that a completed high school education would lead their children to more secure white-collar employment. Also, because they could no longer be certain of their children's future economic contribution, mothers worked to save money for their own old age. After all her children had left home, one Italian daughter went back to work in the textile mill where she had been employed before she was married. Another Italian daughter worked in a jewelry shop after her marriage until the birth of her first child seven years later. She returned to work when her youngest child went to kindergarten and stayed at her job until she was in her late sixties.[103]

Speaking and reading English, educated in the public schools, immigrant daughters had more exposure to American culture than their mothers had. Daughters were often aware of the negative images of working mothers which were a standard part of bourgeois values of domesticity and motherhood. Women had commanded a grudging respect within the ethnic community for their skills as economic providers, and now these skills were caricatured by the stereotype of well-dressed mothers in spotless kitchens supervising clean and quiet children and protecting them from worldly concerns. These values were not without an effect on women, but they often existed in contradiction with the realities of some women's lives— realities that continued to require women's economic contribution.[104]

The Great Depression of the 1930s may have temporarily functioned to intensify the economic interdependence of family members. The economic collapse was severe in Rhode Island. From 1929 to 1931 the number of wage earners employed in cotton textiles fell by 40 percent. Wages dropped drastically: 40 percent for cotton textile workers, 50 percent for jewelry workers, and 55 to 65 percent for foundry and machine-shop workers. In 1939, one out of every

TABLE 2-12.　Family Economy, 1915 and 1935

1915 Household Composition	Italian		Jewish	
Household with one wage earner, one dependent	7%	(12)	6%	(4)
Household with one wage earner, one+ dependents	34%	(55)	44%	(32)
Household with more than one wage earner	57%	(92)	44%	(32)
Single-person households, households with a widow or retired head	2%	(3)	6%	(4)
	100%	(162)	100%	(72)
1935 Household Composition				
Household with one wage earner, one dependent	7%	(7)	12.5%	(5)
Household with one wage earner, one+ dependents	13%	(12)	12.5%	(5)
Household with more than one wage earner	79%	(75)	73%	(30)
Household with a widow or retired head	1%	(1)	2%	(1)
	100%	(95)[a]	100%	(41)[a]

Source: Neighborhood data.
a. From 1915 to 1935, 67 Italian families and 31 Jewish families died, moved, or were not in the records. Of the original neighborhood households, 12% of Italians and 14% of Jews died, and 30% of Italians and 30% of Jews moved or did not appear in the 1935 records.

five families in Providence sought welfare relief, and these numbers included many families on Federal Hill and Smith Hill.[105] The family economy provided an obvious strategy for coping with the extreme and widespread unemployment and income loss that immigrants and their children now faced. Conditions of scarcity gave renewed economic value to women's household work such as canning and sewing. Elsewhere, families testified to a greater interdependency. An Italian mason in Bridgeport admitted that his wife's wage-earning work was now indispensable. With little masonry work available, his wife "have to help supportin' the family." Some masons he knew were able to find jobs in factories to tide them over, but he felt that he was too old for the factory, so his "wife have to work." A Malden, Massachusetts shopkeeper's family found their variety store failing because of the depression, and so the family could only manage on whatever earnings the older brothers and sisters were able to bring home.[106] In 1935 in Providence, the majority of families in both the Italian and Jewish neighborhoods had more than one wage earner (see table 2-12). If the norms of familial economic cooperation had begun to be altered, the effects of the depression on families momentarily masked the changes.

Clearly, then, economic cooperation was a crucial resource for immigrant families. Household strategies that evolved in Europe on the basis of pooling labor and income were transferable to Providence. Men used old skills and developed new ones to take advantage of openings in the local economy, and women and children ingeniously exploited economic opportunities in the neighborhoods to make domestic labor generate an income. Family members helped each other to find work, and in doing so, established kin networks running through neighborhoods and workplaces.

Economic and social change challenged the assumptions of the family economy. Structural economic shifts meant that sons and daughters were more likely to find employment outside of the neighborhood and beyond the experience of their parents. This structural occupational mobility diminished the aspects of parental authority which had been based on the teaching of work skills and the procurement of employment. However, as a high school educa-tion became more important to certain kinds of employment, parents were able to influence their children's job placement in new ways through their control of economic resources for education. And families continued to use the wider resources of their kin networks for finding work because these networks proved to be influential in department stores and insurance companies as well as factories.

The most direct challenge to familial economic cooperation came from children who in the prosperous atmosphere of the 1920s began to question their contribution to the family economy. But the potential loss of children's wages could be made up by mothers, who, as the twentieth century wore on, joined men as the chief supporters of the family. In the 1920s and 1930s mothers were less and less able to find income-generating work that they could combine with housework. The greater ease with which they could find outside employment because of prior work experience gained before marriage was partially offset by the difficulties in balancing housework and child care with employment outside the home. But mothers were able to shift the timing of their employment in order to stay home with small children. Not being sure of the economic contribution of their children, women also stayed at work longer in order to supplement their husband's earnings. However familial economic cooperation may have been changing, the effect of widespread unemployment in the depression years was to renew economic interdependency within the family. At least through 1940, immigrants and their children continued to depend on economic cooperation within their families as a way of life.

Chapter Three

The Bonds of Kinship

IMMIGRANTS CONCEIVED of themselves not as individuals but as members of families. But the contextual meaning of *family* was continuously evolving. Defining the obligations of household members to each other within larger networks of kinship exchange and reciprocity was a constantly shifting process of negotiation, subject to the dictates of regional custom, demographic pressure, and historical change. In late-nineteenth-century southern Italy and eastern Europe, norms of familial interaction were in flux. Increased economic vulnerability drew kin into greater involvement with each other but also undermined the acquisition of resources required to arrange marriages in accordance with family interests. The process of immigration accomplished the goal of family preservation by its short-term dissolution; migration placed kin in new configurations of distance and proximity, and, in doing so, redefined the kinds of assistance kin needed from each other. First the social and economic context of life in Providence, and then the developmental cycle of families and the community in process of settlement, renegotiated patterns of dependency and exchange. In the early years, boundaries between households were blurred as kin who migrated together to Providence became neighbors, and neighbors and friends from the old country acted like kin. But changes in family life, in occupational structure, and in residential geography meant that by 1940, kin reciprocity would no longer be the dominant community ethos. Changing circumstances in the later years would challenge the broader definition of familial obligation and would strengthen families' identities as individual households.

FAMILY AND KINSHIP IN EUROPE

The regions of Europe that would lose a large segment of their population to immigration were diverse in economic structure, as explained in chapter 2. What they shared in the closing years of the nineteenth century was dependence on the individual household as the primary form of economic organization and the experience of being drawn into more complex market relations. The expansion of the market enmeshed smallholders and artisans more deeply in a cash economy. These economic changes created the conditions that prompted the immigration of family groups. Economic change and the stimulus of migration itself also quickened the pace at which traditional cultural norms gave way to new formulations. Josef Barton has referred to the world that peasants left in southern Italy as "a society in disaggregation," and has argued that the splitting apart of the community was everywhere accompanied by the dissolution of the household economy and its rhythms. Within eastern Europe, the move from village to city required by residence laws had already begun to undermine the shtetl culture that had unified the Jewish community for hundreds of years. The explosive ferment of new ideas flourishing in these circumstances broke the automatic link between traditionalism and Jewish life. By obeying the prescriptions of tradition as interpreted by the rabbis, the family had consecrated the rituals of daily life. Now, change in the traditional culture and change in the family were intimately connected. In both southern Italy and eastern Europe, the atmosphere on the eve of migration was a mixture of mounting wretchedness and a sense of new possibilities.[1] It was against this backdrop of economic and social transformation that ordinary family strategies took their shape.

In both southern Italy and eastern Europe, the household was the most important locus of family relationships. Here the most intimate connections existed, and here mutual obligation was most clearly defined. Outside the individual household, there could be varying degrees of involvement between married children and their parents, and between married brothers and sisters. In some parts of southern Italy, entire communities might consist of related families. In contrast, geographical mobility due in large part to residence laws and the search for employment meant that Jewish families were less likely to be residentially concentrated. But whether or not kin were actually neighbors, in both cultures individual households experienced themselves as part of networks of related families.[2]

In most regions of southern Italy, married couples lived most of their lives in households separate from their parents, brothers, and sisters. Even in one southern Italian town where a tradition of patriarchal joint households has been identified, the extended household lasted only for the relatively few years between the marriage of the oldest son and the death of the father; when the father died, the extended household usually dissolved. Bilateral inheritance traditions, providing that both sons and daughters might inherit, meant that any property to be divided held the danger of exacerbating competition between siblings. In general, the economic rivalry between families in the extended kin group, loyalty to one's family, and competition over inheritance all militated against closeness among siblings.[3]

Parents and married children had different amounts of daily contact in different regions of southern Italy and Sicily. In some parts of Sicily, the husband's family supplied the new couple with a house, and here married couples were quite likely to live near the husband's parents. Although marriage rituals emphasized the severance of a daughter from her father's house and her transfer to the jurisdiction of her husband, if a daughter married a man from her own or a neighboring village, her parents were likely to live nearby.[4] Physical proximity allowed various kinds of potential intervention in the new marriage. An immigrant from a village near Foggia in Apulia recalled a situation in which a married daughter's parents lived near enough to defend her against physical violence from her husband. When the young husband would "beat up his wife and curse her family," all the villagers knew what would follow. The young wife would return to her parents complaining about her husband.

> In a short while a crowd would gather around the girl's parents' home. Shortly after, the brothers, cousins, and other male relatives of the beaten girl would go, led by the old mother, toward the home of the girl. And there they pounced upon the husband and beat him up.

In this instance the father was not the arbiter. "He neither laughed nor was he angry; he acted as if he had no right to butt in." The father remained at home while the mother led the procession to defend her daughter. In another instance recalled by an immigrant from Reggio Calabria, proximity to the maternal parents enabled them to reinforce the husband's authority over their daughter. A woman married a man from a neighboring village, and he complained to her father that she was disobedient. One day her father came over and, in the presence of her husband, gave her a "severe beating with his cane." As she remembered:

> In all my life I will never forget it; the brutal looks of my father and the feeble protestations of my husband. Never will I forget how my husband looked pleasantly at me and said: "I am sorry. I see now what fine folks your parents are."

In this case, it was the father who supported the husband's authority as an extension of his own.[5]

In theory, unless they were destitute, southern Italian parents no longer had any actual claims on the resources of married children in separate households, even though the loss of a son and his earnings or the loss of a daughter, her earnings, and her contribution of household work might have brought real hardships to the parents. Families attempted to control and delay marriage in keeping with the needs of the family economy, and the mean age of marriage in late-nineteenth-century southern Italy reflected this concern: the age of marriage was approximately twenty-three for women, twenty-seven for men. In practice, it seems to have been difficult for hard-pressed families to stop considering their children as potential sources of income even after marriage. Supposedly, parents were less likely to make demands on a married daughter because they had no blood claim on her husband's earnings. But there is evidence that parents did continue to expect financial help from their daughters after they married. Older Italians interviewed in the early years of the 1940s who reminisced about the old custom of the father's blessing of the daughter seldom failed to mention the "practical advice" that accompanied the blessing: "Obbedisci tuo marito, ma non dimenticare che hai un dovere verso i tuoi propri genitori" [Obey your husband, but do not forget that you owe a duty to your parents]. The blessing implied that even after their daughters were married, the parents still expected some help from them. Daughters were caught between two sets of obligations, to husband and to parents. The older Italians recalled that it was common for a new bride to "sneak out" and undertake some farm labor for her parents, or to send over some money or produce as an acknowledgment of her obligations to them. Formal familial norms did not sanction such conduct, but according to the immigrants, there was general agreement that a daughter's help was a concession to the father who had to be "sodisfatto per la perdita d'une figlia" [placated for the loss of a daughter].[6]

Oldest sons were expected to be responsible for their parents when they became dependent. Even though male children had the formal obligation to care for their parents as they aged, the fact that women were brought up to feel responsible for taking care of others meant that they were likely to be continually involved with their parents. As a Sicilian proverb suggested: "He who has female children has both daughters and sons, but he who has male children has neither sons nor daughters."[7]

The marriage ritual emphasized that a wife was taken into her husband's family. Her family were considered to be outsiders. A Sicilian folk proverb indicated that relations between families were not always consistent with this principle. "The relatives of the wife are sweet like honey; the relatives of the husband are sour like vinegar." One observer suggested that as a couple got older, the wife's family became increasingly important and familiar to her husband and children. If both parents of children died while the grandparents were still alive, the formal importance of the male lineage was acknowledged in the customary provision that the father's family care for the children. But if the mother of the children survived, she might return with them to her own family. According to one southern Italian immigrant, the wife's family was much more likely to aid her as a widow:

> The father's relatives showed themselves unwilling to assume the responsibility. It was therefore the woman's relatives who usually came to her aid. No such responsibility was ever assumed by the brothers and sisters of the husband.[8]

Married brothers and sisters also had varying amounts of contact in the different regions of southern Italy and Sicily. If patrilocal residence traditions were strong, brothers might be in frequent contact after marriage, while sisters, scattered among different neighborhoods, would rarely see each other. It was acceptable to see one's married siblings no more frequently than at

the parental home on Sunday-afternoon visits. Brothers and sisters
might not have any relationship at all after marriage. In Sicily,
siblings had no absolute expectation of financial aid. A brother was
supposed to give a home to an unmarried or widowed sister, but it
was harder for a sister to render the same assistance, for her home
was not considered to be hers to offer.[9]

Relationships among families in the extended kin group were
clearly limited. The larger kin group existed as a group only from the
point of view of a given individual.[10] Parents consulted members of
the extended kin group only for advice on marriage decisions. The
opinions of kin on this issue were important because their
reputations as persons and as family members were tied in with the
fortunes of the family as a whole. Any marriage plans, involving a
potential alliance between families, would personally affect family
members. Individual households made other kinds of decisions by
themselves, such as whether or not to buy or sell land, or to emigrate.
Informal encounters strengthened the bond between some relatives,
as for example a Sicilian boy who became close to an aunt he saw
"every day as I pass her house on the way to school." Sometimes
relatives visited each other on Sundays or on religious holidays. But
they gathered regularly as a group only for weddings, baptisms, and
funerals.[11]

In times of crisis, households expected kin to step forward with
assistance. Relatives came to call on those who were seriously ill,
bringing food when there was a death. In towns in Sicily, when death
seemed imminent, the closest relatives who were able to do so moved
into the house and remained there until the body was removed. The
female kin took over shopping, cooking, cleaning, and sitting with
the family. Male relatives helped in the fields so that, for example, a
father might sit up with a sick child. In an economy where cash was
scarce, exchange of goods and services was more likely to be
forthcoming than actual financial aid. Informal assistance networks
could also include ritual kin, friends, and neighbors. This emergency
assistance was a kind of insurance adjustment made by people who
knew all too well that they might sooner or later be subject to similar
hardships.[12]

In eastern Europe, households more frequently included several
generations because newly married couples often settled under
parental roofs. Young couples lived with the husband's family unless
the wife's family commanded more resources. Wealthy families who
arranged marriages for their daughters with scholars ordinarily
promised room and board for the new couple as part of the dowry.
Sometimes these extended-family households were arranged for the

benefit of the older generation. One immigrant described how when her grandfather died, her mother took over his business, for which she has been trained since childhood, and with it, the support of her mother. Combining two households had the potential to exacerbate tensions between them. A Yiddish folk song enumerated the grievances from a son's wife's point of view:

> I knead the bread—
>   she says: it lacks consistency!
> I prepare the fish—
>   she shouts: it's bitter!
> I make the bed—
>   she says: too high!
> I heat the stove—
>   she smells smoke.
> I walk slowly—
>   she says: I'm crawling!
> I walk quickly—
>   she's tearing her shoes!

Economic scarcity, which made it hard for most families to support extra people, and the fierce competition for employment meant that households did not ordinarily include married brothers and sisters.[13]

In eastern Europe, as in Italy, an individual gained primary social recognition as part of a family. Obligations of husbands and wives, parents and children to each other were carefully spelled out in Jewish law and shtetl custom. Communities presumed common standards in regard to behavior for children. As one immigrant remembered,

> In the old country, if someone else's child did something naughty, one either complained to the father of the child who then punished the culprit, or one spanked the child himself.

Husbands and wives were to teach their skills to their children and arrange their marriages. Children were to respect their parents, achieve in their name, and support their parents in their old age. Folk proverbs suggested that the expectation of support was directed at sons, but that dependence on sons was socially difficult: "When the father gives to the son, both rejoice: when the son gives to the father, both weep." Being reduced to dependency on one's children was a blow to parental self-esteem, especially for fathers. "Better to beg one's bread door to door than to be dependent on one's sons."[14]

As in southern Italy, marriage was undertaken as part of complex negotiations between families. As one immigrant described the process:

> Parents usually chose their children's mates. Love played a small part in this business-like transaction. The parents met, decided on the size of the dowry to go with a daughter or to be given to a son . . . set the date for the wedding, inform their respective children as to the person with whom they are going to spend their lives, and then marry them.[15]

Economic considerations were wryly acknowledged in a Yiddish proverb: "Love is like butter; it goes well with bread." Daughters in families with property were closely watched before marriage and were supposed to marry in birth order so that parents could fully control the distribution of their resources in the form of dowries. Only those with no property to concern their families were free to arrange their own marriages.[16]

Jewish extended-family groups included all those related by blood and marriage. The in-laws, *machetunim*, claimed and rendered the obligations of kinship. As in southern Italy, extended kin took their most active role in marriage negotiations for young men and women. Before a marriage contract was actually drawn up, the groom's female relatives inspected the person, family, and accomplishments of the prospective bride, and the bride's male kin undertook the same investigation of the prospective groom. One immigrant described how marriage negotiations involved the assembled families of both parties in open discussion, with much haggling over the details of the marriage contract. A poor cousin particularly relished the opportunity to dispute minor details, exhorting her family "to be firm lest their flesh and blood be cheated under their noses." Kin gathered as a group only for wedding festivities, and sometimes for holiday celebrations. Kin who lived nearby got together more informally. One Jewish immigrant from Galicia remembered how female relatives would gather at his house: "Some nights, some nights there were four, five, six women sitting, gabbing, and knitting stockings." He recalled that they would gossip and talk about their ailments. Competition and tension between families in the extended kin group were common; they were ritualized in a wedding dance in which the new mothers-in-law acted out a quarrel and then a reconciliation.[17]

Jewish families also depended on their relatives for assistance in times of need, as southern Italians were accustomed to doing. The patterns of assistance that existed within the nuclear family were followed in attenuated form in the extended family. Kinship ties entitled an individual to expect aid during an illness and to make a claim on any spare family resources to use for education and emigration. A Yiddish proverb suggested that extra resources prompted extra claims: "Rich kin are close kin." Relatives visiting from a different town could expect food, lodging, and support.[18] By the 1880s, kin probably claimed these services with increasing frequency as the moves from familiar villages to large towns and cities, forced by the settlement laws, placed more families in need of temporary lodging and help in finding employment. Like the uncertain effects of the market in southern Italian villages, the unstable economic system of the shtetl made mutual obligations of kin particularly important as a kind of insurance. It was socially valued to help those in need, and it would always be useful to have others indebted to one for past assistance.

Jews might also depend on neighbors in the shtetl to extend the resources of their families and kin. According to anthropologists who studied eastern European community life, the shtetl community was like an extended family, with a similar network of obligations and duties. A Jewish immigrant's experience suggests how immigration may have made families even more dependent on extrafamilial assistance. When this woman was seven, "trouble with her eyes" kept her from immigrating with her family. She first stayed with her grandmother, but she was too lonely in her grandmother's rural village, so she returned to the city, Bialystok, and stayed with a former neighbor for several years until she rejoined her family: "The neighbors, you know in Europe, the neighbors are like in one family."[19]

The increased involvement of southern Italian and eastern European Jewish families in a cash economy in the late-nineteenth-century made them more economically vulnerable. Households became even more economically interdependent, as described in chapter 2. At this time, families looked also to an enlarged network of kinship ties outside the household for help in dealing with the cash and wage nexus of the new economy. According to Josef Barton's research in southern Italy, kin ties replaced crumbling village ties during the 1880s, and broadened practices of dowry and donation bound families in circles of assistance. Barton claimed that the increased economic importance of familial ties was not "preindustrial or traditional" but an innovative response of the poor to the new uncertainties of their village economies.[20] Migration forced by settlement laws in eastern Europe may have set a similar process in motion.

The resources of family and kinship networks may have thus become more important because of increasing economic insecurity. But uncertain market relationships also contained the potential to realign family relationships. For example, a study of inheritance patterns in Potenza in Basilicata found that, as supplementary resources became both more necessary and more numerous for families, a shift from inheritance by sons toward inheritance by both sons and daughters took place.[21]

Orderly marriage arrangements, which preserved and extended family groups through the transmission of property, were particularly vulnerable in times of economic scarcity. Emigration was sometimes directly linked to the disruption of customary marriage provisions, as revealed in a story related by the novelist Mario Puzo about the migration of his mother from the hills near Naples to New York City:

> There had come a time when her father, with stern pity, had told her, his favorite daughter, that she could not hope for bridal linen. The farm was too poor. There were debts. Life promised to be even harder. . . . In that moment she lost all respect for her father, for her home, for her country. A bride without linen was shameful . . . what man would take a woman with the stigma of hopeless poverty?

It was at that moment that Puzo's mother decided to emigrate to America, to marry a man she barely knew, rather than face her bleak prospects in Italy. Once underway, emigration itself began to alter accepted arrangements. The loss of available men meant that the age of marriage and the proportion of women remaining single increased in the areas of southern Italy experiencing heavy emigration. The search for marriage partners began to transcend the boundaries of the village. A study of two villages that produced many emigrants suggested that the custom of endogamy, by which marriage partners had been selected from within the community to avoid scattering properties over a wide area, was beginning to give way to marriages that combined partners from nearby villages.[22]

The severe economic constraints on Jewish families in the Pale similarly interfered with ordinary marriage expectations. For one Jewish family living in a town near Minsk, hard times meant that a son who had hoped to be a rabbi worked instead as a tailor, and his sister who had hoped for training as a seamstress worked as a domestic servant. As the mother assessed the situation, her daughter's chances to marry were "small enough" without a dowry. When the son was forced to leave Russia to avoid conscription into the czar's army, the mother, who had been living with the son's family, realized that she and her husband would now become dependent on their daughter, further limiting her opportunity to make a marriage match.

> Poor Masha . . . what is to become of her? . . . Burdened with an aged father and a blind helpless mother, the best she can expect is a middle-aged widower with a half-dozen children.

Rather than accept such a fate for her daughter, the blind mother sacrificed her own comfort. She would send her daughter with her son to the United States, where surely she would be able to marry, even though it meant that the parents would be alone in old age, separated by oceans from their children. Another Jewish daughter made the decision to emigrate based on her own analysis of her situation: "I'm reaching fifteen or sixteen, what's gonna be, no money, how they gonna buy a husband, *nadan*, a dowry? . . . So I says well, . . . I am going to America!" A Women's Bureau study of immigrant women suggested that many girls came to this country for "a chance to work and to marry."[23] Clearly, there was less and less opportunity in Europe to accumulate the dowry that was virtually a precondition to marriage.

The disruption that poverty and emigration provoked in customary marriage provisions also opened up marriage negotiations to participation by individuals rather than families.[24] The fiction of the period suggests that a challenge to arranged marriage was in the air. In Giovanni Verga's 1890 novel of Sicilian family life, *The House by the Medlar Tree*, the grandfather was outraged, but not surprised, when his grandson resolved to marry without parental approval or regard for family priorities:

> To marry her . . . And who am I? And does your mother count for nothing? When your father married her that sits there, he made them come and tell me first. Your grandmother was then alive and they came and spoke to us. . . . Now these things are no longer the custom, and the old people are of no use. At one time it was said, "Listen to the

old and you'll make no blunders." First your sister must be
married.

In Sholom Aleichem's "Tevye" stories, written between 1892 and
1907, the conflicts between Tevye and his daughters, symbolic of the
disintegration of traditional shtetl culture, took the form of struggle
over his authority to arrange their marriages.[25]

In both southern Italy and eastern Europe, then, variations in
customary family arrangements showed the effects of wide-ranging
economic and social change. Whether the family referred primarily
to parents and unmarried children or to the larger kin group, those
to whom one looked for assistance would become even more
important in the trials of migration and resettlement that lay
ahead.

KINSHIP AND MIGRATION

Migration was particularly a familistic response to the transformation of ordinary life in southern Italy and eastern Europe.
Emigration was an intentional, self-selecting strategy that had
particular appeal in areas dominated by household production.[26]
Individual economic goals for migration were inextricably connected
to survival strategies for family groups.

The bonds of kinship often provided a basis for chain migration,
linking communities in Europe to communities in the United States.
The resources of family and kinship networks were invaluable in
facilitating the actual migration process. Cousins wrote to cousins
still in Europe describing what they found in the United States. Both
men and women guided their kin to specific locations, employment,
and housing; uncles, sisters, brothers, daughters all wrote to urge
other family members to join them in American cities.[27]

Family and kin often provided the financial means for migration. One well-educated daughter of a rabbi in Cleveland was paid by
her neighbors to transcribe their letters home for them, and she
claimed that:

> There was hardly one person near us who did not send to
> Europe some small sum for father or brother or mother, or
> most frequently of all, for wife and children.

The U.S. Immigration Commission found that more than one-
fourth of Italian immigrants and more than one-half of Jewish

immigrants arrived between 1908 and 1910 on tickets prepaid by relatives.[28]

Looking ahead to the strangeness of arrival, family members planned before they left home to make contact with relatives in this country for temporary housing. One Jewish immigrant woman who travelled to New York on her own explained that she had begun to write letters to her mother's family in New York several months before she actually left Russia. She could have stayed with one of her uncles, to whom she had written, but she did not because "I had my mother's sister so I stayed with her." An Italian immigrant woman also recalled that, even before they left Italy, some of her *paesani* "make the arrangement to stay in the house of some relatives." Then "when they stay here for a little bit they used to send for the wife and family." In her eyes, this chain migration of kin was a universal in the community: "This is the way that everybody used to do it that time."[29]

For these reasons, family ties often underlay the provincial ties that linked immigrants from villages in the old country to neighborhoods in this country. Southern Italians deeply valued stable ties to villages. Mario Puzo remembered how his parents spoke of their forebears who spent all their lives farming the arid mountain slopes of southern Italy: " 'He died in the house in which he was born,' they say enviously. 'He was never more than an hour from his village, not in all his life,' they sigh."[30] Jewish families, having been scattered by pogroms, residence restrictions, and the fierce competition for work, were less likely to be settled in a specific community. Forbidden by law to own land, many Jewish families felt that they left behind a kind of community experience rather than a specific place. As one immigrant described it,

> There was no love attachment for home or town as far as my brothers and I were concerned. We lived there because we happened to have been born there. I never even thought of having any kind of attachment for my home, town, or other people. I knew that I had to work in order to live, and that particular town gave me work. If something happened, as it later did, I would leave at a moment's notice without regrets.[31]

Their ties were to fellow Jews in a particular place, not to the community itself.

Though immigrants were likely to be dependent in these ways on family connections, the experience of migration disrupted family relationships. Many families did not relocate completely, and family members often emigrated at different times. A common separation caused by migration was that between husband and wife. These separations, which sometimes lasted many years, could exacerbate divisions within a family. According to a Sicilian folk song, men had great concern over the conduct of their wives in their absence:

> The wives of the Americans [emigrants]
> Eat and drink like dogs.
> They go to the church and pray to God:
> "Send me money, my husband,
> For if you do not send me money,
> I will change your name
> And christen you Pasquale [cuckold]."

In actuality, wives were often anxious to end the separations. One Italian immigrant explained that her husband had made two previous trips to America, but when he wanted to make his third trip, she refused to let him go alone: "Nothing doing, we all go or we all stay." When he argued that they could not afford passage for all to migrate, his wife turned for assistance to her father, who was a landowner. He was able to give them a piece of land to sell, and the family made the third and final trip to America together.[32]

Sometimes separations caused by migration grew out of existing tensions in the household. One Jewish immigrant remembered that his parents "did not get along very well. They never agreed." He was a small boy when his father left for America, so he did not understand the roots of the quarrel between his parents. However, he was able to observe the shift in parental authority made possible by his father's absence. Before the father migrated, he was the "boss of the house." It was after the father left for America that "we got the business and mother took care of it." In other families, men and women were divided by their response to the opportunity for migration. Varying expectations set one Italian husband and wife against each other. In their daughter's words:

> In them days, lots of people was coming over here, and my mother makes up her mind she wants to come here too. My father says, no, I'm all right here, I work on my little farm and I get by pretty good. But you know my mother, she

makes up her mind, and she told my father, if you no go, I
go, see.

The daughter stayed behind with her father while her mother and
sister left for America. Parents and children were frequently divided
by willingness or reluctance to uproot themselves. One Italian
immigrant sent passage money to his parents so that they could join
him and his brother in this country, but they refused. They were both
in their sixties and perhaps they "figure they are too old to come here
now." Even knowing they would probably live and die apart from
their sons, the parents did not want to leave southern Italy: "My
father own his farm and he is satisfied with what he got."[33]
    Because marriage meant that men and women were involved in
two sets of kin relationships, immigrants often had to choose
between them. One Jewish immigrant woman explained the process
by which her entire family settled in America while her husband left
all of his kin in Russia. Her uncle and oldest brother were the first to
leave, and they then sent for family members to join them, one by
one. At some point, all the men in her family decided to emigrate,
planning to send for their families and younger brothers and sisters
as soon as possible. Her father, realizing that her whole family would
be reunited in America while she was still in Russia, asked her
husband to join the group of men. His decision was a difficult one, as
his wife remembered:

> Although my husband did not like his work as a shoemaker
> he hesitated about going to America, probably because it
> would mean leaving behind all of his people.

The only one who could make such a hard choice was someone
outside the family, and so the husband asked his mother-in-law to
speak to the rabbi, and the rabbi advised him to go. Regrouping one
family meant breaking another family apart. Frequently, in fact,
immigration meant permanent separation from parents. One Jewish
immigrant had lived near her own mother in Russia after marrying,
but emigration meant that she left her mother "as one leaves the
dead." She came to America and her mother died without ever seeing
her daughter again.[34] Almost by definition then, the process of
immigration built on ties of kinship and at the same time broke apart
family connections.

FAMILY AND KINSHIP IN PROVIDENCE

Migration and relocation distributed family members in new combinations, and settlement in Providence redefined familial needs for assistance and the norms of family residence. Whichever kin found themselves in Providence joined forces to face the tasks of daily existence in a strange place. Kin networks that rarely expanded into residence in Europe did so frequently in Providence.[35]

Because immigration was a family strategy so often facilitated by kin connections, many of the immigrants who came to Providence had relatives there. Sixty-nine percent of the Italian families in the neighborhood studied, and 42 percent of the Jewish families, had at least one parent or sibling in Providence.[36] Jewish families, more likely to have been separated from kin in eastern Europe, were less likely than Italians to have relatives in Providence. But because of the way in which immigration separated family members and because of separations already endured by Jews in eastern Europe, kin networks of immigrants were rarely completely reconstituted in Providence. Families almost never had both sets of parents, or all brothers and sisters together in one place (see table 3-1). A Providence-area Jewish immigrant in her reminiscences captured this sense of immigration as building on family ties while at the same time separating kin. As she understood the family history, her father came to Providence originally because he had a nephew there, and he himself helped to establish two other nephews and a niece in the area. All those local

TABLE 3-1. Incomplete Immigrant Kin Networks in Providence, Arrival to 1915

	Italian		Jewish	
Kin Relationships of Heads of Households				
Immigrant men with parents in Providence	14%	(23)	13%	(9)
Immigrant women with parents in Providence	30%	(48)	14%	(10)
Immigrant men with siblings in Providence	39%	(63)	22%	(16)
Immigrant women with siblings in Providence	40%	(64)	19%	(14)
Kin Relationships of Immigrants with Kin in Providence				
Families with siblings or siblings-in-law	33%	(37)	33%	(10)
Families with parents or parents-in-law	5%	(6)	4%	(1)
Families with siblings and parents	49%	(54)	53%	(16)
Families with other kin	13%	(14)	10%	(3)
TOTAL	100%	(111)	100%	(30)

Source: Neighborhood data.

relatives got married and had children, but those who were missing made it seem like "rather a small family." According to the daughter, her father's only regrets were those relatives he had lost. He had had "five or six brothers, and their children emigrated all over the world, you know, we don't know where they are." At the same time as her father felt connected to his kin in Providence, he was very conscious of those who were far away.[37]

Lacking the resources of a complete family network but sharing common needs as strangers in a new land, families with kin in Providence were very likely to combine households. If immigrants had parents in Providence, they were likely to live with them at some point. Many left parents in Europe, but 65 percent of the Italian families and 66 percent of the Jewish families who had parents in Providence lived with a parent for some period of time. Usually the doubling up occurred in the first years after migration when immigrants had the least resources and the greatest need for assistance, and then periodically on a short-term basis at other moments of need. Most commonly, widowed parents lived with married children and grandchildren. In one instance, a Jewish couple with two grown sons came to Providence sometime between 1896 and 1897. The older of the sons married in Providence, and he and his wife lived with his parents for about a year until they found an apartment around the corner. When the father died, the older son brought his mother to live with him and his family for fifteen years until she died. During most of these years, the younger son and his wife and children also lived around the corner.[38] As this family history indicates, often the temporary sharing of household space was followed by long-term residential proximity. Whatever relationships family members had created inside the expanded household could persist, although in attenuated form, down the street.

More immigrants were likely to have brothers and sisters in Providence, and they also were likely to live with their siblings at some point. In 1915, brothers or sisters were the most likely candidates to join a household (see table 3-2). For brothers and sisters as well as parents, coresidence was often followed by close residential proximity; brothers and sisters were likely to find their own homes within a few blocks of where they had been sharing living quarters. For example, one Italian immigrant couple came to Providence in 1890. Thirteen years later in 1903, two of the wife's brothers, who had been ten-years and two-years old when she left Italy, came to board with her in Providence. The older of the two brothers married in 1906 and continued to board with his sister for

TABLE 3-2. Composition of Combined Residence, 1915 and 1940[a]

Kin in Household	Italian				Jewish			
	1915		1940		1915		1940	
Siblings	51%	(20)	8%	(5)	40%	(4)	8%	(2)
Married child	8%	(3)	82%	(50)	20%	(2)	80%	(19)
Siblings and parents	18%	(7)	5%	(3)	30%	(3)	—	(0)
Parents	15%	(6)	—	(0)	10%	(1)	—	(0)
Siblings and married child	—	(0)	1.6%	(1)	—	(0)	8%	(2)
Parents and married child	—	(0)	1.6%	(1)	—	(0)	—	(0)
Other kin	8%	(3)	1.6%	(1)	—	(0)	4%	(1)
TOTAL	100%	(39)	99.8%	(61)	100%	(10)	100%	(24)

Source: Neighborhood data.
a. Combined residence in 1915 = in same household or at same address; combined residence in 1940 = at same address.

several years until his second child was born, at which point he and his wife and children moved to an apartment around the corner. The younger brother married in 1912, and he also brought his wife to live with his sister until their first child was born, when they moved half a block away. After their second child was born, the younger brother moved his family back to his sister's house, where they stayed for two years until they moved to a new apartment, across the street from his older brother and a block from his sister.[39] Combining households and living near family served to compensate for incomplete family groups.

Families found that residence in the same building enabled them to offer important kinds of assistance to one another. Property ownership was not necessary for families to live in adjoining apartments, but many immigrants who did own property used their tenements to house relatives (see table 3-3).[40] In 1915, 74 percent of Italian families and 46 percent of Jewish families who owned property in Providence had kin listed at the same address. A Jewish immigrant remembered how her family had divided up the apartments in a Providence triple-decker house that her father bought with his cousins. Her family lived downstairs because they had four children; one cousin lived on the second floor with two children; and the other cousin lived on the top floor because he had no children. An Italian daughter recalled the financial advantage her family gained living in the 1910s and 1920s in a Providence tenement owned by her mother's parents: her parents paid only twelve dollars in rent while other tenants paid fifteen dollars. Living across the hall from parents yielded the family an additional, although less quantifiable, financial benefit—free babysitting. The daughter remembered that she "spent more time with my grandparents than my mother and father when I was little because my mother worked in the bakery when my father opened his own."[41] Residence in the same building was thus particularly important for working women, carrying the responsibility for both household work and employment, because it enabled mothers at home to help daughters going out to work.

TABLE 3-3. Property Ownership and Kinship Networks

	Italian[a]		Jewish[b]	
	Traceable Immigrants Owning Property in Neighborhood	Property Owners with Kin at Same Address	Traceable Immigrants Owning Property in Neighborhood	Property Owners with Kin at Same Address
1915	18% (27)	74% (20)	38% (24)	46% (11)
1935	36% (41)	71% (29)	56% (23)	56% (13)

Source: Neighborhood data linked with Providence Board of Assessors, *Tax Book*, 1915, 1935.
a. $N = 152$ in 1915, 113 in 1935.
b. $N = 63$ in 1915, 41 in 1935.

Brothers and sisters were more likely than parents and adult children to migrate together to Providence, and their rough similarity of age and situation made them particularly well suited for domestic exchange. An Italian daughter remembered how crucial a shared tenement was to the kind of help her family received from her father's brother and sister-in-law in a family emergency. As she grew up, "living conditions were a bit crowded," with her uncle, his wife, his father, and his stepmother in the same tenement as her parents, brother, and sisters, but "no one minded, because we were a family." After her mother died, her aunt helped her to care for the younger children in her family, and she felt "thankful we all lived together." Even in ordinary times, residence in the same building made it possible for mothers of young children to exchange child care. Three young Italian immigrant sisters who lived with their husbands in a tenement house in Federal Hill found many ways in which their parallel life situations and the forced intimacy of their crowded housing could work to each other's advantage, as one of their daughters described:

> Then the babies starting arriving. The three women would share the housework and motherly duties. . . . The sisters bore their children almost at the same time, and often there was more than one baby crying and fussing. There was so much closeness among the growing family that whenever a small baby began to cry, whatever mother happened to be around, would pick up the child and breastfeed it, whether it was hers or not.

In these ways, women immigrants particularly benefited from having relatives nearby, and may have taken an active role in encouraging and organizing residential kin networks.[42]

If the relationship between brother and sister was close, then aunts, uncles, and cousins became important members in a family network. Connectedness to siblings encouraged involvement with a larger number of relatives. Aunts or uncles living in the households had a particular impact. The children who grew up in households extended by aunts and uncles described these extra adults as almost surrogate parents, who were able to give guidance and encouragement outside of the emotional demands and limits of the parent-child relationship. One Jewish daughter in Providence remembered her aunt, who was a nurse and had lived with her family for a number of years, as the person she most admired. Another Jewish daughter felt that her aunt, who had lived with her family, had influenced her more than her parents. "We were like very close sisters. Anything I wanted to know, she was the one I went to." An Italian daughter most looked up to an uncle who was a musician, who had lived with his sister's family after becoming separated from his wife. "He taught me to play the piano. I admired his way of life, his love of life." She would have emulated her uncle's life to the extent of becoming a concert pianist herself, but her mother objected.[43] Clearly the experience of living with kin in the household or across the hall shaped children's lives in ways their parents could not predict or completely control.

Sharing household living space or residing in the same building was thus a common feature in the immigrant neighborhoods of Providence. Between 1900 and 1935, 71 percent of the Italians with kin in Providence and 53 percent of the Jewish families had at least one relative living at the same address for some period of time. Close residential proximity also enabled kin to have involved and important relationships with each other, and almost everyone with kin in Providence had a relative close by. Ninety-two percent of the Italians and 87 percent of the Jewish families with kin in Providence had relatives in the household or within two blocks of where they lived; 87 percent of the Italians and 99 percent of the Jews who had a parent in Providence lived in the same household or within two blocks of a parent for some period of time. Within the household, across the hall, up and down the block, immigrant families spread kinship networks through the neighborhoods. Eighty percent of the Italians and 90 percent of the Jews who had a brother or sister in Providence lived with a sibling or within two blocks of one during these years. Almost all of the immigrants with kin in Providence had relatives living near enough to meet together every day to exchange news, meals, child care, to shop together, to travel to work or walk to church or shul together.

Within the Italian neighborhood, families from the same region who lived near each other were also likely to be kin. Of the 67 percent of the Italian immigrants in the neighborhood whose town or region of origin was recorded, all those from the same town who lived in the same triple-decker or next door were also related by blood or marriage. In these instances, kin ties were the basis of old-country village ties.[44]

Living so close to relatives meant that it was easy and natural to ✓ socialize together. As one Jewish immigrant to Providence described the constant visiting, "Kids would drop in, families would drop in, the men would drop in and chat, play a little cards . . . everyone was in the neighborhood!" One Italian daughter explained the assumptions operating in her family about how often they would visit relatives. She saw her mother's family, whose house she could see from her window, every day, while she saw her father's family, who lived several blocks away, only on weekends. Family visits tended to dominate weekend social life and to divide along sex lines. One Italian immigrant to Providence remembered that in southern Italy and in Providence, men and women gathered in separate groupings. In Federal Hill on a Saturday night, the men in her family would be in one room playing cards, and the women and children would sit in the newly cleaned tenement stairwell listening to night stories, "and I mean stories about ladies of the evening, and everything." Visiting brought the oldest and youngest into contact; in one Italian family in Providence, it was Sunday dinner at the father's parents' house that brought all the family members together. One of the uncles had to build a huge table big enough for everyone to fit around it. The meal was a feast, with homemade bread and wine, olives, fresh cheeses, all kinds of cold cuts, but the dinners seemed very long to a little girl: "The children sat at the table with the grown-ups. We used to stay until my mother and father were ready to come home." Informal visiting was often dominated by the wife's relatives: one Italian daughter recalled that she and her husband took their children visiting to her family, her sisters, her aunts.[45] For these immigrants and their children, visiting kin was the central component of a rich neighborhood social life.

In Providence, then, the exigencies of migration and the dominant multiple-family architecture and crowded street plans of the settlement areas facilitated family linkages. It was both desirable and possible for immigrants who had parents, brothers, or sisters in the city to include them as part of their households, to live close-by in the neighborhood, and to maintain close ties. Living nearby, relatives in Providence sometimes attempted to take the place of missing family. In some instances, brothers and sisters assumed the responsibility of absent parents. An Italian immigrant man assumed he would handle his sister-in-law's earnings since she was in Providence without other family. He resented the fact that she chose to save her money in a bank instead of handing it over for him to take care of. Another Italian immigrant woman took charge of her brother's family after his death. First she arranged work for her brother's wife in the textile mill where she was employed. After her sister-in-law died six years later, the sister single-handedly raised her five nieces and nephews.[46] With parents absent, brothers and sisters took it for granted that, should the need arise, they would step into their parents' shoes.

Immigrants whose families had been scattered by migration often experienced the opposite phenomenon—instead of kin becoming neighbors, neighbors acted like kin. Neighbors from the old country who had already come to the United States were sometimes willing to assume some of the responsibilities of kin. They often served as a wider circle of assistance for those with only one or two close relatives to draw on. At times they went beyond even the traditional role of kin by providing room and board for those without family. One Italian immigrant followed his brother to Bridgeport because his brother said it was "the best place, because there are a lot of people from the old country that we knew in Bridgeport." When he arrived, he was "glad to see all the people that come from my place, and they started to make a good time for me. They made a party, and they had wine and *biscotti* and lots of meat and macaroni." A Jewish immigrant who arrived in New York by himself quickly found a *landsman* "who had lived in our Russian village" and "had known my father since early childhood." The landsman took him home, fed him, and helped him to find work and permanent lodgings.[47] Just as kin often took on new obligations to each other in the new surroundings, so did neighbors.

If boarders were not already relatives, they were often friends from the old country. Although it was not possible to be sure of the relationships between boarders and heads of household in the neighborhoods studied, many boarders were close to the same age as the head of household. Oral histories identified many of the boarders as *paesani* or *landsleit*. When a young Italian couple moved into the husband's father's house after their marriage, there was an Italian immigrant family in the downstairs parlor because "they came from the same part of Italy that Victor's father came from and they had no one in America and they didn't have much money." When a young Jewish immigrant woman got married, her friend moved in with her. The woman recalled the arrangement:

> I took four rooms . . . I wanted to take less than four, I wanted to take three rooms or two, so my friend . . . very close friend from Europe, so she says, Fannie, take four rooms and I'm going to move into you. So I took four rooms and she took a bedroom.[48]

The boarding relationship by definition introduced money into the exchange of goods and services, and there were limits on the amount of responsibility families took on for their boarders. But in certain circumstances, those who kept boarders acted like family in enforcing certain communally accepted norms of behavior. For example, one boardinghouse keeper supervised the courtships of young single women in her house. As one immigrant recalled:

> [Her father] had heard about this nice young girl who had come . . . and asked his sister about her. One day he went to the boarding house to meet her and was formally introduced by the woman running the house. They were never allowed to be alone.[49]

The boardinghouse keeper was as strict as parents would have been.

New neighbors in the ethnically homogeneous areas in Providence also provided assistance to each other. One Italian immigrant explained that "sharing a common background" created a bond such that "you were always ready to lend a helping hand." What this woman defined as a "common background" probably referred to a number of shared experiences—language and cultural references, recent uprooting and resettlement, precarious employment, scarce family resources. Whatever its origins, the common bond enabled immigrants to extend a culture of reciprocity from family to kin to old-country villagers to new neighbors in Providence. Neighbors responded to household emergencies, as this immigrant woman remembered:

> I can recall my father running to a neighbor's house in the middle of the night because a water pipe broke. He must have managed to do a fairly good job since they never did have to call a plumber.

Providence neighbors also attempted to substitute in a more general way for missing or unavailable kin. A young Italian woman who had only one sister in Providence depended on her neighbors for help during childbirth: "The neighbors pitched in, and cooked and cleaned for each other at these times. We Italians say, 'One hand washes the other.'" When her husband died, again the neighbors came to her assistance,

> not with money, but with companionship, advice (sometimes too much advice), and tending the children. . . . Looking back, I know I couldn't have survived those first years without my friends and neighbors.

The assumption of shared values in the neighborhood made her confident that neighbors would watch out for her children, disciplining them as she or an aunt or grandmother would. She was willing to do the same for others. As she explained:

> In our neighborhood, the children were treated as children. They were expected to respect adults, and they did, or else. And if you saw a neighbor's child doing something wrong, you treated him as though he were your own, and his parents were grateful for it.

Her neighbors stood in for family, making her feel cared for and secure amidst a larger group. Like family socializing, friendships among neighbors remained inside lines of gender: women helped out other women, men made contact with other men.[50]

In Providence, then, families compensated for the profound disruptions accompanying immigration in three particular ways.

They brought parents, brothers, sisters, and cousins to crowd together in shared households and in apartments in the same building. They found tenements that allowed kin to gather near each other in the neighborhood. When family members were missing, *paesani* and *landsleit* with common memories of the old country attempted to take their places; so did new neighbors with shared language and immigration experience. The result of these adjustments was to blur the boundaries of the household and the distinction between kin and neighbor. Immigrant families had intense needs for help, for companionship, for resources beyond those commanded by combinations of parents and children alone. Expanding the circle of assistance to include kin, neighbors, and friends enabled immigrants to survive and sink new family roots in Providence. When they would no longer be migrants, when family networks would again be complete, the lines separating households and neighbors would again be redrawn. The configurations of family interaction would then take yet another form.

Changing Patterns of Family Connection

As the years in Providence turned into decades, and as immigrants who had arrived carrying babies discovered themselves to be the parents of adult men and women, the patterns of interaction inside and between households shifted once again. As the immigrants themselves aged and as their own children married and settled nearby, the patterns of mutual assistance between brothers and sisters which had sustained the immigrant generation through the perils of migration and resettlement were replaced by expectations of aid between parents and married children. The connection between aging parents and adult children, which had been broken for the immigrant generation by their distance from parents left behind in Europe, was reestablished between Providence immigrants and their own children.

By 1940, the most likely candidates for residence in the same building were married children, sometimes bringing with them grandchildren (see table 3-2, p. 000). With the maturation of the ethnic settlements in Providence, ties between immigrant parents and married children who lived nearby became closer. Many of the immigrants in the neighborhoods settled married children in the buildings in which they lived. In 1940, 60 percent of the Italian families and 59 percent of the Jewish families with married children had a married child at the same address. Others had married children close by: 78 percent of Italian families and 71 percent of Jewish families with married children had at least one married child at the same address or within two blocks (see table 3-4). Between unmarried children living at home and married children in the same building, 89 percent of Italian immigrant parents and 77 percent of Jewish immigrant parents had assistance within their own families close at hand (see table 3-5).[51]

TABLE 3-4. Parents' Proximity to Married Children, 1940[a]

	Italian		Jewish	
Nearest married child at same address	60%	(53)	59%	(24)
Nearest married child within 2 blocks	18%	(16)	12%	(5)
Nearest married child within 10 blocks	11%	(10)	15%	(6)
Nearest married child in different neighborhood	11%	(10)	12%	(5)
Nearest married child in another city	—	(0)	2%	(1)
	100%	(89)[b]	100%	(41)[b]

Source: Neighborhood data.
a. If both parents were dead by 1940, parent-child proximity was measured in the year before the last parent died.
b. N = total number of families with married children.

In the same years, the likelihood that siblings would live as close to each other diminished. Daily visiting between brothers and sisters was not unlikely, but by 1940 less than half of those families that had lived with brothers and sisters in their households or nearby were still in close proximity. Some remained within the boundaries of the old neighborhoods, but almost one-fourth of the Italian families that had lived close to brothers and sisters, and almost one-half of the Jewish families similarly situated, were now living in different neighborhoods altogether. In one instance, two Italian brothers and a sister who had lived within three blocks of each other for twenty years moved during the 1920s so that by 1940, they each lived in a separate neighborhood. Two Jewish brothers had lived across the street from each other for many years but by 1940 were more than ten

TABLE 3-5. Residential Options for Immigrant Parents, 1940[a]

	Italian		Jewish	
Couple or widow with unmarried child or children at same address	49.5%	(60)	35.5%	(19)
Couple or widow with married child or children at same address	15.5%	(19)	19%	(10)
Couple or widow with both unmarried and married child or children at same address	24%	(29)	22.5%	(12)
Couple or widow apparently alone	9%	(11)	17%	(9)
Widow plus boarders	—	(0)	2%	(1)
Couple or widow with unmarried child or children and coresiding kin	1%	(1)	4%	(2)
Couple with coresiding kin	1%	(1)	—	(0)
	100%	(121)[b]	100%	(53)[b]

Source: Neighborhood data.
a. If both parents were dead by 1940, parent-child proximity was measured in the year before the last parent died.
b. N = total number of families who stayed in Providence.

blocks apart, one of them living next door to his oldest daughter and her husband.[52] As this family history suggests, the loosening of ties to brothers and sisters and the intensification of connection between parents and married children were related phenomenon. With their own married children nearby, immigrants who were themselves aging did not look to other kin and neighbors to exchange assistance as they had earlier, but rather relied on those who owed them the most clearly defined obligations. No longer missing members, immigrant families were not as open to kin, friends, and neighbors. The family networks of immigrants as they grew older were likely to be more vertical than horizontal,[53] more hierarchical than fraternal.

The faint boundary between kin and neighbor which had characterized social life in the immigrant settlements became more sharply defined as the Italian and Jewish communities spread out from the old ethnic neighborhoods over the city as a whole. The real impact of suburbanization on families and neighborhoods would not be felt in Providence until after World War II, when veterans' mortgage insurance and federal highway building encouraged population movement away from the city. But even in the 1920s and 1930s, the process of residential dispersion meant that kin were not as likely to be neighbors, nor neighbors as likely to be related. By 1940, less than half of the Italian families in the neighborhood and one-third of the Jewish families were still living in the areas they settled as new immigrants. Immigrants moved frequently, perhaps prompted by economic stringency, perhaps in search of more space or different surroundings. A Jewish immigrant who lived in New York City explained her family's frequent change of address as worth the hard work of moving, because "even moving from one dingy place to another is a change. And then, too, some were less dingy than others."[54] Those who did remain on Federal Hill and Smith Hill almost never remained in the same building.

Regardless of the reasons for which people moved, moves to far corners of the neighborhood or outside it had the potential of breaking up ties between kin based on residential proximity. Twenty-eight percent of Italian and 34 percent of Jewish families moved to other residential neighborhoods in Providence or to nearby suburbs.[55] Some of this residential movement may have been for the purpose of reestablishing kin ties; several widows left the old neighborhoods to live with their married children who had moved to other parts of Providence. Some families appear to have moved as a group to newer, less-settled areas where they could own or rent several houses or apartments near each other. This seemed to have been the intention of three Jewish brothers, who, after their parents died, moved their families from several scattered residences within several blocks on Smith Hill to three residences next door to each other in a neighborhood a mile to the west. The intention to regroup a family seemed also to explain the pattern of three Italian brothers and their children, who, within four years, moved from residences in Federal Hill to three residences across the street from each other a mile from where they had lived previously.[56] But most moves out of the neighborhood meant that wives left sisters back on Federal Hill, and husbands left brothers behind in Smith Hill. And even moves within the old neighborhoods which left kin ten or twelve blocks apart meant that it would be much more difficult to see each other frequently.

Even with small pockets of related people, the new residential neighborhoods were markedly less ethnically homogeneous than the original neighborhoods had been. Families in the new neighborhoods were less likely to be connected by kinship, less likely to have been neighbors in the old country, less likely to share an immigrant past. The lessening of ethnic homogeneity meant that people no longer assumed a commonality; they regarded their neighbors in the new residential areas as different from themselves, whether in fact they were or not. One Jewish immigrant mourned the loss of sociability based on that assumed common ground:

> I miss that period. I miss that period, because in those days, I would walk out on my porch, and there was somebody across the street I could holler to and talk to, and then there was a relative somewhere a couple of houses up I could talk to, and I met a few people on the corner, or in a candy store, you lived a real social life. Now I don't know my next door neighbor![57]

For many families, residential dispersion continued a process whereby assistance and social needs were more likely to be absorbed within individual families in the interaction between parents and married children than by kin and neighbors. Residential dispersion transformed the community context that had supported and extended kinship networks.

At the same time as the lines between households were being redrawn, the composition of the household itself was being altered. Changing economic and political conditions in Europe and new restrictive laws in this country slowed the pace of migration from Europe dramatically. The flow of kin and boarders, whose need for temporary housing had expanded the membership of the household, virtually stopped altogether. By 1940, ethnic households still contained extra adults, but now these were primarily unmarried sons and daughters (see tables 3-6, 3-7).[58] Nearly 40 percent of the Italian sons between the ages of thirty and thirty-nine and 35 percent of the Italian daughters in the same age group were unmarried and living at home in 1940. In the same age group, 31 percent of Jewish sons and 23 percent of Jewish daughters were unmarried and living at home. A considerable number of the adult children between the age of forty and sixty were also unmarried and at home; 22 percent of Italian sons, 7 percent of Jewish sons, and 11 percent of Italian and Jewish daughters in this age group were living as single adults in their parents' homes.

Many different factors determined the rates of marriage and the ages of marriage in southern Italy, eastern Europe, and Providence; a detailed analysis of these is beyond the scope of this study.[59] But it does seem important to point out that the difficulties which families

TABLE 3-6. Location of Italian Children in Relation to Their Parents, by Sex and Birthdate, 1940

Child's Status	Sons								Daughters							
	1880–1900		1901–10		1911–20		1921+		1880–1900		1901–10		1911–20		1921+	
Single at home	22%	(11)	39%	(33)	80%	(69)	95%	(21)	11%	(7)	35%	(26)	66%	(64)	97%	(33)
Separated, same address	—	(0)	—	(0)	—	(0)	—	(0)	—	(0)	—	(0)	—	(0)	—	(0)
Married, same address	27%	(13)	11%	(9)	9%	(8)	—	(0)	16%	(10)	13%	(10)	9%	(9)	—	(0)
Married, in neighborhood	20%	(10)	28%	(24)	6%	(5)	—	(0)	47%	(29)	27%	(20)	15%	(14)	—	(0)
Married, different neighborhood	12%	(6)	15%	(13)	5%	(4)	—	(0)	10%	(6)	5%	(4)	6%	(6)	—	(0)
Married, different city	16%	(8)	5%	(4)	—	(0)	—	(0)	15%	(9)	11%	(8)	1%	(1)	—	(0)
Inadequate information	2%	(1)	2%	(2)	—	(0)	5%	(1)	1%	(1)	9%	(7)	3%	(3)	3%	(1)
N in age category		(49)		(85)		(86)		(22)		(62)		(75)		(97)		(33)

Source: Neighborhood data.

TABLE 3-7. Location of Jewish Children in Relation to Their Parents, by Sex and Birthdate, 1940

Child's Status	Sons								Daughters							
	1880–1900		1901–10		1911–20		1921+		1880–1900		1901–10		1911–20		1921+	
Single at home	7%	(4)	31%	(11)	88%	(24)	100%	(1)	11%	(4)	23%	(13)	52%	(14)	100%	(2)
Separated, same address	7%	(4)	3%	(1)	4%	(1)	—	(0)	—	(0)	—	(0)	—	(0)	—	(0)
Married, same address	7%	(4)	8%	(3)	—	(0)	—	(0)	14%	(5)	9%	(5)	7%	(2)	—	(0)
Married, in neighborhood	25%	(14)	19%	(7)	—	(0)	—	(0)	20%	(7)	11%	(6)	11%	(3)	—	(0)
Married, different neighborhood	25%	(14)	22%	(8)	4%	(1)	—	(0)	14%	(5)	20%	(11)	4%	(1)	—	(0)
Married, different city	14%	(8)	—	(0)	—	(0)	—	(0)	26%	(9)	9%	(5)	0		—	(0)
Inadequate information	16%	(9)	17%	(6)	4%	(1)	—	(0)	14%	(5)	28%	(16)	26%	(7)	—	(0)
N in age category	(57)		(36)		(27)		(1)		(35)		(56)		(27)		(2)	

Source: Neighborhood data.

faced in arranging marriages in Europe, and which prompted the migration of young men and women, were not completely resolved by that strategy. Single immigrants themselves had married, freed by distance from familial, social, or economic constraints. But as parents, immigrants felt caught between traditional pressures to arrange marriages for their children, thus preserving family continuity, and their own dependence on their children's wages. This conflict increased in intensity in Providence because of the steady availability of wage work for children in contrast to children's important but more precarious economic contribution in Europe. The parents' dilemma sharpened, particularly during the Depression years in Providence which in many cases coincided with the young adulthood of the American-born generation. One Italian father in New York confessed his role in keeping his adult daughter home:

> I am not a strong man any more. My hardworking days are over. . . . One of our daughters is an old maid, causes plenty of troubles. . . . It may be my fault because I always wished her to remain at home and not to marry for she was of great financial help.

Immigrant parents had to balance their conception of family honor against their strategies for economic survival, as one Italian daughter explained. The main expectation both her parents had for their daughters was that they be "safely married," that they not "shame them" by becoming pregnant first but only marry when the family could financially afford it. But the parents only got part of what they demanded from their daughters: "they were never shamed, but each marriage brought loss of wages and the strain of wedding bills." Her parents could not help but view their daughters' marriages with mixed emotions.[60]

Immigrants' children were caught between these conflicting sets of expectations, and a sizeable proportion of both sons and daughters delayed marriage or postponed it indefinitely. The national marriage rate also dropped sharply during the Depression years.[61] Certainly coming of age during the Depression deepened children's sense of economic responsibility to their parents. Sons and daughters who did not go to high school, who worked at sexually segregated jobs, or whose families were relatively isolated from village or kinship networks might not have had the social opportunities to arrange marriages.

Some daughters, supporting themselves and their families with their wages, chose not to marry. One Jewish immigrant mother expressed her high-school-graduate daughter's point of view:

> The other day I was in an argument with my youngest
> daughter. She says, why should she get married? She has a
> nice home, makes $15 a week.[62]

Similarly, an Italian daughter felt free not to marry because she was
working. Of course, she "did have to contribute to the family quite a
bit." After her father died, she was the only one in the family
bringing in an income. Her mother had taken it upon herself to turn
down her daughter's first proposal of marriage:

> My mother once told me that some one wanted to marry me,
> but she told him no I was too young. She never told me who
> it was. I was seventeen at the time.

In her account years later, the daughter affirmed her mother's
intervention: "I wouldn't have gotten married anyway." Her own
feelings about supporting herself and supporting her family stood
between her and marriage: "It's not that I didn't want to get
married, but when you are working and you have your own
money . . . " She did not feel isolated in her decision not to marry,
for her social world was filled with other young men and women who
had the same sense of obligation to their families:

> During all the years I worked, I had a boyfriend, but we
> both had responsibilities at home. . . . Now they say "career
> woman" but at the time you wouldn't call yourself that. It's
> just because you felt you had a responsibility at home,
> too.[63]

The decision not to marry came from some combination of personal
and familial concerns.

Social and emotional as well as financial responsibilities bound
children to their parents. A Jewish daughter in Providence described
the ties to her parents which overrode any longing for her own
household and family:

> I wasn't even thinking of getting married, my mother and
> father needed me. I was going out with a man, but it didn't
> make any difference. . . . I lived with them.

She felt that if she had a family of her own, she could not have been
fully available to meet her parents' needs, even if she lived in an
adjoining apartment:

If I were married and lived upstairs, I could not have been as good a daughter, I'd have other responsibilities. When you're married and have children, you cannot, as much as you want to, you cannot devote your life to your mother and father. I had no difficulty—they were part of me . . . it was good to know that I was with them, and I was just part of their lives.

Her mother was concerned that her daughter was sacrificing her own life; she "used to worry about my not getting married." But for the daughter taking care of her parents was a conscious choice, not "at all a tragedy." As she explained, "I would have liked to have had a husband and children, but—that's how life went and I didn't regret a word of it."[64] Cultural norms which defined marriage primarily in terms of family needs could be adjusted to support the decision *not* to marry because of familial considerations.

The immigrant sons and daughters who did marry increasingly asserted more control over the choice of a marriage partner. Individual initiative began to play an acknowledged part in courtship and marriage decisions. Family deliberations did not disappear, but parental control over marriage partners was partially eroded by the conditions of social life in a big city. Parents postponed the age at which their daughters began to date, insisted on family escorts to high school dances and movies, and placed strict limits on the hours by which their children had to be home. But sons and daughters met their future wives and husbands at dance halls and at work as well as at family celebrations. Very little intermarriage took place, but parents had to settle for prospective spouses who were familiar types—from the same ethnic group or from a similar background—rather than men and women whom they actually selected for their sons and daughters.[65]

Breaking marriage out of the context of familial considerations meant not only greater individual choice of marriage partner but also greater pressure toward individual autonomy from the claims of family responsibility. Although most immigrant parents had been successful at settling at least one married child at the same address, easily available to meet parents' needs, the child might experience conflicting sets of demands in this situation. One Jewish daughter described the difficulties that emerged for her, living after her marriage on the second floor of a triple-decker with her mother on the first floor and her older brother and his family on the top floor. The tensions that arose between the families illustrated how difficult it must have been to sort out conflicting claims on loyalty, and how fragile was the balance between reciprocity and betrayal. When the daughter found her husband and her brother in continual conflict about their children, she thought "it was time we moved away." Her mother became very angry with her for leaving, and wouldn't talk to her again "until they rented the tenement." Even after she moved away, she did all the shopping for her mother, and she and her sister did all the housecleaning, "wash the floors, do everything." She still felt emotionally protective of her mother and yelled at her sister-in-law for arguing with her mother. Both her husband and her sister-in-law accused her of neglecting her own health and her family's needs in order to care for her mother. But her ties to her parents were very strong:

> You know, you're taught in the old country to be respectful to your parents, no matter what, and I was . . . I'll do that as long as I live.[66]

In this case, the daughter's sense of responsibility to her parents caught her in a double bind between her obligations as a daughter and those as a wife and mother.

Although in most families, one single child or married couple seemed willing to stay home to care for aging parents, many other children dealt with the potential conflict of responsibility by moving into neighborhoods in Providence other than those where their parents lived, or following employment opportunities away from Providence altogether (see table 3-8). Living in the same building or nearby meant being able to make claims on family resources, but it also brought complex and conflict-prone negotiations over what one owed to, or was owed by, the family. Some children, willing to forego assistance from parents, found it easier to sort out their obligations to family at a safe distance, away from the parental household and outside the ethnic community where standards of mutual family obligation were supported by community norms.[67]

Comparing the immigrant patterns of proximity to parents, brothers, and sisters to those established by their children reveals a major shift. Although in many cases living on opposite sides of the Atlantic Ocean had broken the automatic bond between immigrants and their own parents, most of those who had parents in Providence managed to organize their lives in such a way that they lived close by. Sharing the traumas and dreams of migration tied together immigrant brothers and sisters in Providence, and they too, appeared to settle themselves in order to be easily accessible to each other. A sizeable and important minority of the children's generation re-

TABLE 3-8.   Location of Married Children in Relation to Their Parents, 1940[a]

	Italian		Jewish	
Same address	26%	(58)	21%	(27)
Within two blocks	21%	(47)	5%	(6)
Within ten blocks	23%	(51)	20%	(25)
Different neighborhood	25%	(56)	35%	(45)
Other city	4%	(9)	16%	(20)
Inadequate information	1%	(2)	3%	(4)
TOTAL (number of married children)	100%	(223)	100%	(127)

Source: Neighborhood data.
a. If both parents were dead by 1940, location of married children to parents was measured in the year before the last parent died.

peated those patterns in their own lives. Married children accepted help, in the form of housing, and the care of their aging parents by living in the same building. Married brothers and sisters, linked by their common public-school exposure to American culture as well as by similar needs for shared resources, settled across the hall or down the street from each other. However, by the late 1920s and 1930s, the decision to live near family was made in the context of an expanded array of alternatives facing the children's generation. The sons and daughters of immigrants were well versed in English and as much at home in the white-collar world of downtown and the single-family blocks of the new suburban areas as in the old neighborhoods. For these children, nearness to family was not the first criterion for locating a residence, and many of them lived in altogether different neighborhoods than parents and siblings (see tables 3-9 and 3-10). What had been a fundamental organizing principle in the immigrant generation was no longer universally accepted. Networks of proximity and reciprocity could no longer be assumed.

The minority of married children who lived with their parents were divided from others in their generation not only by their acceptance of kinship as the central preference of residence but also by gender. It was daughters who were increasingly likely to live with parents (see table 3-9). For Italians, this shift represented an alteration of the norm that a daughter must accommodate herself to her husband's family. Perhaps daughters were looking to their parents for protection,[68] perhaps social and economic change had forced a compromise in traditional patriarchal arrangements. For both Italian and Jewish families, this trend suggests a change from male responsibility to female responsibility for aging parents. Both

TABLE 3-9. Parent–Married Child Proximity Over Time

	Italian				Jewish			
	Immigrants		First Generation		Immigrants		First Generation	
Parental residence in same building	65%	(29)	28%	(59)	66.6%	(10)	26%	(27)
Parental residence within 2 blocks	22%	(10)	22%	(47)	33.3%	(5)	6%	(6)
Parental residence elsewhere in Providence	13%	(6)	50%	(107)	—	(0)	68%	(70)
TOTAL	100%	(45)[a]	100%	(213)[b]	100%	(15)[a]	100%	(103)[b]
Of those who live in the same building								
Parents living with sons	59%	(17)	51%	(30)	50%	(5)	37%	(10)
Parents living with daughters	41%	(12)	49%	(29)	50%	(5)	63%	(17)
TOTAL	100%	(29)	100%	(59)	100%	(10)	100%	(27)

Source: Neighborhood data.

a. Total number of immigrants with parents in Providence.
b. Total number of married children.

TABLE 3-10. Adult Sibling Proximity Over Time

	Italian		Jewish	
	Immigrants	First Generation	Immigrants	First Generation
Sibling residence in household or building	49.3% (38)	20% (13)	58% (11)	24% (8)
Sibling residence within 2 blocks	36.3% (28)	43% (28)	32% (6)	30% (10)
Sibling residence elsewhere in Providence	14.3% (11)	37% (24)	10% (2)	46% (15)
Total number of families with siblings in Providence	100% (77)	100% (65)[a]	100% (19)	100% (33)[a]

Source: Neighborhood data.

a. Total number of families with two married children.

the change in the location of work, from family farms and shops in Europe to large factories and companies in Providence, and the increasing dependence on wages as an exchangeable product of labor, meant that coresidence was no longer a necessity in order for married children to give substantial financial help to their parents. In Providence, both men and women could help financially wherever they lived. Separate from their economic needs, aging parents needed nurturance, and this they could still demand most successfully from their daughters. Domestic exchange made possible by kin proximity had consistently had a great impact on women's household work, and women had been active in organizing and maintaining networks of kin. Perhaps men ceded to women the central role in maintaining contact with parents as a way of resolving the tension between the American cultural ideal of the independent nuclear family and the ethnic culture's practice of mutual dependence on kin.[69] The loss of consensus around standards of kin reciprocity was reflected in the increasing tendency for kin obligations to be shouldered by women rather than men.

The depression in the 1930s may have momentarily expanded the number of families once again sharing household space. As one Jewish son recalled, "people used to double up, brothers and sisters." In 1931, this man moved with his wife into a tenement building his brother-in-law had bought. The two families lived together in one apartment for several months "with three kids, with all the furniture, we had everything on top." Then the two families occupied two apartments in the building for fifteen years. The man's son suspected that his family paid no rent for several years when his father was out of work. An Italian daughter explained that she and her sister shared an apartment self-consciously in order to economize:

> My sister got married during the Depression, and she and her husand moved in with us. It was a large two-bedroom apartment so there was plenty of room. We had just one baby then, and the baby's crib was in our room.

The arrangement was a "great help financially" because the sisters divided all the expenses: "rent, heat, electric, food—were split in half and shared." The sisters also helped each other by dividing the household work.

> [My sister] worked part time as a salesgirl and did all the cooking. I worked part time in the bakery and did all the housework.

But neither sister expected the situation to be long term:

> It worked out fine for about four years. Then she became
> pregnant and I became pregnant and they had to move into
> a place of their own.[70]

In times of particular need, children of immigrants fell back on the
strategies that they knew from first-hand experience could extend
scarce resources. By 1940, ties of kin were still very significant in
explaining the patterns of residence of Italian and Jewish immigrant
children. But the ascendant pattern was indicated by the increasing
number of the children's generation located at a distance from
family.

For an important transitional period, immigrant family and kin
networks had taken on new functions, different from what they had
been in Europe or what they would become as the immigrant
community matured. Late-nineteenth-century social and economic
upheaval in Europe had unsettled ordinary family arrangements,
increasing the interdependency of kin and intervening in familial
control of marriage. Migration built on this interdependency of kin
and at the same time caused both short-lived and permanent
disruption of family groups. The trials of immigrant settlement in
Providence increased families' needs for assistance and redefined
norms of family residence as families brought parents, brothers,
sisters, and even friends in need of temporary housing into expanded
households. Nearby tenements housed other relatives and friends.
The fact that few family groups arrived in Providence fully intact was
the stimulus for kin who did migrate to draw closer together.
Boundaries between households were blurred as kin who were in
Providence became neighbors, and as neighbors and friends from
the old country offered assistance in the role of missing kin. The
bonds of kinship were thus woven through the immigrant neighborhoods. Sharing language and the trauma of relocation made
neighbors in immigrant settlements extend familial norms of mutual
assistance to each other: according to personal testimony, neighbors
always stood ready to help. The ethic of familial reciprocity was in
this way generalized beyond the boundaries of individual households
throughout the immigrant neighborhoods.

The changing developmental cycle of the family began to alter
the forms family networks had taken. Different sets of circumstances
converged to delineate the individual household much more sharply
from the larger network of kin. As immigrants aged and their

families in Providence expanded in the 1920s and 1930s, they turned to their own children rather than to other kin for assistance. Family networks began to lose the particularly fraternal character they had assumed in the early years. As immigrants and their children moved to different areas of the city, neighbors and kin were less likely to be the same people. The new neighborhoods were less ethnically homogeneous and neighbors felt that they no longer shared the common background that had enabled them to act like kin to each other. Households were less likely to be expanded by boarders and relatives and were even more self-contained as unmarried adult children were immediately available for support and assistance.

Some of the children's generation came to challenge the norms of family collectivity by initiating their own courtships and marriages. Some altered their relationship to networks of exchange and reciprocity by moving away to new neighborhoods at a distance from the parental households and from those established by brothers and sisters. However, a significant group of the children replicated the intense kin-dominated social life of their parents. Some of these married children were settled in the same building as parents; others may have established enclaves of ethnic reciprocity in the new neighborhoods by moving close to married sisters and brothers. Kin proximity and reciprocity did not disappear as an organizing principle of ethnic family life. Rather, more of the exchange of services was absorbed in the interaction between parents and children. More fundamentally, kin reciprocity was no longer the dominant community ethos; norms of exchange that had been widely accepted by the immigrants were not universally internalized by their children.

Although in the early years Italians were more likely than Jews to have relatives in Providence, over time Italian and Jewish families came to resemble each other. Both expanded during the period of immigration and early settlement to rely on a wider variety of kin and neighbor connections, and then both appeared to return to older patterns, narrowing reciprocity to an exchange between parents and children. This narrower conception of household more closely approximated the dominant American patterns of the period. Italian children were more likely to cluster within several blocks of parents and brothers and sisters, but both Italian and Jewish children explored new options of living far from kin, turning inward rather than expanding outward for assistance and social contact. The diverging experiences of immigrants and their children defined and then redefined the meaning of family.

Chapter Four

Circles of Assistance: Reciprocity and Associational Life

IMMIGRANT FAMILIES lived amidst coexisting networks of kinship, of neighborhood, and of association. The connections between families which ran through workplaces and neighborhoods were paralleled by the extensive organization of mutual-benefit societies in Providence. The principles of mutual support and reciprocal obligation that governed family relations also bound together nonkin in these associations. Through the collection of weekly or monthly assessments which were then paid out as sick and death benefits, mutual-benefit associations formalized the obligation, normally limited to kin, to give assistance, to accept assistance, and to repay assistance rendered. By participating in this kind of exchange, mutual-benefit members accepted the responsibility of helping people who had helped them. Mutual-benefit associations were the products of men, or sometimes women, whose vision of collectivity extended beyond the boundaries of household and friendship. Women's sharing was most commonly expressed in day-to-day exchanges, and men were the most likely to operate in formal associations, but a separate immigrant women's culture resulting from the traditional sexual division of labor in families and neighborhoods sometimes gave rise to a distinct female associational life.[1]

This form of organization had spread through southern Italy and eastern Europe on the eve of migration as a communal response to the economic and social transformation unsettling village life. Mutual-benefit associations would also prove to be a crucial resource for immigrant families in American cities.[2] In Providence, each society drew friends and neighbors into wider exchanges of mutual assistance. Ethnic solidarity within the associations mirrored the collectivity of the family economy. Fraternal social relations within these organizations echoed the expansive direction and particularly the sibling orientation of immigrant kin networks. As self-generated institutions, mutual-benefit associations were a public expression of the reciprocal culture of the immigrant community. As the link to a provincial past, mutual-benefit associations kept alive regional traditions of southern Italian Catholicism and Jewish Orthodoxy as an alternative to northern Italian Catholic and German Reform Jewish religious ritual. Building on ethnic concentrations within occupations, mutual-benefit associations sometimes underlay the struggle against common economic grievances. The ideology of reciprocal obligation and the assumption of group loyalty justified punishing middle-class members of one's own ethnic group who appeared to be taking advantage of community support. Mutual-benefit associations were thus connected directly and indirectly with conflict resulting from group expressions of solidarity.

But in Providence, the mutual-benefit tradition would begin to weaken by the 1920s and 1930s as the children of immigrants came of age. Reflecting the widening gap between the social and occupational experiences of the immigrant and American-born generations, different kinds of associations would claim the loyalties of young people. The new organizations would substitute social and philanthropic activities for economic cooperation, assuming a population more diverse in occupation and class than the early immigrant community had been. By the 1930s, mutual-benefit associations would lose membership and community visibility to new organizations that defined ethnic interests as embracing a variety of cultural traditions and social concerns. The decline of mutual-benefit associations meant that traditions of mutual support and reciprocal obligation would no longer be a dominant presence in community life. The culture of reciprocity that had permeated immigrant community institutions now operated only inside the boundaries of individual families.

MUTUAL-BENEFIT TRADITIONS IN EUROPE

In southern Italy and Sicily, small landholders and artisans extended the resources of family and kinship networks by organizing mutual-benefit associations. The tradition of association among artisans and small proprietors reached back to the late Middle Ages and the early modern period. Popular religious fraternities which embodied traditions of kinship and communal solidarity served as societies for mutual benefit until the eighteenth century. *Maestranze*, descendents of medieval craft guilds, were prominent in Sicily as late as the end of the eighteenth century; they provided support for members in distress and ensured members a proper burial as well as regulating entry and competition within a trade. In the second half of the nineteenth century, mutual-aid organizations spread through Italy. By 1873, there were approximately 1,400 associations, and by 1894, the number had increased to more than 6,700 with a membership of nearly one million. Changes in the local economy which unsettled ordinary family arrangements prompted villagers in the south as well as the north to revitalize and expand this familiar form. In Palermo, Sicily, there were nine such associations in the 1860s, including groups of fruit vendors, agricultural workers, and master shoe-makers. Organizations appeared in Potenza, Basilicata, as early as 1870. Mutual-benefit associations continued to spread; there were thirty-five mutual-benefit societies founded in Palermo during the 1870s, and ninety-two associations founded in the province during the 1880s. Organizations appeared throughout the southern provinces; in 1885 these regions contained 37 percent of the total Italian population and 30 percent of its mutual-benefit societies. One contemporary government report counted 193 mutual-benefit societies in the Abruzzi and Molise region, 500 in Campania, 78 in Basilicata, 158 in Calabria, and 350 societies in Sicily as of 1 January 1895. The government suppression of the Sicilian *Fasci* in 1894 slowed the growth of mutual-benefit associations in this region, but by 1900 there was still a broad range of associations in nearly every village. Immigration also affected the membership of these societies, but as late as 1917 there were still 259 such organizations in the province of Messina, Sicily.[3]

The wide range of organizational activity in this period reflected the differential effects of a market economy. Organizations of the village elite, proprietors, merchants, and notaries were concerned with a felt lack of deference; they acted to preserve the social hierarchy by promoting their own education and by supporting work houses, orphanages, and pauper children's education. Artisans' organizations, troubled by apparent threats to customary relationships between masters and workmen, proposed educational self-help activities and attempted to guarantee apprenticeships for their sons. Organizations of agricultural workers, whose members included laborers, tenants, and peasant proprietors, defended themselves by sometimes challenging landlords to respect traditional grazing privileges. Both artisans and agricultural workers used mutual-benefit associations to start savings and credit banks, cooperative marketing unions, and night schools. Throughout the south, and especially in Calabria, mutual-benefit associations engaged in a number of different economic self-help activities, lending money to members at low interest, organizing producer as well as consumer cooperatives, and even finding jobs for members in other cities when work became scarce in the home commune. The Sicilian *Fasci* came the closest to acting as labor unions, although their diverse membership of peasants, small proprietors, and unattached laborers was not organized along occupational lines. Rural *Fasci* defended members' interests on land ownership, contracts, and taxes, while urban issues included conventional demands about working conditions, unemployment, and wages.[4] The form of organization provided by mutual-benefit societies could operate in defense of a variety of interests.

Most commonly, the organizations provided sick and death benefits to members, taking over tasks that would previously have been the sole responsibility of family members. Societies themselves used the metaphor of familial assistance to describe their purpose. A workers' society in the mining commune of Villarosa, Sicily, organized in 1888, explained its goals in these terms. According to its statutes, the purpose of the society was:

> the union and fellowship of all the working classes in order
> to unite finally into a single family, so that they can
> reciprocally succor each other materially and morally.

Many *mutuo soccorso* organizations were communewide, and most restricted active membership to working men, offering honorary membership to important local or national figures. Master artisans were eligible for membership only if they worked side by side with their journeymen. Women were not usually members of mutual-benefit societies; they were allowed to serve food at banquets and to receive benefits but they were included more as spectators than as participants. However, women and children constituted a significant proportion of the membership of the rural *Fasci*, and according to one historian, women were a conspicuous and militant part of *Fasci*-led strikes and demonstrations.[5]

Villages characteristically supported a range of associational activity. In some areas, occupational divisions required two local societies: one for town workers who saw themselves as bound by common entrepreneurial interests, and one for agricultural workers. In Alcara Li Fusi, a Sicilian village of 1,800 inhabitants, the mutual-aid association of San Vincenzo was founded in 1889, a religious confraternity was founded in 1891, two confraternities were founded in 1895, two more in 1901, and then three more mutual-benefit associations in 1907. Peasants and laborers took control of the San Vincenzo society, while a group of carpenters, mostly in their twenties and thirties, assumed control of another mutual-benefit society. The proliferation of mutual-benefit societies suggested the process of social fragmentation at work, with each society composed of allied family groups trying to reestablish some measure of social order.[6]

The boundaries distinguishing secular and religious associations were not always sharply drawn. In the late-nineteenth century, the Catholic church attempted to organize religious fraternities to compete with the growing movement of secular mutual-benefit associations. Some village associations were initially connected with the church and then, over time, detached themselves from their church connection, retaining only the responsibility for handling arrangements for feast days in celebration of the local patron saint. The great majority of workers' societies surveyed recently by historian John Briggs showed little evidence of being directly inspired by, or under the significant influence of, the clergy. Many named themselves after heroes of the Risorgimento; most made no provision for a chaplain or pastoral advisor and made no mention in statutes or minutes of ties to the church or religious obligations of members. Although priests were occasionally members of societies, they were usually honorary members. Still, the societies were products of a fundamentally religious society and could not have been totally distinct from popular religion. Even the socialist-led *Fasci* demonstrated the intertwining of religious and secular themes. In the offices of rural *Fasci* were hung pictures of the king and queen, a crucifix, and a picture of Marx.[7] Such a mixture of cultural references was characteristic of a society in the process of social and economic transformation.

Forms of self-organization among Jews in eastern Europe dated from the earliest arrival of Jews in this region. In the late-nineteenth century, however, a combination of expanded economic vulnerability and social and cultural ferment, connected with the move from shtetl to city required by settlement laws, transformed these organizations into mutual-benefit associations that provided some communal protection against family adversity. Men in the same craft had formed themselves into a *chevrah ba'alay melakhah*, an artisan association or guild, to defend their craft interests and to meet the religious prescription that at least ten adult men must pray and read the Torah together at the beginning and end of each day. Shared responsibilities of members began with the collective purchase of Torah scrolls and expanded to include religious duties such as staying all night with sick members and participating in special services for those that died. Facing increasingly uncertain economic circumstances, Jewish artisans extended these agreed-upon obligations to include a collection of dues for the provision of sick and death benefits. Despite the economic decline of artisans in the nineteenth century, the *chevroth* flourished in this period because their combination of social and ritual observance as well as their benefit funds continued to address real needs in the daily life of Jewish artisans. A traveller to Vilna in 1882 counted over twenty of these *chevrah* organizations. The wealthier organizations maintained their own synagogues, where members would congregate to study and pray; groups with more modest resources would raise only enough money to purchase their own Torah, symbol of the group's independence within the community and of the unity of its members.[8]

As working conditions deteriorated and the competition for work intensified in the overcrowded economies of the cities and towns in the Pale, journeymen found that their economic interests were becoming more sharply distinguished from the concerns of the masters. Some *chevroth* split into separate organizations of master craftsmen and journeymen. As early as 1841, a group of Minsk journeymen tailors broke away to form their own association, and a similar society of journeymen tailors was established in Bialystok. This splitting of *chevroth* was increasingly common in the late-nineteenth century. In Mogilev in these years, there were separate *chevroth* for ladies' tailors, carpenters, dyers, and stove builders, with the journeymen signalling their independence by purchasing their own Torah. Masters and journeymen continued to meet together in *chevroth* of shoemakers, jewelers and watchmakers, tinworkers, roofers, and locksmiths. The separate workingmen's *chevroth* often acted as unions, negotiating for hours and wages.[9]

Forms of association also included *chevroth* organized in each community to assist the poor, old, sick, and infirm, whose needs went beyond what could be provided by participation in exchanges of mutual assistance. These varied in number and extent of resources from community to community, but most villages and towns included groups whose task was to raise money to provide clothes, medical care, funeral and burial expenses, and Passover matzoth for impoverished Jews. A particular group took responsibility for raising money for dowry and wedding expenses for Jewish women whose families could not provide them. Women were often active in these kinds of organizations. In addition, communities attempted to support a Talmud Torah to provide free schooling for orphans and children who could not afford to pay for an education, a home for orphans, and a home for the aged who could not be helped by their families. Jewish tradition held that receiving aid from this kind of organization was one's right as a member of the community.[10] And as the rising number of Jews in the context of limited resources meant greater and more widespread immiseration, this kind of organization became more important.

The *chevrah* was a form of organization that could be transplanted despite the short-term migration forced on many families by the settlement laws. Moving from smaller villages to larger cities and towns, Jews reconvened their *chevroth* on the basis of older communal loyalties. The Yiddish novelist I. B. Singer described how, after his family moved from the town of Radzyim to the city of Warsaw in Poland, the men naturally turned to the Radzyim study house for services and sociability. The men especially appreciated the familiar faces in their hometown study house when circumstances forced them to go to the Minsk study house one Passover; there they were invited to pray, but in lonely anonymity. Reorganizing a familiar associational life was of great importance in coping with the disruptions of migration, within eastern Europe or across the ocean. The social content of associational life was a real part of its meaning.[11]

The move from shtetl to city speeded the disintegration of the traditional shtetl culture that had unified the Jewish community for hundreds of years. But new ideas flourished in the vacuum: the religious enthusiasm of Hasidism, the modern enlightenment thought of Haskalah, the development of a secular Yiddish literary and cultural movement called *Yiddishkeit*, the political ideology of socialism, the notion of a Jewish rebirth through Zionism. This intellectual and cultural ferment loosened the grip of religious traditionalism. Secular self-help organizations divorced from religious ritual also spread through the cities of the Pale in the late-nineteenth century. By 1888–89, mutual-benefit organizations called *kassy* had been formed by stocking makers, ladies' tailors, printers, carpenters, locksmiths, and cigarette makers in Vilna, and a similar array of organizations had appeared in Minsk. Although these early *kassy* expressed self-help aims identical to those of the journeymen's *chevroth*, the *kassy* were more radical organizations, making a clear break from a traditional and religious orientation. Because of their exclusion from religious ritual women were not members of *chevroth*, but as an increasing percentage of the knit-goods and cigarette-manufacturing labor force, women workers could participate in the mutual-benefit funds of *kassy*.[12]

In the context of the beginnings of trade union organization and the wave of strikes in the Pale in the years from 1895 to 1904, many *kassy* became underground unions, devoting their weekly or monthly dues entirely to supporting members during strikes. Building on this varied experience of association, the Bund, the major Jewish labor movement in the Pale, helped to organize trade unions outside the traditional crafts. Aided by such organizations, draymen in Pinsk and Berdichev, boatmen in Kovno, hotel attendants in Pinsk and Slonim, and domestic workers in Warsaw, Grodno, Mogilev, Bobruisk, Pinsk, and Dvinsk struck for shorter hours, strictly defined and respectful relationships between workers and employers, and higher and more consistent wages. The strike movement was broader than the membership of the *kassy*, which never included more than 20 to 30 percent of the workers in a trade. In practice, the trade union movement occasionally revealed religious roots. During one strike, for example, bristle workers swore on a Torah scroll that they would not serve as strikebreakers. Another time, Jewish tanners swore by a pair of phylacteries that they would stand firm and support workers who had been fired. The tanners then confirmed their religious vows with the singing of the official and of course defiantly secular song of the Bund.[13] The mixture of religious forms of organizations with economic urgency and socialist militancy proved to be an emotionally powerful means of collective self-defense.

Experiencing increasing economic vulnerability in a market economy, both Italians and Jews thus developed an associational life with a primary focus on collective defense. This active organizational response to uncertainty would play an extremely important role in immigrant resettlement in Providence. The mutual-benefit associations that Italian and Jewish immigrants would organize in Providence were not identical to their European counterparts. Although based on familiar exchanges of reciprocal economic assistance, Providence associations would also incorporate other

functions appropriate to the situation of their immigrant constituency. The tradition of self-help institutions nourished the rich
collective life immigrants would build in Providence.

ASSOCIATIONAL LIFE IN PROVIDENCE

The earliest societies founded by Italian immigrants in Providence
provided an opportunity for all Italian immigrants in the city to
develop mechanisms for collective security. The Unione e Benevo-
lenza was organized in 1882 for the purpose of dispensing emergency
aid in the Italian community, in addition to the familiar sick and
death benefits. The Roma Society was founded in 1888, and the
Società Fratellanza Militare Italiane Bersaglieri was organized in
1890. An Italian immigrant from Salerno to Bridgeport, Connecticut
interviewed in the late 1930s explained the rationale for building an
Italian mutual-benefit association, the Court of Rome Society, in
1898:

> I helped to found it because I felt that the Italian people of
> this city should have some security from death and acci-
> dents. The Italian people of this time didn't trust the big
> insurance companies because they thought they would get
> cheated. They felt that if some organization was Italian that
> it was all right.

Faced with other self-conscious ethnic groups, Italian immigrants
experienced themselves as a group in a new way: "In those times, the
Italian was hated by the Irish and other nationalities, and by
organizing, we got better respect from those people." These societies
emerged at the point when enough Italians had settled in Providence
to support such an organization and when a sense of commitment to
the community and increasing family responsibilities made association necessary.[14]

As immigrants from particular areas began to become numerous
in Providence, they formed mutual-benefit societies based on local or
provincial associations. By the early-twentieth century, immigrant
families from certain regions in Italy settled in Providence and began
to congregate on certain blocks. Families from Marzano Appio,
Roccamonfina, Ischia, and Pietravairano near Naples, and Frosolone and Isérnia near Campobasso comprised a majority of the
families on Federal Hill: Frosolonese on Dean, Cedar, and Spruce
streets, Pietravairanese on Spruce, Cedar, Acorn, and West Exchange

streets. Italians from other southern regions settled into other sections of Providence. Immigrants from Fontegreco and Venafro near Campobasso moved into the Italian North End on Charles Street, and into Eagle Park. Immigrants from Fornelli, Campobasso went to Natick, in West Warwick, south of Providence. Farmers from Capriati al Volturno and Prata Sannita, Campobasso went to rural areas west of Providence. In 1908, immigrants formed the Società Fratellanza Abbruzzese, Società Marzano Appio, and MS Trinacria from Termini Imerese, Sicily. In 1910, the Circolo Frosolone was initiated, and in 1911, Cittadini di Pico. By 1919, there were one hundred Italian societies in Providence, seventy of them identified by provincial loyalties and a common dialect, patron saint, and local social and religious customs. All provincial societies were formally named with the letters MS, standing for *mutuo soccorso*.[15] The organization of mutual-benefit funds, of such importance in expanding the resources of individual families in southern Italy, was also a common response to the new kinds of uncertainty in the American urban environment.

The societies provided sick and death benefits, as they had in Italy, and also sponsored feast days which intensified shared local loyalties. The societies made weekly or monthly payments to sick or unemployed members, often furnishing a society doctor. In the event of a member's death, the smaller societies insured that there would be proper pomp and ceremony at the funeral by guaranteeing the expenses of the band. The larger and wealthier societies paid the entire funeral expenses. Feast days celebrated the patron saint with band concerts, colorful parades, and dramatic fireworks. The provincially based mutual-benefit societies drew on deep traditions of localism, as one contemporary observer noted:

> A great number of organizations such as the Societa Arcese, Societa Teanese, Circolo Frosolone, and others initially constitute tiny provinces of their own in the community. To attend their meetings and listen to their business conducted in a characteristic dialect is like crossing from one Italian province into another.[16]

The formation of local societies after the organization of broader citywide associations suggested the complex process of development of Italian immigrant self-definition. (See map 4-1 for the location of the mutual-benefit associations in the Federal Hill neighborhood between 1915 and 1919.)

Local provincial loyalties were also important in determining

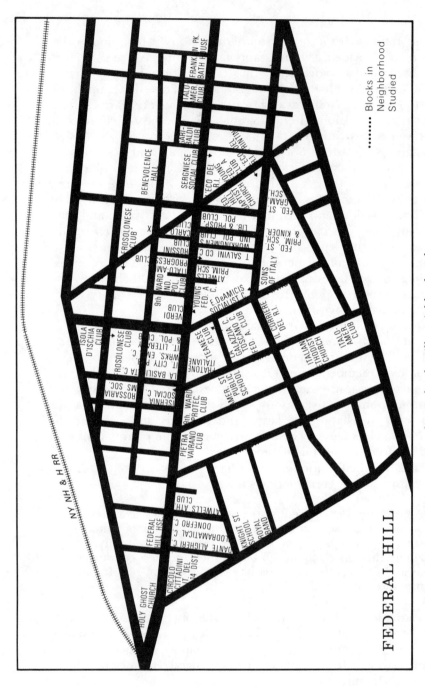

FEDERAL HILL

Map 4-1. Community Associations in the Federal Hill Neighborhood,
1915–19

Federal Hill Community Organizations in the Neighborhood, 1915–1919

Acorn

146 Rossaria MS Society

America

    America Street Public School

62 First Italian Methodist Church

100½ Italo-American Club

Arthur

36 Isola D'Ischia Club

68 Frosolonese Club

74 Teanese Club

    La Galazzia Club

88 Toscano Club

    Federal A. Club

109 E. De Amicis Socialist Club

111 Sons of Italy Club

Atwells

    Franklin Park Bath House

120 Italo-American Club

142 Garibaldi Club

173 L'Eco Del Rhode Island

189½ Sergniese Social Club

200r Liberty and Prosperity Political Club

206 Carlo Marx Club

207 Workingmen's Independent Political Club

    T. Salvini CD Club

    Rossini Club

209 Italo-American Progressive Club

    Atwells Avenue Primary School

213½ Young Federal A Club

221 Ninth Ward Independent Political Club

238 Verdi Club

296 Fratone Italiane

    Italian Literary and Political Club

298 Italian City Public Works Employees Club

    La Basilicata Club

300 Isernia Social Club

    Ninth Ward Protective Club

331 Pietra Vairano Club

393 Atwells Athletic Club

397 Donefro Club

    Filodramatical Club

399 Dante Alighieri Club

400 Federal Hill House

433 Circolo Cittadini Italian del 14 Dist.

472 Holy Ghost Church

Dean

71 Frosolonese Club

139 Federal Hill Baptist Church

140 Young Federal A Club

151 L'Eco Del RI Printing

Federal

    Federal Street Grammar School

    Federal Street Primary School and Kindergarten

146 Il Corriere Del Rhode Island

Knight

40 Royal Band

    Knight Street School

Spruce

    Benevolence Hall

Sources: *Sanborn Insurance Atlas, 1899 Corrected to 1918* (Providence: Sanborn and Perris, 1899), vol. 1; *Providence Street Directory 1915, 1917, and 1919* (Providence: Sampson and Murdock, 1914, 1916, 1918).

patterns of eastern European settlement and the subsequent development of Jewish mutual-benefit associations. Jews from Lithuania,
Poland, and White Russia tended to collect in the Jewish North End
and in the Smith Hill neighborhood, while Jews from Galicia in
Austria, from Roumania, and from the Ukraine tended to move to
the Jewish community around Willard Avenue in south Providence.
The first eastern European *chevrah* to appear in Providence was
organized by Smith Hill immigrants in 1875 as a prayer group
named B'nai Zion. Over the next eighteen years, B'nai Zion grew to
include separate *chevroth* responsible for maintaining the special
rituals for the dead and care of the sick and two *chevroth* dedicated to
the study of different portions of the Talmud. In 1888, Roumanian
immigrants formed their own congregation, and Polish Jews left
B'nai Zion in 1889 to organize their own prayer group. The
organizational purposes of one *chevrah* formed in 1896 clearly
defined the mixture of religious ritual and mutual-benefit activities
in these congregations:

> to promote and maintain worship of Almighty God accord-
> ing to the faith and practice of the Hebrew congregation, to
> furnish free medical attention, weekly benefits, and to
> maintain a free burial ground for members and their
> families.

By 1914, immigrants had organized twenty-four different religious
congregations, among them several different Austrian and Roumanian groups.[17]
    In the early years, congregations met for worship in the tenement
apartments of members. As the volume of immigration increased,
some congregations expanded in membership and resources, and
they began to meet in rented halls and rooms. In time, some acquired
the means to buy or build permanent structures. At most times, the
chevroth remained inconspicuous, perhaps because the recent experience of religious persecution in eastern Europe still remained a part
of collective memory. Yet the expansion into permanent quarters was
an occasion for public acknowledgment and celebration of immigrant success in the reestablishment of their communal organization.
Huge parades and bands accompanied members of B'nai Zion in
1893 and Sons of Jacob in 1906 as they took possession of their own
buildings on Orms Street and Douglas Avenue. According to the
newspapers, thousands were in the streets to celebrate the transfer of
the Torah from temporary to permanent quarters, cheered on by
lively Russian music and, in 1906, carrying red, white, and blue

4-1. Congregation Sons of Zion on Orms Street near Charles Street, Smith Hill, 1903. The congregation moved their Torah scrolls into this building in 1893. Photograph courtesy of the Rhode Island Historical Society (RHi X3 4809).

4-2. Congregation Sons of Jacob, 24 Douglas Avenue, Smith Hill, 1920. The congregation moved its Torah scrolls to the first story of this building in 1906. The building was enlarged in 1912, and the superstructure was completed in 1920. Photograph courtesy of the Rhode Island Historical Preservation Commission.

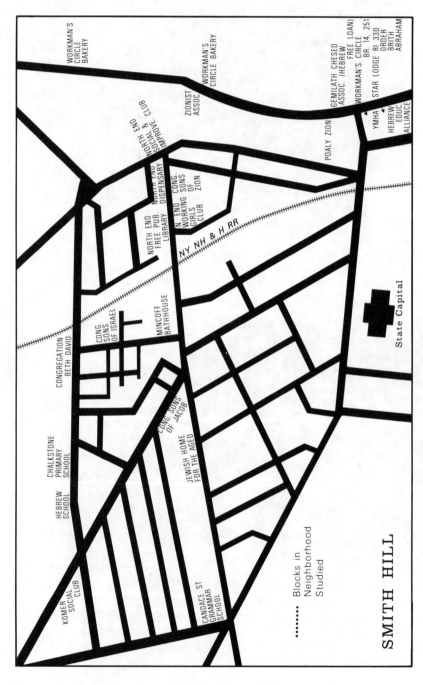

SMITH HILL

WORKMAN'S CIRCLE BAKERY

WORKMAN'S CIRCLE BAKERY

ZIONIST ASSOC.

NORTH END SOCIAL & CLUB IMPROVE.

NORTH END DISPENSARY

NORTH END FREE PUB. LIBRARY

N. END CONG. WORKING SONS GIRLS OF CLUB ZION

NY NH & H RR

CONGREGATION BETH DAVID

CONG. SONS OF ISRAEL

MINCOFF BATHHOUSE

CHALKSTONE PRIMARY SCHOOL

HEBREW SCHOOL

CONG. SONS OF JACOB

JEWISH HOME FOR THE AGED

KOMER SOCIAL CLUB

CANDACE ST GRAMMAR SCHOOL

GEMILATH CHESED ASSOC. (HEBREW FREE LOAN)

WORKMAN'S CIRCLE BR. 14, 251

STAR LODGE RI 330

ORDER BRITH ABRAHAM

POALY ZION

YMHA

HEBREW EDUC ALLIANCE

State Capital

.... Blocks in Neighborhood Studied

Map 4-2.   Community Associations in the Smith Hill Neighborhood, 1915–19

Smith Hill Community Organizations in the Neighborhood,
1915–1919

Chalkstone
  161   Congregation Beth David
  277   Chalkstone Primary School
  299   Hebrew School
Charles
  111½ North End Social and Improvement Club
Douglas
  10   Congregation Sons of Jacob
North Main
  128   Hebrew Educational Alliance
         YMHA
         Star Lodge RI 330, Order Brith Abraham
         Workman's Circle Branches 14, 251
  299   Gemilath Chesed Association (Hebrew Free Loan)
  344   Poaly Zion
  391½ Workman's Circle Bakery
  470   Zionist Association
  593   Workman's Circle Bakery
Orms
  45   Congregation Sons of Zion
  49   North End Dispensary
         North End Free Public Library
         North End Working Girls Club
  191   Jewish Home for the Aged
  287   Candace Street Grammar School
Shawmut
  16   Congregation Sons of Israel
  38   Tillie and Hyman Mincoff Bath House

Sources: Sanborn Insurance Atlas, 1899 Corrected to 1918 (Providence: Sanborn and Perris, 1899), vol. 2; *Providence Street Directory, 1915, 1917, and 1919* (Providence: Sampson and Murdock, 1914, 1916, 1918).

streamers along with Zionist and American flags.[18] (See map 4-2 for the location of the four congregations in the Smith Hill neighborhood between 1915 and 1919.)

Eastern European Jews also organized secular mutual-benefit associations in Providence, frequently on the basis of regional or craft loyalties. Several of these mutual-benefit associations were local lodges affiliated with the Independent Order of Brith Abraham, a national order organized by eastern European immigrants in 1887. One of these local lodges limited its membership to Jews from Elizabethgrad. Nine other regional mutual-benefit associations were organized in Providence between 1902 and 1916, and these served Jews from the Ukraine, Lublin, and Odessa among other areas. Twenty-one workingmen's mutual-aid associations served tailors, shoemakers, cigar makers, and junk peddlers. Providence Jewish workingmen also organized several branches of the Workmen's Circle, *Arbeiter Ring*. These were affiliated with the national organization founded in New York City in 1892 by twenty-five cloak makers. The national organization was chartered as an insurance society, published two newspapers along with various books and pamphlets, and maintained a summer camp for members in New York State. Dues accumulated toward burial plots, funeral expenses, medical costs, and sick and death benefits. The Providence branches also supported a school, two cooperative bakeries, forums and speakers, and other kinds of cultural events. Providence Jewish businessmen benefited from nine free-loan associations and dealers' organizations. Twenty-four other general-membership mutual-benefit associations served other parts of the Providence Jewish community.[19] The tradition of collective protection had generated a wide array of self-help associations in Providence.

For male immigrants, mutual-benefit associations functioned as actual extensions of kin ties and as a community parallel to kinship networks. Since family-based migration chains were often the underpinning of village chains in Providence, family connections were interwoven with village loyalties in the associations. Evidence from immigrants to various northeastern cities suggested the range of family and familylike affiliations in mutual-benefit societies. One immigrant to Boston described the actual overlap of regional, occupational, and family bonds in a society to which he belonged:

> It was an association formed by all the people who were [tool] grinders from this area [in Italy]. It was sort of like a trust association where they would meet and have dues and if somebody would lose a husband they would give expenses

for the funeral. Also it was like a union because you wouldn't take another person's customers. You would sell customers to another person. Respect for one another, in other words, and since they were all related, it was like a family organization. . . . They used to talk about different peoples' routes, sort of try to patch up disagreements and arguments. . . . When somebody would die, the women would go in and cook in the home and care for the kids and the men are usually the pallbearers at the funeral because they are relatives, too, at the same time.

For a Jewish immigrant to New Haven, mutual-benefit members substituted for absent family; he discovered people in his society who had been his playmates in his old village and whose parents had been friends of his parents. He described his association meetings as "like a family gathering." A Jewish immigrant from Lithuania who had come to New Haven without his family felt that his contact with other Lithuanians at mutual-benefit-society meetings was "a family reunion" of substitute kin.[20]

Mutual-benefit societies also integrated friendship networks with social life. One Italian immigrant to Providence was persuaded to join a society by his friends: "the only way I got into it was a lot of friends of mine in it, and they kept talking to me to get into it, and so finally I got into it." The society was a way of making sure that old-world loyalties could be maintained: "See, they knew themselves in the old country, so they wanted to keep up the friendships and all that, and so they joined the society of their town." Friendships took on extra social importance in the ritualized form of fraternal brotherhood, and shared participation in the societies gave new content to everyday discussions. One Jewish daughter of a poor New York garment worker remembered that it was his friends' consultations with him on issues of concern to their burial society that made him lift up his head and feel important. On nights when the society met in their front room, she recalled smoke-filled, unpleasant air and late nights without sleep as heated arguments over the location of a burial plot, an extra dollar assessment, or the hiring of a society doctor resounded through their small apartment. But her father, "if he had succeeded in carrying a point, and in the knowledge that he had served the society in giving the room, went to bed smiling."[21] Clearly the societies infused existing relationships with new meaning.

As in Europe, women's participation in mutual-benefit societies in Providence was ordinarily limited to passive support and the receipt of benefits. Burial plots were intended for husband and wife and any unmarried children, and sick and death benefits were an important resource added to a family budget customarily handled by women. But southern Italian and eastern European Jewish immigrant women may have also brought with them slender threads connecting them to European organizational traditions. A few Sicilian women may have been active in strikes and demonstrations called by the rural *Fasci*, and a few Jewish women may have had experience in strikes and organizations connected with the Bund. More women were probably active in associations concerned with female religious ritual or observance. At any rate, in Providence some women were active in female associations, most commonly connected with parish or religious congregation.[22]

Little more than fragmentary evidence still exists to document the working of these female organizations. Reflecting the importance of women's economic roles in family survival, some female organizations assessed their own dues and paid out their own benefits. Some of the Jewish women's mutual-benefit organizations combined fundraising for their own insurance with collecting money for those in need of extra resources, such as the aged and the orphans. The short distances between home and meeting places may have made it easier for women to take part in associational life. One Bridgeport Italian woman's description of the Holy Rosary Society, a mutual-benefit organization connected with the Catholic church, suggests the appeal similar organizations may have had for Italian Catholic women in Providence:

> The only society I belong to is the Holy Rosary, made up of all women. I like it because it is a Catholic society, and because when any member dies, they give the family . . . cash. Then the society sends as many members as possible to the funeral to pray for the salvation of the departed soul. All the members wear a black sash with the name of the society and a picture of the Madonna. They also send one large ("ghirlanda") wreath of flowers and hire some cars to go to the funeral. And the society pays for the funeral mass, too. When a member dies we all pay one dollar extra apiece. This they call the "Tassa Mortuaria," it means death assessment. Otherwise we just pay fifty cents a month for regular dues, and no more.[23]

Members must have felt a great security knowing that the funeral mass, the presence of mourners, and a lump sum of insurance money for their families were guaranteed by their participation in the society.

Female mutual-benefit associations potentially competed with household and family responsibilities as claims on women's time and energy. For women, the associations appeared not so much to extend kin ties as to rival them. As has been well documented for nineteenth-century American women, activity in voluntary associations that appeared to be extending the domestic concerns of women in the family to the community at large had the effect of broadening women's self-definition, sometimes at the cost of family concerns. Married women with young children simply may have been unable to participate. One Jewish immigrant wife was very involved in organizations as a young woman: "I was always active. . . . I think I belonged to a lot of organizations. . . . Some of the times I was the chairlady." But later, as the wife of a struggling baker and the mother of small children, she literally could not leave the house. "I couldn't afford to leave the kids alone and I couldn't get a sitter, I didn't have the money for it, so I used to stay home." Finally, when her daughters were old enough to share the domestic labor, she could return. She left her twelve-year-old daughter to watch the younger children and she "started to be active again."[24] During the years when family obligations were at their most demanding, most women's participation in associations must have been limited.

Because of the link between female mutual-benefit associations and activity in a social and public sphere potentially more compelling than the claims of family, men sometimes opposed women's participation. One young Italian woman in Providence described how first her parents and then her husband prohibited her participation in a church society. She initially wanted to join an association when she was in her teens and working in her family's bakery, but her parents "would not hear of it." In their opinion, "a church was only a place to pray, and an organization might lead to an uprise" in her character. After she had married, had children, and her children were grown, she again wanted to join a church society, but this time it was her husband who "would not allow his wife to do any such thing."[25] In this case, even a church organization seemed to be too great a step outside of familial patriarchal authority.

Mutual-benefit associations carried with them a complex European inheritance of religious culture and secular experience. In Providence, the Orthodoxy of some of the religious *chevroth* and the dedication to the veneration of saints of some *mutuo soccorso* societies brought these associations into conflict with existing German Jewish and Irish Catholic religious institutions. The reinterpretation of tradition taking place in the villages and towns of southern Italy and eastern Europe continued to unfold in American cities. In Providence, the practice of association sometimes had the effect of heightening immigrant commitment to a European religious culture that provided an alternative to pressures toward conformity and assimilation.

The Orthodox rituals of worship familiar to eastern European immigrants differed sharply from the religious service used in German Jewish congregations already established in Providence. Guided by the Reform movement in Germany, German Jewish settlements in the United States modified the Orthodox service and substituted English for Hebrew as the language of prayer. The altered service was highly unsatisfactory to the new immigrants. As well, class and linguistic differences between the Americanized, English-speaking German-born merchants and the newly arrived, often unskilled and impoverished Russian and Polish immigrants made joint congregations impossible. No formal or structural obstacles blocked the formation of separate congregations, however. As soon as a few eastern Europeans had settled in Providence, they organized a familiarly Orthodox congregation, B'nai Zion, described above. The fact that twenty-four different congregations were established in Providence between 1874 and 1914 suggested that regional groups followed the example of B'nai Zion and organized separate congregations to allow maximum autonomy in structuring their services as they chose.[26]

Although the autonomous regional congregations enabled Orthodox *chevroth* to control the content of their services, the fragmentation of Orthodox Jews as a group left them with little ability to influence the course of development of community-wide Jewish institutions. When issues of Jewish religious practice entered into the public sphere, the more assimilated Reform Jews were successful, out of proportion to their numbers, in establishing their position as accepted policy. One instance of the public weakness of Orthodoxy was a legislative debate over the legality of the Orthodox Jewish divorce. Although Orthodox ritual provided certain grounds for a religious divorce, in 1906 the Rhode Island legislature proposed legislation to prohibit rabbis from granting religious divorces until civil procedures had been satisfied, in effect undercutting the legitimacy of the Jewish divorce. Both Orthodox and Reform Jews testified at the hearings before the legislative vote. Prominent Jews, including North End politician Jacob Eaton and the jewelry manufacturer Harry Cutler, testified in favor of the bill, arguing that civil laws were adequate to grant divorce to Jews as well as to other applicants. The principal of the Hebrew Free School tried to discredit those in favor of the bill by arguing that allowing non-Orthodox

Jews to testify on this bill was like allowing Protestants to testify on Catholic church regulation, and a junk peddler joined him in "speaking warmly against the men who wanted the bill." When another prominent Jewish businessman, Simon Jersky, rose to speak in favor of the bill, declaring that he was an Orthodox Jew, a "voice from across the room behind a hat" vehemently disagreed with his self-identification, saying, "He [Jersky] is nothing!" Of course, Reform Jews, making their case in English, had a linguistic advantage over the Orthodox spokesmen, dependent on translators to interpret their Yiddish. In any case, the legality of the Jewish divorce could not have persisted for long in view of the direction of twentieth-century legal decisions and the accommodations Judaism would make to twentieth-century American norms. Predictably, the bill became law.[27] Still, the incidence demonstrated the weakness of the Orthodox spokesmen relative to the more credible Reform Jews, and provided an example of how the autonomy of individual congregations lessened the impact of Orthodoxy as the Jewish community came to be publicly identified and defined.

The option of forming autonomous congregations was not available to southern Italians who came to Providence, bringing with them a complex history in regard to the Catholic church which set them in an antagonistic relationship to the church in Rhode Island. Traditionally, the church in Italy had been allied with large landowners in opposition to peasant interests. The recent attempts of late-nineteenth-century Catholic reformers to involve the church more in the lives of the peasants and to counteract the appeal of socialism through organizing trade unions, cooperatives, and welfare agencies had met with mixed success in the southern countryside. The high point of religious life of the village, the feast day of the patron saint, was administered by a lay committee not under the control of the church. The church had played a vital role in peasants lives by marking with rituals such important events as baptism, marriage, and burial. But the church's role was often limited to such once-in-a-lifetime events. Southern Italian immigrants would fail the tests of commitment put to them by American Catholics—regular attendance at mass, confession, Holy Communion, and financial support of the parish.[28]

As the organizers of annual celebrations for patron saints in Providence, the provincially based mutual-benefit societies kept alive the residual expression of peasant, folk Catholicism outside of the church. Societies also demanded the acknowledgment of saint veneration within the Providence church, thus placing provincial societies at the center of the struggle to reconcile southern Italian

4-3. Holy Ghost Catholic Church, 472 Atwells Avenue, Federal Hill. Ground was broken for the church in 1890, the basement was completed in 1901, and in 1910, the church structure was completed. Photograph courtesy of the Providence Public Library.

Catholic culture with American Catholicism. All aspects of southern Italian saint veneration and attitudes toward Catholicism seemed foreign, pagan, and sacrilegious to Irish parishioners and priests. In an attempt to win Italian loyalties to the church, the Providence bishop Matthew Harkins established an Italian national parish, Holy Ghost, on Federal Hill in 1889, even before heavy emigration from southern Italy had begun. But the succession of northern Italian missionary priests whom Harkins invited to head the parish, chosen from the newly established Society of St. Charles Borromeo, proved little better than the Irish leadership in bringing southern Italians into active participation in the church. The missionary priests appeared to share a vision of Catholicism that was compatible with the standards of American Catholics but worlds apart from that of their southern Italian parishioners. As southern Italian immigrants began to congregate in Providence and as village groups began to organize mutual-benefit societies, conflict developed between the northern Italian priests and southern Italian parishioners. The divergence between the official worship service of the church and the mutual-benefit associations' celebration of patron saints was too great.[29]

When a northern Italian priest challenged the special prerogatives claimed by mutual-benefit-society members in Providence, the mutual-benefit association countered with a strong attack. In 1906, members of the church-affiliated Società Di Mutuo Soccorso Maria SS Del Carmine voted unanimously to "prefer charges unbecoming a priest" against Father Domenico Belliotti, the pastor of Holy Ghost parish on Federal Hill. In their letter of complaint to Bishop Harkins, members of the society implied that the issue at stake was no less than who had the right to determine the content of southern Italian Catholicism. The letter explained that in July, members of the society had made arrangements with Belliotti to have seats reserved in a special area in the church on the feast day of Santa Maria Del Carmine later that month, "but when the day came, despite our prior arrangements, the members were compelled to stand up and be scattered all over the church." Moreover, when the members of the society brought the image of the saint into the church, Belliotti "became irritated, and cursed her name, and also the day that he donned the priestly garments." When members heard this, they asked him to explain, and "he replied in substance that we did not control him and that if we said another word, he would not let us enter the church." Belliotti heightened his insult when he belittled the uniqueness of the society's patron saint, arguing that "he saw no difference between the blessed Virgin and St. Rocco and any of the saints that were in the church." The members concluded by asking

4-4. Società Di Mutuo Soccorso Maria SS Del Carmine members parade down Atwells Avenue, Federal Hill, 1906. This society was affiliated with Holy Ghost Church but in 1906 members unanimously complained to Bishop Harkins that their priest, Domenico Belliotti, should be removed for ignoring the special interests of the mutual-benefit societies. Photograph courtesy of the Rhode Island Historical Society (RHi X3 1782).

Harkins to remove Belliotti from the parish. The day after writing the letter, a delegation of Italians visited Harkins to complain about Belliotti in person; another mutual-benefit society, Society of La Madonna Del Carmento lodged similar complaints against Belliotti two weeks later. Harkins found grounds on which to ignore these complaints, and took no action against Belliotti.[30]

The struggle between southern Italian immigrants and the Providence church escalated to a new level in 1907 when Father Antonio Bove, the already controversial priest of St. Ann's parish in the Italian North End whose contact with Providence southern Italians had been marked by discord since his arrival to the city in 1901, took the offensive against the societies. He stopped a man from collecting funds for fireworks for the St. Rocco Society's August feast-day celebration. Bove was quite explicit that his action was prompted by antagonism to the saints'-day celetrations in general and that he particularly disapproved of "using so much money for fireworks and firecrackers." Bove's concern was that "at these celebrations money is collected in the name of the church and used for fireworks and other useless things." Bove had other aspirations for the collection: "I want them to give the money to some good institution, either the church or the hospital or some such enterprise." This time, rather than complain unavailingly to the bishop, the parishioners demonstrated with their feet. One Sunday later, several thousand Italians gathered in a park opposite St. Ann's Church with the intention of taking the church keys from the sexton and closing the church to show their opposition to Bove's stance. Practically the entire neighborhood turned out, hoping to overrule Bove's action "by closing up the church forcibly and by driving away the priest."[31] In response to Bove's attempt to belittle saint worship and redirect financial support from festas to the church, the demonstraters demanded that Catholicism be defined in ways that were consistent with familiar southern Italian practices.

As immigration continued to swell the numbers of southern Italians in Providence, the mutual-benefit societies continued to increase in membership and confidence with regard to their claims on the church. Informally, at least, southern Italians appeared to have gained some concessions. In 1910, the Marzano Appio Society (whose members came from a town near Naples that sent a steady stream of immigrants to Providence) and its supporters filled Holy Ghost Church to witness the religious christening service of the society's newly made Italian and American flags. The silk flags, each of which was sponsored by an honored couple serving as godparents, were sanctified "amidst the most profound silence" with a sprinkling of holy water by a visiting priest, Father Domenico Galluppi. The flag christening was then celebrated with a large parade which followed the church service. The day's festivities were concluded with a mass meeting held at the Italian-built Benevolence Hall.[32]

When Bishop Harkins heard that the christening ceremony had taken place, he immediately communicated to Father Belliotti his objections to the practice and told him that no such ceremony could be repeated in the church. A committee from the Frosolonese Society, which had scheduled the christening of their new flags in Holy Ghost Church for later that month, visited Harkins several times, but failed "to obtain the necessary permission." The christening of the Frosolonese Society flags was performed in Benevolence Hall instead. Several hundred people "filled every corner of the hall," while hundreds of others who could not get inside waited in the streets. Bowing to what must have been tremendous popular pressure, Belliotti did officiate at the christening and sprinkle the flags with holy water which he had brought from the church. He got much public credit for his appearance: "Father Belliotti was given an enthusiastic reception, every man standing up and cheering him as he withdrew from the hall into the reception room."[33] For the moment, the church responded to the societies' initiative.

As in Italy, the church in Providence attempted to counter the expanding presence of mutual-benefit associations by establishing a church-related network of societies that would compete for membership and influence with the secular societies. A contemporary church historian observed that in St. Ann's parish, Father Bove was active in establishing organizations for each sex and for every age— "Holy Name societies for the men and boys, sodalities for women and girls." But there were indications that Bove's attempt was not fully successful. In 1918, Bove tried to stop the affiliation of mutual-benefit societies with the Sons of Italy by publishing a pamphlet under the imprint of Bishop Harkins, labelling the order "an enemy of the Catholic Church" and calling its constitution "offensive to the Catholic conscience." The Sons of Italy leadership responded that Bove's real concern was that "four societies in his parish have affiliated with the order, and . . . Father Bove fears that as a result, he will lose a certain control over them." If in fact, these were Bove's concerns, his pamphlet was counterproductive, for within one week of its publication, three more societies from his parish applied for affiliation with the order.[34] In these years, mutual-benefit associations were too numerous and self-directed, and the credibility of the church in the immigrant neighborhoods was too weak, for the societies to be damaged by such an attack.

Despite the concessions made by Belliotti to the mutual-benefit societies in 1910, his stance toward immigrant culture in general continued to provoke antagonism. And even the church-affiliated mutual-benefit societies, like those that Bove had hoped would support the parish, continued to oppose northern Italian leadership that seemed at odds with southern Italian culture. In 1920, continuing to assert their right to some voice in church affairs, mutual-benefit societies, including the church-affiliated Holy Name Society at Holy Ghost, were at the forefront of a campaign to remove Belliotti from Holy Ghost Church. They hoped to have Belliotti replaced by his assistant, Vincenzo Vicari, who had grown up in the southern Italian neighborhood in Providence and so understood and shared the cultural background of his parishioners. Various parishioners wrote to the bishop complaining of Belliotti's high-handed treatment and comparing him to Vicari—"everybody's friend and also a friend to the poor." Some 1,175 women of the parish petitioned the bishop making similar charges against Belliotti, adding the specific complaint that he had ignored the mutual-benefit societies and refused "repeatedly to hold devotional services in honor of the sacred heart and also other services, although they may have been in great demand by hundreds of parishioners." Twelve mutual-benefit societies joined together and wrote to the bishop demanding Belliotti's removal. The bishop responded to the outpouring of complaints and petitions in a manner that minimally acknowledged the parishioners' complaints while reaffirming the power of the church hierarchy. First he ordered Vicari to another parish and then finally relieved Belliotti of his responsibilities at Holy Ghost. Belliotti's replacement, Angelo Strazzoni, was another priest from the same northern Italian order from which Belliotti had come.[35]

Within two months of Strazzoni's arrival, mutual-benefit societies had begun to organize for his removal. Four women and three men were arrested for disrupting a Sunday mass by shouting for Strazzoni's resignation. The arrested parishioners were careful to state the intention of their protest. They objected less to Strazzoni himself than to the cultural tradition of the order from which he came. The protest was intended to "end the administration of the church by priests of the St. Borromeo Society." Several mutual-benefit societies formed a committee of protesting parishioners to defend the arrested people and to continue to complain to the bishop, the chancellor of the diocese, the cardinal in Boston, and the apostolic delegate in Washington, D.C. Writing a letter to the prefect of the Congregation of the Council, protesting parishioners spelled out the tensions between their version of Catholicism, which Vicari had embraced, and the version practiced by the northern Italian missionary priests. The parishioners objected to the priests' opposition to saints' days, their inaccessibility, and their use of cultural references that separated them from their parishioners. Vicari's example emboldened them and made them feel entitled to make their demands.

> [Vicari] always cited the Gospels and the Fathers of the Church while the Scalabrini Fathers were accustomed to embellish their homilies with citations from Philosophers, Poets, and even from modern Novelists. . . . [Vicari] was the true guardian and depository of divine science and orthodoxy such as is contained in the Gospels, in the writings of the Fathers, in Tradition.[36]

Again, the heart of their protest was the parishioners' insistence on defining Catholicism in such a way that it affirmed rather than denied their cultural background.

Strazzoni stayed at Holy Ghost only a year-and-a-half. The next priest in the parish, Flaminio Parenti, was also from the same northern Italian order, but he had had extensive pastoral experience in southern-Italian immigrant neighborhoods in the United States. He seemed able to accommodate southern Italian culture within the parish. Also, by the 1920s the American-born generation was becoming more active in the church, and their presence may have shifted the orientation of associational life toward the Catholic mainstream.[37] Prior to this point, protesting parishioners had waged a long and sustained struggle for acknowledgment of their cultural traditions within the church. Mutual-benefit societies had played a key role, both in defining the elements of an alternative southern Italian Catholicism and in providing an organizational structure that could be used to mobilize opposition to threats against familiar southern Italian cultural norms.

Mutual-benefit associations also brought with them traditions of craft organization and defense of workers' interests central to many European *mutuo soccorso* societies and *chevroth*. Because immigrants were grouped in certain trades and excluded from others, the trades where they constituted a significant number were starting places for mutual-benefit organizations. As unskilled workers, many immigrants were excluded from the craft unionism dominant in the period, and for these workers, mutual-benefit associations provided the only protection against the economic uncertainties of urban and industrial life.[38] In some occupations, particularly those in which there were large numbers of their compatriots, Italians and Jews were able to transform mutual-benefit associations into craft locals. Even when not unified by a single occupation, mutual-benefit members often shared a common economic status, and their mutual-benefit associations could sometimes reflect common class concerns.

Just as they had settled into distinct neighborhoods, immigrants tended to group themselves in certain trades—partly because of skills they brought from the old country, partly because of their reliance for their first job on kin and neighbors who had arrived earlier. Tight exclusionary controls exercised by some skilled-craft unions combined with the preference of immigrants for working with familiar people distributed the immigrants unevenly in the city's occupational structure. The preimmigration experience of southern Italians and Jews may have been responsible for the large numbers of men and women working as tailors in Rhode Island. In 1905, 27 percent of the garment makers in the state were Italian, and nearly 14 percent were Jews. Reflecting prior commercial orientation, 36 percent of the peddlers in the state were Jewish, and 12 percent were Italian. In 1905, Jews and Italians were just beginning to be hired in the jewelry industry; where 3 percent of the workers were Italian and nearly 4 percent were Jewish. Italians also comprised nearly 32 percent of all barbers, 25 percent of all laborers, and almost 14 percent of all bakers in the state.[39]

By 1915, ethnic concentrations within certain occupations were even more marked. According to local labor statistics collected from that year, 8 percent of Providence's population were born in Italy, and over 3 percent were Jews from eastern Europe. Both groups continued to be substantially overrepresented in the needle trades. Sixty-two percent of the tailors in the city were Italian and another 18 percent were Jewish. Both Italians and Jews found work in large numbers in the jewelry industry. According to one local historian, some jewelry companies recruited immigrants "right off the boats of the Fabre Line and put them to work." In 1915, the jewelry work force was 24 percent Italian and 9 percent Jewish. Sixty-two percent of all laborers in the city were born in Italy, and 31 percent of those employed in the building trades, especially those working as hod carriers, were Italian. Six percent of the building-trades workers were Jewish. These occupational concentrations, once established, generated ethnic dynamics of their own. As within families, shared occupational experience could mean similar economic status and common social and economic interests. Occupational concentrations reinforced a sense of group solidarity. The small organizations of Italian and Jewish socialists in Providence also played a role in popularizing issues in the broadest terms of common class interest within their respective communities.[40]

Reflecting these concentrations and their impact on the immigrant communities, between 1905 and 1915 Italian workers organized locals of barbers, building laborers and hod carriers, and cement workers. Jewish workers organized locals of bakers, peddlers, and hat and cap makers. Italians organized an Italian-language local of the Carpenters and Joiners Union, and Jewish carpenters established a Yiddish-language local of the same union.[41] Most of these locals probably began as mutual-benefit associations, and many of them seemed to have lasted only a few years as unions, reflecting the precarious state of the craft labor movement in this period. Still, the very existence of these ethnic local unions testified to the associational strength of European loyalties in Providence. Overlapping ties of birth and craft also sharpened Italian and Jewish self-identities as cohesive communities laced through with interconnections.

Building on a sizeable concentration within the lowest ranks of the building trades, Italian building laborers drew on mutual-benefit traditions to successfully mobilize broad-based community support for their strike in 1910. Sixteen hundred hod carriers led their newly organized building-laborers union out on strike on May Day, demanding a new wage scale and a shorter working day. The building laborers organized a saints'-day-type parade through the city, beginning and ending in the Italian neighborhoods, followed by an open-air strike meeting. While winding through Federal Hill, the parade combined secular and socialist, Italian and American references, expressing the contradictory late-nineteenth-century southern Italian culture that mutual-benefit traditions were heir to. As the *Providence Journal* reporter described it:

> The Italian Royal March was succeeded by the Socialist Anthem, and the American National Anthem by the Garibaldi March. Whenever the band struck up the well-known strains of the Garibaldi March, all the marchers took their hats off and applauded enthusiastically. Along Knight Street the band played the Socialist hymn "Internationale" but as the members passed in front of the Church of the Holy Ghost, the majority of them uncovered and remained so until they had swung into Atwells Avenue. The march was headed by laborers with Italian flags, followed by men with American flags, followed by the Savoia Band, followed by [Boston organizer Felice] D'Allessandro, followed by the officers of the union.[42]

The building laborers generated support for the strike by tapping already existing social networks. According to the newspaper, the strikers packed the room used as strike headquarters and spilled out into the streets below, but the Federal Hill neighborhood as a whole was "alive with men, collarless, and in some cases coatless, who gathered on street corners and discussed the situation." The strikers needed to close down construction sites all over the city in order to pressure the rest of the building-trades unions to join the strike and gain the considerable influence of the Building Trades Council in support of their demands. The building laborers assumed community solidarity and mutual interests as they persuaded other Italians to support the strike. In one incident at a construction site where a new factory was being built, Italian strikers "interviewed" the

Italian foreman. As the newspaper reported with customary euphemism, the foreman, "who is gifted with a fine sense of humor, told the interviewers that they might go if they saw fit to a place which is a good deal warmer than Providence is at the present time." The foreman's verbal abuse did not deter the strikers: they "simply lifted him off his feet and carried him to a position on the opposite side of the road where they initiated him, willy nilly, into the mysteries of their union." The foreman at length "found a dollar which he did not need in his pocket, handed it over to the secretary of the union, and signed the roll of the organization." Now that he had rejoined the community by virtue of his new support of the strike, "the men gave him three cheers." Then the strikers made sure that the foreman faced no additional temptations to return to work: "they escorted him to a city-bound car." Attempts to enforce the strike against strikebreakers were critical to its success, and according to the newspaper reports, the scenes of strikers defending themselves against strikebreakers and police "surpassed any since the streetcar strike of 1902"—a strike that had similarly involved a well-mobilized community. A total of thirty-seven people were arrested during the strike. By the end of the week, the determination of the building laborers to close down construction sites finally prompted the Building Trades Council to support the strike and several individual carpenters' locals to go out in sympathy strikes.[43] This additional pressure ended the strike with a settlement favorable to the building laborers. The community support on which the strikers were able to draw was a crucial factor in their success.

Unanimous community support which ethnic unions could draw on proved to be a more limited resource in situations that depended on cross-ethnic cooperation, such as the strike in the needle trades in 1913 and the strike in the jewelry industry in 1917. Both of these industries employed large numbers of Italians and Jews. The structure of both industries, built around small independent contractors and dependent on homeworkers, made them extremely hard to organize. The organizing drive in the garment industry in Providence met bitter opposition from the local AFL hierarchy, and the union campaign in jewelry faced well-organized and staunchly antiunion manufacturers. Still, it appears that neither the largely Italian leadership in the 1913 garment strike nor the principally Jewish leadership in the 1917 jewelry strike was capable of reaching across ethnic lines and mobilizing the broad community support necessary to enforce the strikers' demands.[44]

Mutual-benefit associations that were not organized as unions still shared economic concerns as well as ties of origins, because the sizeable ethnic concentrations within occupations produced common work-related and economic grievances. Under these circumstances, mutual-benefit societies could sometimes be activated to express class solidarity within the ethnic community. Forty-seven mutual-benefit associations joined together to organize a parade of more than two thousand people to support the 1912 textile strikers in Lawrence, Massachusetts and to protest the imprisonment of the Italian strike leaders Arturo Giovanitti and Guiseppe Ettor. According to the newspaper, "practically every Italian organization on Federal Hill and in the Hopkins Park [North End] and Silver Lake districts had turned out." The societies led the parade, and a socialist delegation formed at the end of the procession. Police disrupted the parade, trying to seize the red flags carried by socialist demonstrators, and six policemen were injured in the riot that ensued. The broad sympathies that united the diverse mutual-benefit societies extended to the defense of the socialist demonstrators. The parade's organizers, including the representative of the committee of participating mutual-benefit associations, issued a public statement in which "they laid full blame for the affair on the police."[45] National identification as Italians and a shared cause as workers underlay the enthusiasm with which Providence Italians took up the Lawrence strike as their own issue.

The tradition of mutual benefit and its implicit assumption that the ethnic community was shot through with webs of reciprocal obligation also justified attacks against middle-class representatives of one's own ethnic group when they were seen as taking advantage of community support. When ethnic retailers raised their prices, immigrants viewed such acts as an abandonment of the principles of community justice and particularly as a breach of reciprocity. An increase in the price of necessary commodities was an injury to a customer loyally patronizing a *paesano* or *landsman*. Neighborhood customers expected special consideration in exchange for their patronage, and they were outraged when instead they were offered what they considered to be unfairly high prices. In this case, the high prices fell most severely on women, the managers of the family budget, who were expected to stretch a meager family income to feed and house a family despite changing prices at the marketplace. Women, not surprisingly, were among the most furious avengers against neighborhood retailers who betrayed their trust by charging what appeared to be inflated prices.[46]

In 1910, Jewish women in Providence "declared war against the kosher butchers" because of price increases. The women planned to boycott meat sold by the kosher butchers in their community until "the meat has come down to the prices people could afford." The women picketed the shops and dissuaded shoppers from buying meat. The butchers responded by trying to mobilize a house-to-house canvass intended to drum up business, in some cases bringing meat to families who had not ordered it. The women strikers sent delegations to the houses to explain the boycott and to persuade the families to rescind their orders, and "in every case, it was said, the butchers were instructed to send after the meat." More was at stake than simply prices. The boycott demands included "respectable treatment of the customers," echoing the protests of Dvinsk domestic servants for private rooms and Kishinev shop workers for "polite treatment of employees." Other demands insisted on "fresh meat wrapped in clean paper, and not newspapers, as has been the custom in some of the shops," as well as a reduction in the price of all cuts of meat. Police were called out to keep women picketers from blocking entrances and biting prospective customers. The women won their protest when another butcher shop opened in the neighborhood, offering meat at the lower prices they demanded. The other butchers reluctantly lowered their prices in self-defense.[47] Community solidarity in opposition to the right of retailers to profit without limit returned peace as well as lower prices to the neighborhood.

In 1914, Federal Hill Italians participated in a similar collective punishment of a prominent Italian retailer who appeared to have raised his prices without concern for the effect of his action on his compatriots. On Federal Hill, the consumer protest seems to have been orchestrated by men, suggesting their close involvement with the workings of the family economy and the requirements of the family budget. In August, neighborhood men attended two mass meetings protesting the high price of food before they took to the streets one Saturday night to mete out special punishment to a pasta wholesaler who had raised prices. The wholesaler, Frank P. Ventrone, was a well-known and successful businessman in the Italian community who had come to Providence in the 1880s from Isérnia, a city from which many Italians had emigrated to Providence. Over a thousand people marched through Federal Hill, shattering the windows in a block of property owned by Ventrone and then dumping the stock of macaroni and staples from his store into the street. The participants insisted that this was a matter between Ventrone and themselves and resisted the intervention of the police. According to a newspaper account, "jeers and catcalls greeted the police as they tried to clear the area." The police used their nightsticks freely but "every time the patrol was sent to the Knight Street station with a prisoner, it was a signal for the mob to hurl at the police anything they could grab." When police returned to Federal Hill the next afternoon, ostensibly to arrest someone on a nonsupport charge, Italians again resisted outside intervention in a three-hour struggle that a newspaper called "the worst riots in the annals of the city." The issue was resolved on Monday, when representatives of the Italian Socialist Club met with Ventrone's representatives and secured a substantial decrease in the price of pasta. The Italian newspaper, in its editorial the following week, articulated the basis on which community sanctions had been applied, arguing that "Signor Ventrone . . . owes everything to our colony," and thus had a responsibility to the community which he did not meet until pressure was brought to bear on him. "Our brave colony, when we all stand together, will be given justice."[48] Shared experience of economic grievances turned the ethnic community against its own middle class. The protesters could take the community's unanimous support for granted, and with it they won the desired results.

Mutual-benefit associations had assumed a multitude of functions in immigrant community life. For men, mutual-benefit associations had extended certain familial responsibilities to a wider network of men and their families. For women, associations sometimes had expanded neighborhood patterns of sharing and sometimes had developed into a combination of activities that competed with the claims of household and family. As repositories of shared ethnic, regional, and occupational loyalties, mutual-benefit associations had played a central role in the maintenance of immigrant culture and the solidarity of the ethnic group. The community food protests, drawing on the same norms of reciprocity that ruled family relations, suggested how widespread a shared familial culture of mutual support and reciprocal obligation was in the immigrant community. But, just as the shapes of family networks had changed, the particular associational life created by the immigrant generation was not replicated by their children. The decline of mutual-benefit associations meant, among other things, the decline of a community institution through which familial values were articulated.

THE WANING OF THE MUTUAL-BENEFIT TRADITION

Mutual-benefit associations had coexisted since the early days of settlement with other types of organizations within immigrant neighborhoods. But in the 1920s and 1930s, other kinds of organizations came to dominate community life, and mutual-benefit associations began to recede from prominence. A number of factors diminished the appeal of mutual-benefit societies. For Italians, Mussolini's attacks on provincialism in the name of Italian nationalism were influential. For both Italians and Jews, immigration restriction in the 1920s cut off a potential supply of new members, and widespread depression-related unemployment placed greater demands on the associations' shrinking resources while alternative forms of life insurance, pensions, and social security payments emerged after 1935. As the American-born children of immigrants came of age, they brought new needs, new priorities, and a new constituency to community associational life.

Some mutual-benefit associations continued to exist on a smaller scale, but the organizations increasingly important in the ethnic communities were those centered around Americanization activities and philanthropic goals. The new organizations, often citywide rather than drawing on neighborhood networks, reflected the widening gap between the social and occupational experience of the immigrant and American-born generations, as well as the age segregation increasingly common in American cultural and social institutions. Oriented toward defining hyphenate Americanism, these organizations looked forward to asserting a place for Italians and Jews within American society rather than toward maintaining European cultural loyalties. The Catholic parishes in Providence and the synagogues that persisted as viable congregations consolidated their hold on Italian and Jewish religious activities, while making whatever accommodations to American culture were necessary to induce the American-born generation to be active participants in redefined religious ritual.[49]

The principles of mutual support, reciprocal obligation, and economic self-help were largely absent from the community agenda. In contrast, philanthropic activities gave notice that an ethnic middle class had emerged to take care of its own. There had always been class divisions in the ethnic communities, once partially obscured by regional distinctions, but now social mobility sharpened divisions among eastern European Jews and among southern Italians. The new organizations were part of the process of charting a new definition of ethnicity to describe the fragmented community. Unique cultural and common economic interests could no longer be assumed. The new meaning of ethnicity would be an identification that might serve as an alternative to a class identity. For the most part, ethnicity was no longer descriptive of a geographically unified, occupationally concentrated group shot through with ties of kinship, but a more diffuse identity covering a broader spatial and social territory.[50]

By 1936, there were still 120 Italian mutual-benefit organizations in the state of Rhode Island, and 70 of these were provincial organizations. But the societies were suffering from depleted membership which they attributed to the deaths of the immigrant generation, the differing interests of their own children, and the antiprovincial campaign of the Fascist government in Italy. Provincial societies responded to their membership crisis by admitting members' friends who were not *paesani* or by opening up their membership generally. The societies tried to argue that altering their provincial base did not in any way weaken the mutual-benefit tradition, but their membership and influence continued to decline. Funds for mutual benefit similarly disappeared from Jewish organizations. Both Italian and Jewish organizations were also affected by the redistribution of families and neighbors as ethnic communities spread out to new neighborhoods. The effects of widespread suburbanization were not really felt in Providence until the 1940s, but the population movement in the 1920s and 1930s described in chapter 3 played a part in unsettling the automatic connection between family, neighbor, and compatriot which had facilitated the formalization of these relationships in mutual-benefit associations. Commercial amusements joined with public schools to popularize sex-integrated socializing among peers and competed with mutual-benefit associations as a center of ethnic social life.[51]

Mutual-benefit associations were further undermined when their economic benefits could no longer compete with alternative forms of life insurance that began to appear in the 1920s and 1930s. Life insurance plans, group plans, company pensions, and finally government-initiated social security all offered broader and more secure coverage, although at the expense of family policies and self-help principles. As sociologists have argued, the provision of benefits through public channels of distribution operated formally to exclude those gifts that could be obtained through other means, and in doing so, had the effect of contracting social networks. The Jewish Workmen's Circle attempted to expand its membership in the 1920s by reaching out to native-born and English-speaking Jews, women, and youth groups, but the Providence branch lost membership in the 1930s and finally disbanded in the 1940s when its insurance policies lost subscribers to these alternative plans. One Italian woman interviewed in Bridgeport in the late 1930s explained why she and her friends had turned to standard life insurance policies, and perhaps her experience can explain what happened in Providence. As she recalled, "That time they had all the societies that give you the money if you die, and that's another thing why all the women they were belonging to these societies." But times had changed. "Now they don't do this so much, they get the insurance from the Metropolitan and the other companies." She and her friends had grown accustomed to the role segmentation of modern life: "When we want to have the insurance, we get it from the Metropolitan, when we want to see Italian people, we see our friends." She took pride in leaving the old ways behind, in coming to more closely approximate the lives of her American neighbors: "Now us Italian people we are more 'Americanizata.'" The final evidence of Americanization was in terms of social life: "My children, like a lots of their friends, they belong to the American clubs."[52] Leaving behind mutual-benefit funds in this case also meant turning away from associations closely identified with Europe and with peasant cultural traditions.

New community organizations, often specifically designed for young people alone, signified the reorientation in associational values, as they did for the woman quoted above. In the Italian community, young people's organizations included numerous clubs begun between 1910 and 1920. The Young Federal Hill Athletic Club, for example, promoted sports activities for young men and boys who had grown up without the physical "benefits" of manual labor. The Garibaldi Club sponsored the first Boy Scout troop on Federal Hill and worked with younger boys at the local settlement house, the Federal Hill House. The Dante Alighieri Club, which sponsored Italian and English classes for citizenship, supported Americanization activities and helped to popularize a particular definition of Italian culture as the language of poets and artists and the literature of intellectuals, rather than the dialect of folk proverbs and peasant accounts of saints' miracles. One Providence resident described how a newer organization like the Garibaldi Club came to dominate associational life, replacing an orientation toward European bonds of loyalty with an American identity. He remembered the merger of the Italian-American Club, founded in 1896, with the Garibaldi Club as the most important event on Federal Hill in the 1920s. As he described their differences, the members of the Garibaldi Club were younger men, "largely representing the viewpoint of the American-born Italian." He recalled the club as "almost a father-son group after the merger," but clearly the sons had the upper hand, because after that date "English supplanted Italian as the language spoken in the club." In the Jewish community, parallel organizations for young people included the Young Men's Hebrew Association, founded in 1912, and the Young Women's Hebrew

Association, appearing in 1914. The Hebrew-American Club was organized in 1910 and addressed itself explicitly to goals of Americanization and citizenship. The focus on Hebrew rather than Yiddish was an explicit repudiation of eastern European cultural traditions. Activities of all these organizations for young people were social, recreational, and educational; they emulated American cultural activities and abandoned economic concerns.[53]

The reorientation of Italian associational life was symbolized in Providence, as it was elsewhere, by the emergence of the national order of Sons of Italy. The first Sons of Italy chapter appeared in Rhode Island in 1914, and by 1918 the order claimed over five thousand members and forty-three affiliated lodges in the state, including many formerly independent provincial societies. Affiliation may not have changed the inner workings of the societies, but it certainly altered public statements of purpose. Closely connected with tests of loyalty stemming from World War I, the Sons of Italy called itself a patriotic organization whose object was to "make better American citizens out of those of Italian lineage, and to teach them that this country was to come first in their thoughts, even when it comes to giving their lives in its defense." A statement from one of the order's Rhode Island officials sharply distinguished the order from provincial mutual-benefit organizations: "The Sons of Italy is not a mutual aid society, nor, in the strictest sense of the word, an order. It is an Italian-American institution." The Sons of Italy linked its dedication to Americanization with a commitment to its members' advancement, loosely defined. The wives of prominent professional and business leaders in the Italian community in Providence formed female auxiliaries of the order to add their voices in teaching "the American way of life," particularly in the context of groups to "bring together the better Italian elements." The women's auxiliaries dedicated themselves to the "moral and cultural progress of their members" and to the "advancement of the Italo-American." The women's auxiliaries were particularly active in promoting classifically defined Italian culture. Fund-raising activities for the "needy" betrayed the particular class orientation of the Sons of Italy. In mutual-benefit associations, the distinction between benefactor and recipient was temporary at most, but the Sons of Italy membership intended to be in the permanent position of benefactor. The 1921 announcement of plans to raise money for an Italian orphanage was a concrete commitment from the Sons of Italy in the direction of public philanthropy.[54]

Philanthropic organizations in the Jewish community had been organized by wealthy German Jews in the same years that eastern

European immigrants shared the comradeship of minimal resources in mutual-benefit associations. As eastern European Jews began to accumulate wealth, they began to be included in the leadership of these organizations. Wives of rising businessmen were instrumental in organizing Jewish philanthropy in Providence. A variety of organizations provided general relief to the poor, including the German Montifiore Ladies Hebrew Benevolent Association, begun in 1877, the Young Ladies Hebrew Aid Society, founded in 1894, and the Rhode Island Aid Society, chartered in 1911. The goals of other organizations like those which founded and supported a Jewish hospital, orphanage, and old age home, were to provide Jews who needed institutional care with daily access to Jewish ritual observance. Efforts toward the systematization of Jewish philanthropy began as early as the 1920s and were finalized in 1945 with the founding of the General Jewish Committee of Providence, later renamed the Jewish Federation of Rhode Island.[55] The decline of mutual-benefit activities in the Jewish community in the 1920s and 1930s occurred at the same time as the institutionalization of community-wide philanthropic organizations.

The conflict between philanthropic and mutual-benefit orientations was revealed clearly in the Italian community in 1932. A group of unaffiliated Italian provincial societies, organized into a loose coalition called the Columbus Central Committee, challenged the Sons of Italy to give a public accounting of its orphanage fund, which the order had been amassing for ten years. Arguing from a mutual-aid orientation, the provincial societies proposed that the Sons distribute the fund to Italian families hit hard by the depression. The Sons of Italy responded to the challenge by publishing an account of the money, most of which was extended in mortgage loans, but apparently the organization was otherwise unmoved by the committee's request.[56] The Sons of Italy continued to interpret its community responsibility in terms of such philanthropic activity as building an orphanage rather than in the more direct and reciprocal terms of mutual aid.

Italian women continued to be active in Sons of Italy auxiliaries, and many Jewish women took leadership roles in philanthropic organizations. Because of residential dispersion and increasing participation in wage labor outside the home by married women, it was often hard for women to be as active as their mothers had been. Many of the women active in the labor movement in the 1930s were still single and living at home, and many of the married women active in community-wide organizations found that they were only able to do so if they had the freedom from domestic responsibilities granted by grown children or full-time household help. The full history of women's associational activities remains hidden from view, but surely the changing configurations of family, work, neighborhood, and community organizations explains part of that history.

Mutual-benefit associations had extended the resources of families in dealing with the transformation of the local economy in nineteenth-century Europe and in coping with urban and industrial life in Providence. The associations embodied the familial culture of the immigrant community, ordinarily perpetuating the separation between male and female social life. They drew friends and relatives into circles of assistance that operated on the principles of mutual support and reciprocal obligation, indicative of relations inside families. Gathering together members on the basis of regional and occupational loyalties, the associations served as actual extensions of kin ties and as a community parallel to kinship networks.

From 1905 to 1920, mutual-benefit societies honeycombed the Italian and Jewish neighborhoods, serving as both symbols and organizational force in the attempt to maintain immigrant cultural traditions in Providence. As the locus of shared regional loyalties, mutual-benefit associations asserted European religious traditions as an alternative to existing Providence religious institutions. Building on ethnic concentrations within certain occupations, mutual-benefit societies were sometimes mobilized to express common class interests within the ethnic community. The ideology of reciprocal obligation justified the community food riots to punish ethnic middle-class shopkeepers who were seen as taking advantage of ethnic loyalty.

The waning of mutual-benefit associations by the 1930s meant the decline of community institutions that had articulated the familial values of economic cooperation and reciprocity. The children of immigrants founded and joined organizations whose bias was toward integration into mainstream American society rather than the maintenance of old-world culture. The economic benefits of the societies were undermined by the widespread availability of new kinds of corporate and state insurance, whose policies protected individuals rather than families. Community economic assistance was increasingly likely to be provided by philanthropic institutions rather than self-help organizations. Particularistic mutual-benefit associations were eclipsed by the new organizations, drawing on a varied occupational constituency. No longer would ethnic organizations represent the concerns of one neighborhood or one trade. The new organizations redefined the meaning of ethnic culture to refer to an Italian corpus of universal poetry, literature, and art rather than local dialects and peasant folk tales, to the ancient Hebrew of scholarly and religious writings rather than the Yiddish of the shtetl and the Bund. The new organizations were part of the process of designing a new meaning for ethnicity.

The new definition of ethnicity referred to a more diffuse identity as a member of a nationality rather than to concrete experience with common work, shared neighborhood, and overlapping social connections. Workplaces and neighborhoods were no longer identifiable as the province of a particular ethnic group, and the way was cleared for new cross-ethnic associations like the industrial unions of the 1930s and 1940s and neighborhood associations and tenants unions in the 1950s and 1960s to lay claim to loyalties once divided by mutual-benefit associations. But little public space was left to support familial norms of reciprocity—earlier a model for community relations, now an archaic relic in a society that had become much more privately oriented.

Conclusion

IMMIGRANT FAMILIES were not doomed in American cities, nor did they remain unchanged by the world they found there. From the possibilities presented in Providence neighborhoods, shops, and factories, they made new family lives for themselves. Facing the mingled promise and instability of the local economy, families held tightly to strategies of economic interdependence, altering but not abandoning them in the face of technological and occupational change. The disruptions of migration led them to expand their households with kin, to enlarge the networks of kin who owed each other assistance, and to lean on neighbors and friends as substitute kin. Mutual benefit organizations reflected these values of economic collectivity and expanded exchange. Fraternal associations were particularly resonant with the dominance of siblings in networks of immigrant kin.

Over the years in Providence, assertions of individual priorities sometimes threatened the values of family collectivity. These occurred in various circumstances, most often when adolescents tried to reconcile familial traditions with the peer culture they discovered in public school, when young men and women had to steer a course between personal romantic inclinations and familial interest in marriage decisions, or when co-residing married children (increasingly likely to be daughters) found themselves caught between conflicting sets of obligations to parents and their own husbands and children. These kinds of tensions were heightened in the prosperous years of the 1920s and muted in the return to more familiar hard times in the 1930s. By 1940, structural changes in the economy, the distance from migration and the early days in Providence, and the geographical dispersion of the ethnic communities had altered the shape of most families' kin networks. Previously broadened norms of obligation to a wider range of kin and friends were narrowed and mutual benefit associations which had expressed these norms had begun to disappear. Although aid still flowed across houshold lines, kin networks were increasingly focused internally toward parent-child interaction rather than externally among siblings, neighbors, and friends.

Ethnic families present a dramatically different picture in 1940 than immigrant families in 1900. The search for job security had replaced the identification of work with inherited skills and independence. Rather than following familial patterns of work and dreams of self-employment, many Italians abandoned the trades for the factory, and many Jews left neighborhood shops for larger workplaces. For those in the children's generation who had some education, white collar work was increasingly common. With proficiency in English and even limited access to public education, children acquired a familiarity—inconceivable for their parents— with American cultural norms that were potentially at odds with the values of family collectivity. Parental authority over job choice, the timing of marriage, and the selection of marriage partners had noticeably diminished, although it had not disappeared altogether. The place, timing, and familial significance of women's wage-earning had changed from domestic labor in the home (replaced when possible by children's labor as children reached working age) to public labor force participation as one of the family's two primary wage earners. Responsibility for assisting kin, earlier spread among wider networks of exchange, was now principally a woman's burden made more difficult by distances between families separated by changing patterns of residence. But the result of this transformation was not the isolated nuclear family, rampant individualism, or the shedding of a generalized ethnic identity, stereotypically defined as the fruits of modernization and Americanization. As Italian and Jewish families faced the 1940s, they renegotiated participation in family economic collectivity, they redefined but did not abandon responsibilities for families across household lines, and they reinterpreted the meaning of ethnicity to embrace a community no longer economically or geographically unified. Refashioning their family lives in the currents of historical process while preserving cherished traditions at the center was a striking accomplishment.

By 1940, the direction of familial change for Italian and Jewish families was remarkably similar. Despite the many differences between them, particularly in the extent of kinship networks in Providence and in general economic orientation, it was the particular economic skills and resources that each group brought with it together with the circumstances of their migration and the dynamics of twentieth century economic change that explain the divergence of their experience in Providence, not ahistorical ethnic differences. By 1940, many aspects of Italian and Jewish family patterns looked alike.

As they shaped their family lives and in response to many of the same pressures, Italian and Jewish immigrants and their children also made and remade ethnic identities for themselves. Immigrants came to Providence from different areas, and in the years of immigration these areas were in the throes of cultural upheaval. Initially, immigrants did not share identities as southern Italians or eastern Europeans but as townspeople and provincials: Pietravairanese and Teanese, Neapolitans and Sicilians, Jews from Mogilev, Jews from Berdichev, Litvaks and Galitzianers. An identity as southern Italians and eastern European Jews began to be forged in Providence. First shaped by contrast with those few northern Italians and German Jews who had preceded them as immigrants and who occupied very different economic and cultural space, this identity was expressed through regionalism as the number of immigrants from specific towns and regions formed a critical mass that supported provincial mutual-benefit associations and *landsleit* congregations. Regional identities merged to proclaim ethnic immigrant identities in the common workplaces and neighborhoods, made available to the newcomers by their arrival at a time when industrial expansion opened up new kinds of jobs and streetcar lines created new neighborhoods, leaving certain job classifications and downtown neighborhoods to be dominated by immigrants. As they arrived in Providence via family and village chains and then found work and housing for each other and later arrivals, immigrants staked out particular workplaces and neighborhoods as their own. Occupational and residential concentrations defined distinct ethnic identities for southern Italians and eastern European Jews, based on common experience of uprooting, language, economic status and occupational interests, housing and neighborhood lifestyles—all strengthened by overlapping sets of relationships among relatives, friends, co-workers, neighbors. Mutual-benefit associations owed their appeal to these overlapping relationships and their connection with common European roots. These ethnic identities and this sense of ethnic solidarity were expressed in flourishing alternative cultures that supported familial collectivity rather than individualism, old-world cultural celebration rather than American acculturation.[1]

Over time, the conditions that had supported immigrant definitions of ethnic identity changed. In the 1920s and 1930s, occupational and residential movement dispersed ethnic concentrations, and the nearly universal acceptance of English as a language made common background less important as a basis of connection. Small groups of Italians and Jews continued to replicate the conditions of immigrant settlement, sharing ties of occupation, kinship, and neighborhood. For these families, definitions of ethnicity drawing on patterns of frequent association and common origins, economic status, and residence were still meaningful. But the American-born generation as a whole reformulated the content of ethnicity. It now became an identity that was more symbolic and broadly inclusive, capable of crossing wide economic and geographical distance. The children's generation had no interest in mutual-benefit associations, but they did not cast off an ethnic identification altogether. Instead they supported new kinds of organizations that not only crossed class boundaries to embrace a community scattered in different jobs and neighborhoods but appealed to common origins as an aspect of a distant past rather than a concrete shared experience.

I have argued that between 1900 and 1940 the relationship between ethnicity and class underwent a significant alteration that was at the basis of the different ways that immigrants and their children defined their communities. Important institutions in twentieth-century life drew people together across ethnic boundaries: newer residential neighborhoods that were economically but not ethnically homogenous, larger workplaces, the labor movement, the Democratic party, commercial amusements, and public high schools.[2] But at the same time, immigrants and succeeding generations responded to these circumstances by reconstructing the meaning of ethnicity. The potential for reconstruction explains the powerful meaning of ethnic identification and its persistence in common consciousness. Family boundaries also played a part in defining the community. In immigrant families, the sense of family unified private experience and confrontation with the public world, and in time, as immigrant lives became American ethnic lives, that history modified the meaning of family. We see anew the process of change that shapes our own family lives as we glimpse the past through the history of immigrant families.

Appendix

The population studied included all Italian-headed households within a six-block area on Federal Hill and all eastern European Jewish-headed households within a six-block area on Smith Hill, as enumerated by the 1915 Rhode Island State Census. Ninety-two percent of the households within the enumerated blocks on Federal Hill were headed by Italian immigrants, and 74 percent of the households within the enumerated blocks on Smith Hill were headed by eastern European Jewish immigrants. The six-block areas were identified by contemporary observers as centers of Italian and Jewish life in their respective neighborhoods, and each area contained a neighborhood school, a central shopping area, and residential streets. The Italian families included all the Italian-headed households on the west side of Dean Street, both sides of Barker, Weeden, Albro, Messenger, Falls Place, and the east side of Arthur between Federal Street and Atwells Avenue; the southern side of Atwells

Avenue and the northern side of Federal Street between Dean and Arthur. The Jewish families included all eastern European Jewish-headed households on the north side of Orms Street and the south side of Chalkstone Avenue between the railroad tracks and North Davis Street, and both sides of May, Shawmut, Lopez, Rebecca, Kane, and Ambrose south of Chalkstone.

All members of 1915-census households were traced to the *Providence House Directory*, 1915, in order to clarify possible spelling of names, and then were traced through the *Providence City Directory* backwards year by year from 1915 to the year in which they first appeared to be listed as a Providence resident, and then forward year by year to 1940.

All members of 1915-census households were also traced through the *Alphabetical Index of Births, Marriages, and Deaths Recorded in Providence*, 1880–1940, and then to marriage licenses and death certificates in the Rhode Island State Records Center. Children born after 1915 were also traced through city directories.

All the people with the same last name who lived at the same address were traced, and kinship was determined through a) relationships defined in the 1915 census which indicated the relationship of each resident of a household to the head of household; b) having the same parents as indicated on a marriage license or death certificate. Brothers, sisters, and parents related to but not living in the 1915-census household were then also traced through the city records. Categories of kin remaining unidentified by this method include: a) brothers or sisters of the male and female heads who did not live in the census household in 1915, or who did not marry or die in Providence between 1880 and 1940; b) parents of women who did not live with their daughters in 1915, or whose daughters did not marry or die in Providence between 1880 and 1940; c) the parents of men who did not live with their sons in 1915, or die in Providence between 1880 and 1940; d) other kin, for example, cousins, nephews, aunts, and uncles who did not live in the census household in 1915; e) ritual kin, defined by godparentage.

Members of 1915 households were traced to street addresses as identified by the city directories through the 1925 Providence Street Index to the 1925 Rhode Island State Census, which was enumerated, like the 1915 state census, by neighborhood.

Members of 1915 census households were traced by name to the 1935 Rhode Island State Census, which was enumerated by individuals on alphabetically arranged cards.

As sons and daughters in the 1915-census households married, they were traced, and their husbands' and wives' parents were also traced, through the city directories and 1935 state census.

EXPLANATION OF OCCUPATIONAL CATEGORIES

Categories for immigrants include:

Laborer
  unskilled construction worker
  city laborer
  railroad laborer
Factory operative
  machinist
  foundryman
  other factory operatives
Skilled
  mason
  plumber
  pipefitter
  carpenter
  foreman/woman
Craftsperson, artisan
  blacksmith
  typographer, printer
  tailor
  barber
  watchmaker
  stonecutter
  shoemaker
  musician

Retail employee
  driver
  peddler
  clerk
Retail self-employed, employer
  grocer
  fruitseller
  saloonkeeper
  butcher
  baker
  contractor
  banker
Professional
  doctor
  lawyer
  druggist
  rabbi

Categories for children of immigrants include these additional occupations:

SONS
Professional
  engineer
  architect

DAUGHTERS
Craftsperson, artisan
  hairdresser
Retail employee
  saleswoman
  cashier
Clerical Worker
  stenographer
  bookkeeper
  telephone operator

Notes

INTRODUCTION

1   For a description of Lewis Hine's Rhode Island photographs, see
     Stephen Victor, "Lewis Hine's Photography and Reform in Rhode
     Island," essay accompanying the exhibit of Hine's Rhode Island
     photographs, "Things to Be Corrected, Things to be Appreciated:
     Photographs by Lewis Hine," Slater Mill Historic Site, Museum of
     Rhode Island History, Spring 1982.
2   Recent studies that have stressed the critical role families played in the
     migration process include: Josef Barton, *Peasants and Strangers:
     Italians, Roumanians, and Slovaks in an American City, 1890–1950*
     (Cambridge: Harvard University Press, 1975); Caroline Golab,
     Immigrant Destinations (Philadelphia: Temple University Press, 1977);
     Virginia Yans-McLaughlin, *Family and Community: Italian Immigrants in
     Buffalo, 1880–1920* (Ithaca: Cornell University Press, 1978); John
     Briggs, *An Italian Passage: Immigrants to Three American Cities* (New
     Haven: Yale University Press, 1978); Miriam Cohen, "From Work-
     shop to Office: Italian Women and Family Strategies in New York
     City, 1900–1950," Ph.D. dissertation, University of Michigan, 1978;
     Elizabeth H. Pleck, *Black Migration and Poverty: Boston, 1865–1900*

(New York: Academic Press, 1979); Tamara K. Hareven, *Family Time and Industrial Time* (Cambridge and New York: Cambridge University Press, 1982); John Bodnar, Roger Simon, and Michael P. Weber, *Lives of Their Own: Blacks, Italians, and Poles in Pittsburgh, 1900–1960* (Urbana: University of Illinois Press, 1982); Donna R. Gabaccia, *From Sicily to Elizabeth Street: Housing and Social Change Among Italian Immigrants, 1880–1930* (Albany: State University of New York Press, 1983).

3   Important essays on the social and historical construction of family forms include: Lutz Berkner, "The Stem Family and the Developmental Cycle of the Peasant Household: An Eighteenth Century Austrian Example," *American Historical Review* 77 (1972), pp. 398–418; idem, "The Use and Misuse of Census Data for the Historical Analysis of Family Structure," *Journal of Interdisciplinary History* 5 (1975), pp. 721–38; Elizabeth H. Pleck, "Two Worlds in One: Work and Family," *Journal of Social History* 10 (Winter 1976), pp. 178–95; Lise Vogel, "The Contested Domain: A Note on the Family in the Transition to Capitalism," *Marxist Perspectives* 1 (1978), pp. 50–73; Rayna Rapp, Ellen Ross, and Renate Bridenthal, "Examining Family History," *Feminist Studies* 5 (Spring 1979), pp. 174–200; Mary Ryan, "The Explosion in Family History," *Reviews in American History* 10 (December 1982), pp. 181–95; Louise Tilly and Miriam Cohen, "Does the Family Have a History?" *Social Science History* 6 (Spring 1982), pp. 131–79

4   For examples of the argument that family change resulted from the separation of home and work that accompanied industrialization, see John Demos, *A Little Commonwealth: Family Life in Plymouth Colony* (New York: Oxford University Press, 1970); Bernard Bailyn, *Education in the Forming of American Society* (Chapel Hill: University of North Carolina Press, 1960); Richard Sennett, *Families Against the City: Middle Class Homes of Industrial Chicago, 1872–1890* (Cambridge: Harvard University Press, 1970); Edward Thompson, *The Making of the English Working Class* (London: Penguin, 1963). See Vogel's critique of this view, "Contested Domain," pp. 58–62. For the historical argument that family forms changed independently of the effects of industrialization, see Peter Laslett, *The World We Have Lost: England Before the Industrial Age* (New York: Charles Scribner's Sons, 1965); Philip Greven, *Four Generations: Population, Land, and Family in Colonial Andover, Massachusetts* (Ithaca: Cornell University Press, 1970); Berkner, "Stem Family," pp. 398–418; idem, "Use and Misuse of Census Data," pp. 721–38. For a critique of the claim that industrialization eroded the relationship between the family and work, see Pleck, "Two Worlds in One," pp. 181–82. For instances of the connection between industrialization and the rise of cottage industry, see Gareth Stedman-Jones, "Working-Class Culture and Working-Class Politics in London, 1870–1900," *Journal of Social History* 7 (Summer 1974), pp. 484–85; Alan Dawley, *Class and Community: The*

Industrial Revolution in Lynn (Cambridge: Harvard University Press, 1976), pp. 29–30, 46–50, 73–77; Gary Kulik, "Pawtucket Village and the Strike of 1824: The Origins of Class Conflict in Rhode Island," *Radical History Review* 17 (Spring 1978), p. 13. For the argument that industrialization increased the opportunity for family members to find employment for one another, see Michael Anderson, *Family Structure in Nineteenth-Century Lancashire* (Cambridge: Cambridge University Press, 1971); Tamara Hareven, "The Dynamics of Kin in an Industrial Community," in *Turning Points*, ed. John Demos and Saranne Boocock (Chicago: University of Chicago Press, 1978), pp. 151–82; idem, *Family Time and Industrial Time.*

5   For examples of the argument that family forms changed in response to assimilation and modernization, see Oscar Handlin, *The Uprooted* (1951; reprint, Boston: Little Brown, 1973), esp. pp. 205, 228; Caroline Ware, *Greenwich Village, 1920–1930: A Comment on American Civilization in the Post-War Years* (1935; reprint, New York: Harper and Row, 1965), esp. p. 413. The case for the continuity of family values has been made by Rudolph Vecoli, "Contadini in Chicago: A Critique of *The Uprooted*," *Journal of American History* 51 (1964), pp. 404–17; Virginia Yans-McLaughlin, "Patterns of Work and Family Organization: Buffalo's Italians," *Journal of Interdisciplinary History* 2 (Fall 1971), pp. 299–314, esp. p. 301; idem, "A Flexible Tradition: Immigrant Families Confront New Work Experiences," *Journal of Social History* 7 (Summer 1974), pp. 429–45. See the critiques of Yans-McLaughlin by Alice Kessler-Harris and Louise Tilly, "Comments on the Yans-McLaughlin and Davidoff Papers," *Journal of Social History* 7 (Summer 1974), pp. 446–59.

6   Many of the new studies have been influenced by the work of Herbert Gutman, who argued in "Work, Culture, and Society in Industrializing America, 1815–1919," that immigrants made use of non-industrial culture and work habits to resist the imposition of industrial discipline, and the work of David Montgomery, who has argued that immigrants entering industrial society learned critical techniques of survival and struggle from American-born experienced industrial workers. See Gutman's essay in *Work, Culture, and Society in Industrializing America: Essays in American Working-Class and Social History* (New York: Vintage, 1977), pp. 3–78. Montgomery's essay is "Immigrant Workers and Managerial Reform," in *Workers' Control in America: Studies in the History of Work, Technology, and Labor Struggles* (New York: Cambridge University Press, 1979), pp. 32–47, esp. pp. 42–43. Studies that stress the cultural change taking place in Europe on the eve of migration and the active role of European villagers in creating that culture and recreating it in American cities include Barton, *Peasants and Strangers*; idem, "Religion and Cultural Change in Czech Immigrant communities, 1850–1920," in *Immigrants and Religion in Urban America*, ed. Randall M. Miller and Thomas D. Marzik (Philadelphia:

Temple University Press, 1977), pp. 3–24; idem, "Southern and Eastern Europeans," in *Ethnic Leadership in America*, ed. John Higham (Baltimore: Johns Hopkins University Press, 1978), pp. 150–75; Briggs, *An Italian Passage*; Gabaccia, *From Sicily to Elizabeth Street*. Studies that describe how immigrants transformed traditional cultural values into American working-class behavior include John Bodnar, "Immigration and Modernization: The Case of the Slavic Peasant in Industrial America," *Journal of Social History* 10 (Fall 1976), pp. 47–71; John Bodnar, Roger Simon, and Michael P. Weber, "Migration, Kinship, and Urban Adjustment: Blacks and Poles in Pittsburgh, 1900–1930," *Journal of American History* 66 (December 1979), pp. 548–65; Bodnar, "Immigration, Kinship, and the Rise of Working-Class Realism in Industrial America," *Journal of Social History* 14 (Fall 1980), pp. 46–65; Hareven, *Family Time and Industrial Time*. Hareven's work has been criticized for downplaying the industrial assault on immigrant families; see Wini Breines, Margaret Cerullo, and Judith Stacey, "Social Biology, Family Studies, and Anti-Feminist Backlash," *Feminist Studies* 4 (February 1978), pp. 43–67, esp. pp. 51–57. Other studies that share this general approach are Caroline Golab, "The Impact of the Industrial Experience on the Immigrant Family: The Huddled Masses Reconsidered," in *Immigrants in Industrial America, 1850–1920*, ed. Richard L. Ehrlich (Charlottesville: University Press of Virginia, 1977), pp. 1–32; Miriam Cohen, "Changing Education Strategies Among Migrant Generations," *Journal of Social History* 15 (March 1982), pp. 443–66; John Modell, "Patterns of Consumption, Acculturation, and Family Income Strategies in Late Nineteenth Century America," in *Family and Population in Nineteenth Century America*, ed. Tamara Hareven and Maris Vinovskis (Princeton: Princeton University Press, 1978), pp. 206–40; idem, "An Ecology of Family Decisions: Suburbanization, Schooling, and Fertility in Philadelphia, 1800–1920," *Journal of Urban History* 6 (August 1980), pp. 397–417. See also Tilly and Cohen, "Does the Family Have a History?" pp. 152–53.

7   Several scholars of Rhode Island ethnic and women's history collected family-history interviews that were of central importance to this study. Priscilla Long and her students in the Continuing Education Division, University of Rhode Island, developed a women's history interviewing project in 1972. The women's history papers and tapes resulting from this project are collected in the Schlesinger Library, Radcliffe College. Sharon H. Strom and several graduate students at the University of Rhode Island developed a women's history questionnaire that she has used every year since 1974 as the basis of a required family-history assignment for her women's history course. The family histories resulting from this assignment have been collected as the Rhode Island Women's Biography Project at the University of Rhode Island. James Findlay and Valerie Quinney also sponsored the collection of

ethnic family histories as part of the Rhode Island Oral History Project. Sonya Michel did a number of interviews in connection with the Rhode Island Jewish Historical Society which formed the basis of her article, "Family and Community Networks Among Rhode Island Jews: A Study Based on Oral Histories," *Rhode Island Jewish Historical Notes* 7 (1978), pp. 513–33. The tapes and transcripts are deposited at the Rhode Island Jewish Historical Society Library. Jessann Dunn DeCredico did an interview with her family in conjunction with Quinney's class on oral history techniques given at the University of Rhode Island. In conjunction with the histories of the families that I interviewed, these sources provided rich materials detailing immigrant and first-generation daily family life. The Rhode Island oral histories were supplemented by the unpublished life histories of Italian and Jewish immigrants collected by the WPA Federal Writers' Project on Ethnic and Social Life in Connecticut. The Project on Ethnic and Social Life is briefly discussed in Jerre Mangione, *The Dream and the Deal: The Federal Writer's Project, 1935–1943* (Boston: Little Brown, 1972), pp. 277–85. Most of the material collected for this project is at the Library of Congress in the Folk Song and Manuscript Collection, and remains unpublished. Ann Banks has edited a collection of the life histories gathered by the Federal Writers' Project, *First Person America: Life History Narratives from the Archives of the Federal Writers' Project* (New York: Random House, 1980). Willliam D'Antonio found the unpublished materials gathered by members of the Federal Writers' Project in Connecticut and collected them at the University of Connecticut at Storrs as the Peoples of Connecticut Ethnic Heritage Project.

CHAPTER ONE   THE HISTORICAL SETTING

1   Frank Thistlethwaite, "Migration from Europe Overseas in the Nineteenth and Twentieth Centuries," in *New Perspectives on the American Past, 1877–Present*, ed. Stanley Katz and Stanley Kutler (Boston: Little Brown, 1969), pp. 75–78.
2   Josef Barton, "Eastern and Southern Europeans," in *Ethnic Leadership in America*, ed. John Higham (Baltimore: Johns Hopkins University Press, 1978), pp. 151–54; John Briggs, *An Italian Passage: Immigrants to Three American Cities, 1890–1930* (New Haven: Yale University Press, 1978), pp. 8–9; Ezra Mendelsohn, *Class Struggle in the Pale: The Formative Years of the Jewish Workers' Movement in Tsarist Russia* (Cambridge: Cambridge University Press, 1970), pp. 3–15; Henry Tobias, *The Jewish Bund in Russia from Its Origins to 1905* (Stanford, Calif.: Stanford University Press, 1972), pp. 6–9; Simon Kuznets, "Immigration of Russian Jews to the United States: Background and Structure," *Perspectives in American History* 9 (1975), pp. 83–93;

Arcadius Kahan, "Economic Opportunity and Some Pilgrims' Progress: Jewish Immigrants from Eastern Europe to the United States, 1890–1914," *Journal of Economic History* 38 (March 1978), p. 236. See also John Bodnar, "The European Origins of American Immigrants," paper presented at the Lowell Conference on Industrial History, April 1983.

3   Josef Barton, *Peasants and Strangers: Italians, Roumanians, and Slovaks in an American City, 1890–1950* (Cambridge: Harvard University Press, 1975), pp. 41–42, 47; idem, "Southern and Eastern Europeans," pp. 8–12; Rudolph Bell, *Fate and Honor, Family and Village: Demographic and Cultural Change in Rural Italy since 1800* (Chicago: University of Chicago Press, 1979), pp. 151–209; Irving Howe, *The World of Our Fathers* (New York: Harcourt Brace Jovanovich, 1976), pp. 15–29; Kuznets, "Immigration of Russian Jews," pp. 83–93, 100–12; Marc Lee Raphael, *Jews and Judaism in a Midwestern Community: Columbus, Ohio, 1840–1975* (Columbus: Ohio Historical Society, 1979), pp. 95–99.

4   On Rhode Island's economic development in this period, see Peter J. Coleman, *The Transformation of Rhode Island, 1790–1860* (Providence: Brown University Press, 1963); Kurt Mayer, *Economic Development and Population Growth in Rhode Island* (Providence: Brown University Press, 1953); Kurt Mayer and Sidney Goldstein, *Migration and Economic Development in Rhode Island* (Providence: Brown University Press, 1958); Gary Kulik, "Introduction," in *Rhode Island: An Inventory of Historic Engineering and Industrial Sites*, by Gary Kulik and Julia C. Bonham (Washington, D.C.: Government Printing Office, 1978), pp. 1 –21. The figures on the state's expansion in the late-nineteenth and early-twentieth century are in Mayer and Goldstein, *Migration and Economic Development*, p. 9. On Providence, see Division of Industrial and Municipal Research, Massachusetts Institute of Technology, *Industrial Survey of Metropolitan Providence for the Year 1926* (Providence: Akerman Standard Company, 1928), pp. 1–24; John H. Cady, *The Civic and Architectural Development of Providence, Rhode Island, 1636–1950* (Providence: Bookshop, 1957), pp. 171–75; Kulik, "Introduction," pp. 12–16; Patrick T. Conley and Paul Campbell, *Providence: A Pictorial History* (Norfolk, Virginia: Donning, 1982), pp. 99–101, 143–46; William G. McLoughlin, *Rhode Island: A Bicentennial History* (New York: Norton, 1978), pp. 164–66. Providence's claims for its industrial greatness may be found, among other places, in Rhode Island Bureau of Industrial Statistics, *Annual Report, 1906* (Providence: E. L. Freemen, 1907), pp. 95–96.

5   For women's employment in Providence, see Joseph Hill, *Women in Gainful Occupations, 1870–1920*, census monograph 9 (Washington, D.C.: Government Printing Office, 1929), p. 31. For women's employment in Rhode Island, see U.S. Department of Labor, Women's Bureau, *Women in Rhode Island: A Study of Hours, Wages, and Conditions*, bulletin no. 21 (Washington, D.C.: Government Printing

Office, 1922); U.S. Congress, Senate, *Report on Women and Child Wage Earners: Cotton Textile Industry*, vol. 1, document no. 645 (Washington, D.C.: Government Printing Office, 1910), p. 132; Sharon Hartman Strom, "Old Barriers and New Opportunities: Working Women in Rhode Island, 1900–1940," *Rhode Island History* 39 (May 1980), pp. 43–56. For figures on Providence's population, see Sidney Goldstein and Kurt Mayer, *Metropolitanization and Population Change in Rhode Island*, publication no. 3 (Providence: Rhode Island Development Council, 1961), p. 8. For a description of Providence's changing physical development, see Cady, *Civic and Architectural Development of Providence*, pp. 161–217, 223.

6   For figures on Rhode Island's foreign-born majority, see Niles Carpenter, *Immigrants and Their Children, 1920: A Study Based on Census Statistics Relative to the Foreign Born and the Native White of Foreign or Mixed Parentage*, census monograph 7 (Washington, D.C.: Government Printing Office, 1927), pp. 308–9; Mayer and Goldstein, *Migration and Economic Development*, p. 19. Figures on the percentage of foreign-born and their children in Providence are in Rhode Island Bureau of Industrial Statistics, *Annual Report, 1908* (Providence: E. L. Freemen, 1909), pp. 220–21, 224–25; Rhode Island Bureau of Industrial Statistics, *Annual Report, 1916* (Providence: E. L. Freemen, 1917), pp. 98–99; Lester Burrell Shippee, "Some Aspects of the Population of Providence," in *Report of the Commissioner of Labor to the General Assembly for the Years 1916–1919* (Providence: E. L. Freemen, 1920), pp. 210–29, plates and tables, pp. 246–49, 254–57, 264–68, 272–84.

7   On Federal Hill, see Rhode Island Historic Preservation Commission, *The West Side: Providence: Statewide Preservation Report* P-P-1, 1976, pp. 37–41; Peter J. Caldacone, "I remember Federal Hill," *Providence Journal*, 7 December 1947, sec. 6, p. 1; M. Family Interview, Providence, 1975, interviewed by Judith E. Smith. Father born in Caserta, Italy, in 1904; moved to Providence in 1913. On the number of Italians and their children in Providence, see Shippee, "Some Aspects of the Population of Providence," pp. 214–15. On housing in Federal Hill, see Rhode Island Historic Preservation Commission, *West Side*, pp. 21, 37; John Ihlder, *The Houses of Providence: A Study of Present Conditions and Tendencies* (Providence: Snow and Franklin, 1916), pp. 65–66. The observation of Federal Hill was made by William McDonald, "Population," in *A Modern City: Providence, Rhode Island and Its Activities*, ed. William Kirk (Chicago: University of Chicago Press, 1909), p. 51.

8   On Smith Hill, see Rhode Island Historical Preservation Commission, *Smith Hill, Providence: Statewide Preservation Report P-P-4*, 1980, pp. 11, 13–14. For the number of Jewish immigrants and their children, in Providence, see Shippee, "Some Aspects of the Population of Providence," p. 217. Also for Smith Hill, see Bessie Bloom, "Jewish Life in Providence," 1910, reprinted in *Rhode Island Jewish*

Historical Notes 5 (1970), pp. 386–408; Eleanor Horowitz, "Pushcarts, Surreys with Fringe on Top: The Story of the North End," *Rhode Island Jewish Historical Notes* 8 (1979), pp. 9–50. The observation of Smith Hill was made by Lester Bradner, "Religion," in *A Modern City: Providence*, pp. 329–30.

9 Goldstein and Mayer, *"Metropolitanization and Population Change*, pp. 8–10, 33–36, 56; Rhode Island Historical Preservation Commission, *West Side*, pp. 41–42; Rhode Island Historical Preservation Commission, *Smith Hill*, p. 29; Francis R. North, *A Recreation Survey of the City of Providence, Rhode Island* (Providence: Providence Playground Association, 1912), p. 26.

10 Unemployment statistics were listed in Rhode Island Bureau of Industrial Statistics, *Annual Report, 1908*, pp. 28–35; Rhode Island Bureau of Industrial Statistics, *Annual Report, 1915* (Providence: E. L. Freemen, 1916), pp. 94–107. On Rhode Island's weakening economic position, see Mayer, *Economic Development and Population Growth*, pp. 49–59; Robert Eisenmenger, *The Dynamics of Growth in the New England Economy, 1870–1964* (Middletown, Conn.: Wesleyan University Press, 1967), pp. 8–21; Robert J. Paulis, "The Changing Rhode Island Industrial Base," *Rhode Island Business Quarterly* 5 (1969), pp. 1–9; U.S. Employment Service, Labor Market Survey, *The Demand For Labor*, sec. 5, "Preliminary Report on the Cotton and Other Textile Industries in Rhode Island," and "Preliminary Report on Jewelry and Silverware Manufacture in Rhode Island," prepared by the Providence Community Center under the joint sponsorship of the Standards and Research Division of the U.S. Employment Service and American Youth Division, 1939; McLoughlin, *Rhode Island*, pp. 195–96; Kulik, "Introduction," pp. 16–23.

11 Mayer, *Economic Development and Population Growth*, pp. 59–63; Mayer and Goldstein, *Migration and Economic Development*, pp. 13–17; Paulis, "Changing Rhode Island Industrial Base," pp. 7–9; Edward F. Gerish, *The Commercial Structure of New England* (Washington, D.C.: Government Printing Office, 1929), p. 32; *Providence Journal Almanac, 1936*, p. 79; McLoughlin, *Rhode Island*, p. 217. See also U.S. Employment Service, Labor Market Survey, *The Demand for Labor*, sec. 5.

CHAPTER TWO A FAMILY CULTURE OF WORK

1 Richard Gambino, *Blood of My Blood* (Garden City, N.J.: Doubleday, 1975), p. 101. Louise Tilly and Joan Scott develop the concept of the family economy in *Women, Work, and Family* (New York: Holt, Rinehart, and Winston, 1978). See also Basil Kerbay, "Chayanov and the Theory of the Peasant Economy as a Specific Type of Economy," in *Peasants and Peasant Societies: Selected Readings*, ed. Teodor Shanin

(London: Penguin Books, 1971), pp. 150–60; Olwen Hufton, "Women and the Family Economy in Eighteenth Century France," *French Historical Studies* 9 (Spring 1975), pp. 1–22; Louise Tilly, "The Family Wage Economy of a French Textile City: Roubaix, 1872–1906," *Journal of Family History* 4 (Winter 1979), pp. 381–94. James Henretta has argued that a familial rather than an individualistic orientation towards property also characterized early American settlements; see Henretta, "Family and Farms: *Mentalite* in Pre-Industrial America," *William and Mary Quarterly* 39 (January 1978), pp. 3–32.

2   Sydel Silverman, "Agricultural Organization, Social Structures, and Values in Italy: Amoral Familism Reconsidered," *American Anthropologist* 70 (1968), pp. 6–11; J. S. MacDonald, "Agricultural Organization, Migration, and Labor Militancy in Rural Italy," *Economic History Review* 16 (1963), pp. 65–69; David I. Kertzer, "European Peasant Household Structure: Some Implications from a Nineteenth Century Italian Community," *Journal of Family History* 2 (Winter 1977), pp. 333–49; Leonard Covello, *The Social Background of the Italo-American School-Child* (1944; reprint, Leiden: E. J. Brill, 1967), p. 43. Silverman's argument that social and economic conditions in the south led to nuclear-family households has been criticized by William A. Douglass in "The South Italian Family: A Critique," *Journal of Family History* 5 (Winter 1980), pp. 338–59. Basing his argument on a historical analysis of patrilineal joint families in Agnone, a town in the province of Isérnia, region of Molise, Douglass contends that Silverman somewhat simplistically equated the high incidence of nuclear-family households with social structure, failing to take into account contextural issues such as family ethos, cultural values, and demographic process. When these are considered, Silverman's findings of nuclear-family households can be reinterpreted to reflect "specific stages of the developmental cycle of the fully elaborated joint family form" (p. 355). Douglass also argues that in Agnone there were pragmatic, economic reasons for all classes to form joint households. Peasant households could respond more flexibly to the full range of local economic opportunities, sending some members out to do day labor, using others to work additional rented or owned land, while still others might be able to engage in herding. Pooling the resources of several adult males allowed artisans to maintain a larger and more varied inventory in their workshops. Joint professional households in which sons pursued their fathers' occupations enabled family members to monopolize a profession and to minimize competition (pp. 345–48). The demographic realities of high mean age at marriage and low life expectancy for males in premigration Agnone made it statistically less likely for a man to found a joint family domestic group (pp. 348–51).

3   Silverman, "Agricultural organization," pp. 11–14; MacDonald,

"Agricultural Organization," pp. 68–69; Covello, *Social Background*, pp. 78–84.

4 Silverman, "Agricultural Organization," pp. 13 –14; Walter Gold-schmidt and Evalyn J. Kunkel, "The Structure of the Peasant Family," *American Anthropologist* 73 (1971), p. 1060. As mentioned above, Douglass in "The South Italian Family" explained the process by which demographic factors limited the frequent for-mation of joint family households in one southern town (pp. 348–51). Douglass cited other findings as well to argue that Agnone was not a unique exception in the Italian south; in particular, he mentioned J. Davis's finding of the existence of "pseudo-extended paternal households" in Pisticci, a town in the region of Basilicata, and C. G. Chapman's description of the Sicilian *famiglia* and the patrilineal clan *robba* in Milocca, p. 354, n. 15).

5 Rhode Island Women's Biography Project no. 232 (hereafter cited as RIWB); Interviewed by a family member in 1975. Interviewee born in St. Pier Niceto, Messina, Sicily in 1896; moved to Providence in 1914.

6 Charlotte Chapman, *Milocca: A Sicilian Village* (1935; reprint, Cam-bridge, Mass.: Schenkman, 1971), pp. 32, 62; Covello, *Social Background*, pp. 81, 210–12. Rudolph Bell's research documented the considerable role women played in the local economy of three towns in southern Italy and Sicily. See Bell, *Fate and Honor, Family and Village: Demographic and Cultural Change in Rural Italy since 1800* (Chicago: University of Chicago Press, 1979), tables on pp. 124, 129, 134. See also Louise Tilly, "Comments on the Yans-McLaughlin and Davidoff Papers," *Journal of Social History* 7 (Summer 1974), pp. 452–59; Miriam Cohen, "From Workshop to Office: Italian Women and Family Strategies in New York City, 1900–1950," Ph.D. dissertation, University of Michigan, 1978, pp. 35–38. According to Thomas Kessner and Betty Boyd Caroli, southern Italian women also worked at home embroidering tablecloths, knotting fringes, and construct-ing military uniforms for extra income; "New Immigrant Women at Work: Italians and Jews in New York City, 1880–1905," *Journal of Ethnic Studies* 5 (Winter 1978), p. 22.

7 Mr. C., Bridgeport, interviewed by Vincent Frazzetta in 1940. Interviewee born in Monte Verna, Sicily in 1900; moved to New York City in 1921. This is a WPA Federal Writers' Project interview recorded in 1938–40 as part of the national project on ethnic and social life, collected at the University of Connecticut at Storrs as the Peoples of Connecticut Ethnic Heritage Project, box 23 (hereafter cited as WPA-Conn).

8 Covello, *Social Background*, pp. 196–97, 229–32, 265; Chapman, *Milocca*, pp. 31–32; Constance Cronin, *The Sting of Change: Sicilians in Sicily and Australia* (Chicago: University of Chicago Press, 1970), pp. 92–93.

9 Silverman, "Agricultural Organization," p. 12; Donna Gabaccia,

"Housing and Household Work: Sicily and New York: 1890–1910," *Michigan Occasional Papers in Women's Studies* 20 (1981); Joan Scott and Louise Tilly, "Women's Work and the Family in Nineteenth Century Europe," Center for Research in Social Organization (October 1973), pp. 9–18, published in *Comparative Studies in Society and History* 17 (1975), pp. 36–64; Chapman, *Milocca*, pp. 35, 79; Cronin, *Sting of Change*, p. 98. See also Gabaccia, *From Sicily to Elizabeth Street: Housing and Social Change Among Italian Immigrants, 1880–1930)* Albany: State University of New York Press, 1983), chap. 3.

10   Mr. DiMartino, Bridgeport, interviewed by Vincent Frazzetta in 1940, WPA-Conn, box 23. Interviewee born in Sicily.

11   Covello, *Social Background*, pp. 91–96; Phyllis Williams, *South Italian Folkways in Europe and America* (1938; reprint, New York: Russell and Russell, 1969), pp. 25–30, 68–69. For an incident depicting the diminished craft of the shoemaker-peddler, see Guiseppe Pitre, *Biblioteca della tradizioni popolari sicilane* (Palermo: A. Reber, 1913), vol. 25, pp. 246–47, as quoted in Williams, *South Italian Folkways*, pp. 29–30. Chapman argues that the classification *artisan* extended over a wide range of wealth and status. See Chapman, *Milocca*, pp. 59–60.

12   Mr. Amore, Bridgeport, interviewed by Vincent Frazzetta in 1940. Interviewee born in Italy in 1875; moved to New Jersey in 1905). Mr. Merlo, Bridgeport, interviewed by Vincent Frazzetta in 1940. Interviewee born in Sicily in 1885; moved to Bridgeport in 1904. Both from WPA-Conn, box 23. Josef Barton, *Peasants and Strangers: Italians, Roumanians, and Slovaks in an American City, 1890–1950* (Cambridge: Harvard University Press, 1975), p. 40.

13   I. M. Rubinow, "The Economic Conditions of the Jews in Russia," in *Report of the Immigration Commission: Emigration Conditions in Europe*, U.S. Congress, Senate, 61st Congr., 3d sess., Senate document 748 (Washington, D.C.: Government Printing Office, 1911), p. 287; Simon Kuznets, "Immigration of Russian Jews to the United States: Background and Structure," *Perspectives in American History* 9 (1975), pp. 68–72; Ezra Mendelsohn, *Class Struggle in the Pale: The Formative Years of the Jewish Workers Movement in Tsarist Russia* (Cambridge: Cambridge University Press, 1970), pp. 3–5.

14   Rubinow, "Economic Conditions," p. 293; Mendelsohn, *Class Struggle in the Pale*, p. 6; Kuznets, "Immigration of Russian Jews, pp. 72–77.

15   U.S. Congress, Senate, *Report of the Immigration Commission*, pp. 276–77. See also Kuznets, "Immigration of Russian Jews," pp. 53–62.

16   Mary Antin, *The Promised Land* (1912; reprint, Boston: Houghton Mifflin, 1969), p. 22.

17   Rubinow, "Economic Conditions," pp. 333–34; Henry J. Tobias, *The Jewish Bund in Russia from Its Origins to 1905* (Stanford: Stanford University Press, 1972), pp. 9–10.

18   Ruth Rubin, *Voices of a People: Yiddish Folk Song* (New York: Thomas Yoseloff, 1963), pp. 280–81.

19   Mark Zborowski and Elizabeth Herzog, *Life Is with People: The Culture of the Shtetl* (1952; reprint, New York: Schocken Books, 1962), pp. 254–56; Hanan J. Ayalti, ed., *Yiddish Proverbs* (1949; reprint, New York: Schocken Books, 1963), p. 55.

20   Rubinow, "Economic Conditions," p. 306; Mendelsohn, *Class Struggle in the Pale*, pp. 6–7; Zborowski and Herzog, *Life Is with People*, p. 241.

21   Zborowski and Herzog, *Life Is with People*, p. 66.

22   Rubin, *Voices of a People*, pp. 112–13.

23   Rubinow, "Economic Conditions," p. 305.

24   Fannie Savage Schindler, interviewed by Jill Grossberg in 1972. Interviewee born in Bialystok, Russia in 1889; moved to New York City in 1900. This taped interview was a student project for a women's history course at the University of Rhode Island and was collected with other taped interviews and written family histories by Priscilla Long in the Manuscript Collection, Schlesinger Library, Radcliffe College (hereafter cited as Long Coll.).

25   Zborowski and Herzog, *Life Is with People*, p. 241; Rose Cohen, *Out of the Shadow* (New York: G. H. Doran, 1918), p. 10.

26   Cohen, *Out of the Shadow*, pp. 23 –24; Letter to "Bintel Brief" column, *Jewish Daily Forward*, 1909, in *A Bintel Brief*, ed. Isaac Metzker (New York: Ballantine Books, 1972), p. 99. KG, New Haven, interviewed by Rahel Mittelstein in 1939, WPA-Conn, box 58. Interviewee born in Orlov, Pobelov, White Russia in 1891; moved to New Haven in 1921. Zborowski and Herzog, *Life Is with People*, pp. 298–99.

27   Morris Kavitsky, Hartford, interviewed by Morton Tonken in 1938, WPA-Conn, box 61. Interviewee born in Kachinovitch, Grodno, Russia ca. 1873; moved to New York City in 1914. Antin, *Promised Land*, p. 52.

28   Morris Kavitsky, Hartford, WPA-Conn, box 61.

29   Barton, *Peasants and Strangers*, pp. 27, 39–40; Bell, *Fate and Honor, Family and Village*, pp. 195, 198; Robert F. Foerster, *The Italian Emigration of Our Times* (Cambridge: Harvard University Press, 1919), pp. 102–5, 122–26; Edwin Fenton, "Immigrants and Unions: Italians and American Labor, 1870–1920," Ph.D. dissertation, Harvard University, 1957, pp. 2–7; John Bodnar, Roger Simon, and Michael P. Weber, *Lives of Their Own: Blacks, Italians, and Poles in Pittsburgh, 1900–1960* (Urbana: University of Illinois Press, 1982), pp. 44–45. See also, Frank Thistlethwaite, "Migration from Europe Overseas in the Nineteenth and Twentieth Centuries," in *New Perspectives in the American Past, 1877–present*, ed. Stanley Katz and Stanley Kutler (Boston: Little Brown, 1969), pp. 73–78.

30 Pascal D'Angelo, *Son of Italy* (New York: Macmillan, 1924), p. 48–49.

31 Tobias, *Jewish Bund*, pp. 6–7; Mendelsohn, *Class Struggle in the Pale*, pp. 9–15; Kuznets, "Immigration of Russian Jews," pp. 83–93.

32 Barton, *Peasants and Strangers*, pp. 27, 34–35; MacDonald, "Agricultural Organization," pp. 62, 68–70; Robert F. Foerster, *Italian Emigration*, pp. 103–4.

33 Kuznets, "Immigration of Russian Jews," pp. 83–93, 100–12; Mendelsohn, *Class Struggle in the Pale*, p. 15; Irving Howe, *World of our Fathers* (New York: Harcourt Brace Jovanovich, 1976), pp. 24–29; Marc Lee Raphael, *Jews and Judaism in a Midwestern Community: Columbus, Ohio 1840–1975* (Columbus: Ohio Historical Society, 1979), pp. 95–99.

34 For occupations of Italian emigrants, see Foerster, *Italian Emigration*, p. 531; John Briggs, *An Italian Passage: Immigrants to Three American Cities, 1890–1930* (New Haven: Yale University Press, 1978), pp. 12–13; for occupatons of Jewish emigrants, see Kuznets, "Immigration of Russian Jews," pp. 101–2.

35 To compare Providence as a port of entry with New York City, see Thomas Kessner, *The Golden Door: Italian and Jewish Immigrant Mobility in New York City, 1880–1915* (New York: Oxford University Press, 1977), chaps. 1, 3, 4; Cohen, "From Workshop to Office," chap. 3. For Boston, see Stephen Thernstrom, *The Other Bostonians: Poverty and Progress in an American Metropolis, 1880–1970* (Cambridge: Harvard University Press, 1973), chaps. 6, 7. For Cleveland, see Barton, *Peasants and Strangers*, chaps. 1, 5. For Buffalo, see Virginia Yans-McLaughlin, *Family and Community: Italian Immigrants in Buffalo, 1880–1930* (Ithaca: Cornell University Press, 1977), chap. 1. For Pittsburgh, see Bodnar, Simon, and Weber, *Lives of Their Own*, pp. 57–58, 61–64, 66–68. For the Italian experience in several smaller cities, see Briggs, *An Italian Passage*, chap. 5. For the eastern European Jewish experience in smaller cities see Raphael, *Jews and Judaism*, chaps. 7, 9; William Toll, *The Making of an Ethnic Middle Class: Portland Jewry over Four Generations* (Albany: State University of New York Press, 1982), chaps. 1, 4. For additional analysis of the occupations of Providence Jews and Italians, see Joel Perlmann, "Education and the Social Structure of an American City: Social Origins and Educational Attainments in Providence, Rhode Island, 1880–1915," Ph.D. dissertation, Harvard University, 1980, chap. 2, especially tables on pp. 205, 250.

36 M. family interview, 1 December 1975, Providence, interviewed by Judith E. Smith. A. born near Caserta, Italy in 1904; moved to Providence in 1913; M. born in Italy in 1907; moved to Providence in 1909; V. born in Providence ca. 1910. RRC and JCD family interview, 1976, Providence. This interview was conducted by Jessann DeCredico during November and December 1976 for a

course in oral history taught by Dr. Valerie Quinney. Part of the interview was published as Jessann Dunn DeCredico, "Josephine DeCredico," *Mirror* 3 (1977), pp. 31–34. RRC born in Pontecorvo, Latium, Italy in 1891; moved to Boston in 1912. JCD born in Providence, Rhode Island in 1914.

37   Anna Frucht, 1978, Providence. This interview was conducted by Sonya Michel as part of a special project for the Rhode Island Jewish Historical Society Library, hereafter cited as RIJHSL. Interviewee born in Odessa, Russia, in 1902; moved to Central Falls, R.I. in 1905.

38   Marcus family manuscript. Father born Russia 1876; moved to New York in 1883. Syd Marcus shared this manuscript with me.

39   Kuznets, "Immigration of Russian Jews, pp. 105–12, esp. 105–7; Arcadius Kahan, "Economic Opportunities and Some Pilgrims' Progress: Jewish Immigrants from Eastern Europe to the U.S., 1890–1914," *Journal of Economic History* 38 (March 1978), pp. 245–46. Kuznets argues that because commercial skills, such as knowledge of local agricultural markets, and local credit arrangements were hard to transfer, and because businessmen in the pale had little liquid capital, they were less likely to emigrate. To compare Providence Jews' commercial activities with those of Jews in other cities, see Joel Pearlmann, "Beyond New York: The Occupations of Russian Jewish Immigrants in Providence, Rhode Island and in Other Small Jewish Communities, 1900–1915," *American Jewish History* 72 (March 1983), pp. 369–95; Toll, *Making of an Ethnic Middle Class*, chap. 1; Raphael, *Jews and Judaism*, chaps. 7, 9.

40   Sixty-eight-year-old Italian housewife (as identified by interviewer) Bridgeport, interviewed by Vincent Frazzetta between 1938 and 1940, WPA-Conn, box 22. Intervieweee born in Italy ca. 1870; moved to Bridgeport ca. 1890.

41   Mr. DiMartino, Bridgeport, WPA-Conn, box 23.

42   Ibid.

43   Immigrants describe the critical importance for family survival of these neighborhood credit arrangements. See Joseph Julianelle, Bridgeport, interviewed by Frank Nolan in 1940, WPA-Conn, box 23. See also Agnes Gertsacov, interviewed by Paula Cove, 1972, Long Coll., folder 3, box 175 and tape. Interviewee born in Providence in 1900.

44   N. family interview, 2 September 1976, Providence, interviewed by Judith Smith. Interviewee born in Providence in 1901.

45   Maiorano, Sghelli, and Abbenante families, neighborhood data.

46   Mr. Amore, Bridgeport, WPA-Conn, box 23.

47   RRC and JCD family interview, 1976, Providence.

48   RIWB no. 228, interviewed by a family member in 1975. Interviewee born in Pietra, Italy in 1907; moved to Providence in 1911.

49   RRC and JCD family interview, 1976, Providence.

188   *Family Connections*

50   Mr. Amore, Bridgeport, WPA-Conn, box 23.
51   Mr. C., Bridgeport, WPA-Conn, box 23; see also Mr. Amore,
      Bridgeport, WPA-Conn, box 23.
52   See Tony Marrocco, "The Federal Hill Story," *Echo*, 1970–73,
      particularly 27 November and 4 December 1970; 4 June and 7
      October 1971; 27 January 1972.
53   MH, New Haven, interviewed by Rahel Mittelstein in 1939, WPA-
      Conn, box 58. Interviewee born near Kiev, Ukraine, Russia ca. 1895;
      moved to Baltimore in 1914.
54   KG, New Haven, WPA-Conn, box 58.
55   Rosen family, neighborhood data.
56   Leon Kobrin, *A Lithuanian Village* (New York: Brentano's, 1920), pp.
      21–24. Christina Simmons brought this book to my attention.
57   Wolfe Baron, New Haven, interviewed by Rahel Mittelstein (?) in
      1939, WPA-Conn, box 58. Interviewee born in Liepāja, Lettwija
      (Lithuania) in 1897; moved to Philadelphia in 1899.
58   Virginia Yans-McLaughlin has argued that as an expression of
      patriarchal values, Italian families kept wives and daughters from
      engaging in paid labor outside the home in southern Italy and in
      early-twentieth-century Buffalo. See Yans-McLaughlin, "Patterns of
      Work and Family Organization: Buffalo's Italians," *Journal of
      Interdisciplinary History* 2 (1971), pp. 299–314; idem, "A Flexible
      Tradition: Immigrant Families Confront New Work Experiences,"
      Journal of Social History 7 (Summer 1974), pp. 429–45; idem, *Family
      and Community*, chap. 7. Louise Tilly has pointed out that Yans-
      McLaughlin has failed to take into account evidence that con-
      siderable numbers of young unmarried women in certain regions of
      southern Italy did engage in wage work as domestic servants, textile
      workers, and garment workers, particularly in urban areas. See Tilly,
      "Comments on the Yans-McLaughlin and Davidoff Papers," *Journal
      of Social History* 7 (Summer 1974), pp. 452–54. Rudolph Bell's figures
      on three towns in southern Italy and Sicily also support Tilly's
      contention that considerable numbers of women played a role in the
      local economy, although his tables do not show marital status. See
      Bell, *Fate and Honor, Family and Village*, pp. 123–24, 129, 134. Miriam
      Cohen's evidence on Italian immigrant women in New York City
      also challenged Yans-McLaughlin's argument. Her findings have
      indicated a considerable rate of labor-force participation of Italian
      daughters, responding to the multitudes of job opportunities for
      unskilled females in the city. See Cohen, "From Workshop to
      Office," chaps. 2, 3. Cohen's findings are similar to those of Louise
      Odencrantz, who studied Italian working women in New York City
      in 1919. See Odencrantz, *Italian Women in Industry: A Study of
      Conditions in New York City* (New York: Russell Sage, 1919), pp. 12–27.
      In Tampa, Florida, in 1900, considerable numbers of Italian women
      went to work in cigar factories. See Gary P. Mormino and George E.
      Pozzetta, "Immigrant Women in Tampa: The Italian Experience,

1890–1930," *Florida Historical Quarterly* 61 (January 1983), pp. 296–312, esp. pp. 302–7. Providence had many employment opportunities for unskilled women, and Italian women were active in pursuing these. In Providence, as in New York City and Tampa, Italian wives and daughters do not seem to have been deterred by patriarchal values from working. Recent historians of women's work have argued that women's work patterns are explained by a combination of factors such as age, marital status, position in the household, race, ethnicity, and the occupational and demographic structure of particular cities. See Tilly and Scott, *Women, Work, and Family*, pp. 123–45; Susan J. Kleinberg, "Technology and Women's Work: The Lives of Working-Class Women in Pittsburgh, 1870–1910," *Labor History* 17 (Winter 1976), pp. 58–72; idem, "The Systematic Study of Urban Women," *Historical Methods Newsletter* 9 (December 1975), pp. 14–18; Barbara Klaczynska, "Why Women Work: A Comparison of Various Groups—Philadelphia, 1910–1930," *Labor History* 17 (Winter 1976), pp. 73–87; Elizabeth H. Pleck, "A Mother's Wages: Income Earning Among Married Italian and Black Women, 1896–1911," in *The American Family in Social-Historical Perspective*, 2d ed., ed. Michael Gordon (New York: St. Martin's Press, 1978), pp. 490–510; Kessner and Caroli, "New Immigrant Women at Work," pp. 19–31; Mary Lou Locke, "The Impact of Three Urban Environments on Working Women: San Francisco, Portland, and Los Angeles, 1880," paper presented at the American Historical Association, December 1981. Hal Benenson brought Mary Lou Locke's paper to my attention.

59   For an example of a mother bringing a nursing baby with her to the fields in the Abruzzi region, see D'Angelo, *Son of Italy*, pp. 21–22; however, Rudolph Bell has argued that in most areas of southern Italy and Sicily, the lack of shade and the blades of flying scythes would have made harvest fields a dangerous place for a baby, and that working mothers left their children at home under the care of people too old or too young to work in the fields. See Bell, *Fate and Honor, Family and Village*, p. 40. For general overviews of Providence working women, see Kate Dunnigan, Helen Kebabian, Laura Roberts, and Maureen Taylor, "Working Women: Images of Women at Work in Rhode Island, 1880–1925," *Rhode Island History* 38 (February 1979), pp. 3–21; Sharon Hartman Strom, "Old Barriers and New Opportunities: Working Women in Rhode Island, 1900–1940," *Rhode Island History* 39 (May 1980), pp. 43–56.

60   RRC and JCD family interview, 1976, Providence.

61   For a discussion of the p articular importance of immigrant women's unpaid work in the home, see Riva Krut, "The Women of the Johannesburg Jewish Ladies Communal League," typescript, University of London, 1984; my formulation of the economic value of immigrant women's household work is based on her insights. For evidence of the changing dependency of the family in a market

economy, see Cohen, *Out of the Shadow*, p. 73. For a description of the
economic importance of bargaining, see Iola Lombardi Ansuini,
interviewed by Lola Marot in 1972, Long Coll., folder 4, box 175.
Interviewee born in Providence in 1904. Marxist and Marxist-
feminist theorists have written extensively on the question of the
economic value of women's household labor. See Lise Vogel, "The
Earthly Family," *Radical America* 7 (1975), pp. 9–50; Ira Gerstein,
"Domestic Work and Capitalism," ibid., pp. 101–20; Juliet
Mitchell, "Women: The Longest Revolution," *New Left Review* 40
(December 1966), pp. 11–37; Margaret Benston, "The Political
Economy of Women's Liberation," *Monthly Review* 21 (1969), pp.
13–27; Mariarosa Dalla Costa, "Women and the Subversion of the
Community," *Radical America* 6 (1972), pp. 67–102; Wally Secombe,
"The Housewife and Her Labor Under Capitalism," *New Left Review*
83 (1974), pp. 3–24; Eli Zaretsky, *Capitalism, the Family, and Personal
Life* (New York: Harper and Row, 1976); Heidi Hartman, "Capi-
talism and Women's Work in the Home, 1900–1930," Ph.D.
dissertation, Yale University, 1974.

62   These figures probably do not describe the full extent of immigrant
women's paid work in the family economy because the quantitative
sources that historians have used to measure men's labor-force
participation have not recorded women's work completely. On the
problem of the reliability of the census for the measurement of
women's work, see Margo Conk, "Accuracy, Efficiency, and Bias:
The Interpretation of Women's Work in the U.S. Census of
Occupations, 1890–1940," *Historical Methods Newsletter* 13 (Spring
1981), pp. 65–71: idem, "Labor Statistics in the American and
British Census: Making Some Invidious Comparisons," *Journal of
Social History* 16 (Summer 1983), pp. 83–102.

63   KG, New Haven, WPA-Conn, box 58; Kushner family, neighborhood data; R. family interview, 13 December 1977, Providence,
interviewed by Judith E. Smith. Interviewee born in Providence in
1892.

64   Zborowski and Herzog, *Life Is with People*, p. 303.

65   Sixty-eight-year-old Italian housewife, Bridgeport, WPA-Conn., box
22.

66   U.S. Department of Labor, Women's Bureau, *Industrial Home Work in
Rhode Island*, bulletin 131 (Washington, D.C.: Government Printing
Office, 1935); U.S. Department of Labor, Children's Bureau,
*Industrial Homework of Children: A Study made in Providence, Pawtucket,
and Central Falls, Rhode Island*, bulletin 100 (Washington, D.C.:
Government Printing Office, 1922).

67   U.S. Department of Labor, Children's Bureau, *Industrial Homework of
Children*, pp. 48, 24. See also Susan P. Benson, "Women, Work, and
the Family Economy: Industrial Homework in Rhode Island,
1934," paper presented at the Social Science History Association,
November 1979.

68   As suggested above, married women's work was rarely recorded by
       the census (see n. 61). For information on wives' employment
       historians have had to depend on other kinds of contemporary
       surveys such as Caroline Manning, *The Immigrant Woman and Her Job*,
       Department of Labor, Women's Bureau, bulletin 74 (1930; reprint,
       New York: Arno, 1970), p. 74; Odencrantz, *Italian Women in Industry*,
       pp. 17–21. For this study, evidence gathered in oral history
       interviews directly contradicted census enumeration. None of the
       women whose long work histories were recounted by their sons and
       daughters were recorded by state census or city directories as having
       been employed. According to one daughter, her mother, never listed
       as having had a job, had always worked. See N. family interview, 2
       September 1976, Providence; M. Family interview, 1 December
       1975, Providence; R. family interview, 13 December 1977, Provi-
       dence. For analyses of Italian and Jewish married women's employ-
       ment, see Cohen, "From Workshop to Office," pp. 98–120; Pleck,
       "A Mother's Wages," pp. 490–510; Kessner and Caroli, "New
       Immigrant Women at Work," pp. 18–31; Bodnar, Simon, and
       Weber, *Lives of Their Own*, pp. 98–101; Mormino and Pozzetta,
       "Immigrant Women in Tampa," pp. 301–7.
69   Fannie Savage Schindler, 1972, Long Coll., tape; Mrs. L. Salanto,
       Bridgeport, interviewed by Vincent Frazzetta in 1940, WPA-Conn,
       box 23. Interviewee born in Italy in 1911; moved to Pennsylvania in
       1929.
70   N. family interview, 2 September 1976, Providence; M. family
       interview, 1 December 1975, Providence; Italian Immigrant
       Women—1920, interviewed by a family member in 1972, Long Coll.,
       folder 7, box 175. Interviewee born in southern Italy in 1896; moved
       to Providence ca. 1920.
71   RIWB no. 161; interviewed by a family member in 1976; born in
       Providence in 1904. RIWB no. 172, interviewed by a family member
       in 1973; born in Providence in 1905. U.S. Department of Labor,
       Children's Bureau, Providence Study Correspondence File, 1919,
       National Archives Industrial and Social Division, Record Group
       102, box 979. See also U.S. Department of Labor, Women's Bureau,
       Industrial Home Work in Rhode Island; Benson, "Women, Work, and
       the Family Economy."
72   S. family interview, Cambridge Mass., interviewed by Judith E.
       Smith on 9 September 1976; interviewee born in Providence in 1939.
       Iola Lombardi Ansuini, Long. Coll., folder 4, box 175; N. family
       interview, 1976, Providence.
73   S. family interview, 1976, Cambridge, Mass.; Iola Lombardi
       Ansuini, Long Coll., folder 4, box 175; RRC and JCD family
       interview, Providence.
74   RIWB no. 231, interviewed by a family member in 1976. Interviewee
       born in Luca, Italy, in 1897; moved to Providence in 1899.
75   Fannie Savage Schindler, 1972, Long. Coll., tape; Perlmann,

"Education and the Social Structure of an American City," p. 18.

76   Work in family shops, more common in the Jewish neighorhood, may have been underrecorded. Studies describing the differential rates of school attendance between Italian and Jewish children include Michael Olneck and Marvin Lazerson, "The School Achievement of Immigrant Children, 1900–1930," *History of Education Quarterly* 14 (1974), pp. 454–82; Cohen, "From Workshop to Office," chap. 5; idem, "Changing Educational Strategies Among Immigrant Generations: New York Italians in Comparative Perspective," *Journal of Social History* 15 (Spring 1982) pp. 443–66; Perlman, "Education and the Social Structure of an American City." Both Cohen and Perlmann also discuss the gender differentials in school attendance rates within the ethnic groups.

77   For a discussion of the importance of family networks among French-Canadian textile workers in Manchester, New Hampshire, see Tamara Hareven, "Family Time and Industrial Time: Family and Work in a Planned Corporation Town, 1900–1924," *Journal of Urban History* 1 (May 1975), pp. 365–89; idem, "The Laborers of Manchester, New Hampshire, 1912–1922: The Role of the Family and Ethnicity in Adjusting to Industrial Life," *Labor History* 16 (Spring 1975), pp. 249–65; idem, "The Dynamics of Kin in an Industrial Community," in *Turning Points: Historical and Sociological Essays on the Family*, ed. John Demos and Sarane Boocock (Chicago: University of Chicago Press, 1978), pp. S151–82; idem, *Family Time and Industrial Time: The Relationship Between Family and Work in a New England Industrial Community* (New York: Cambridge University Press, 1982), chaps. 5, 8. Bodnar, Simon and Weber have argued that the ability of Polish and Italian immigrants in Pittsburgh to obtain work for children had a critical impact on the shape of the family after migration. Institutional racism, which made it difficult for black migrants to similarly provide for their children, shaped black families and black familial values in a different direction. See Bodnar, Weber, and Simon, "Migration, Kinship, and Urban Adjustment: Blacks and Poles in Pittsburgh, 1900–1950," *Journal of American History* 66 (1979), pp. 548–65; Bodner, Weber, and Simon, *Lives of Their Own*, chaps. 2, 3.

78   RIWB nos. 228, 197.

79   Liberto Dattolo, Bridgeport, interviewed by Vincent Frazzetta in 1939, WPA-Conn, box 23. Interviewee born in Monte Castel, Villina Province, Italy, 1899; moved to Bridgeport in 1914. Letter from I. M. to "Bintel Brief" collumn, *Jewish Daily Forward*, 1906, in *A Bintel Brief*, ed. Isaac Metzker (New York: Ballantine Books, 1972), p. 31; Liberato Dattolo, Bridgeport, WPA-Conn, box 23.

80   Cohen, *Out of the Shadow*, pp. 94–95.

81   For other studies that have been documented the interchangeability of the labor of mothers and children, see Tilly and Scott, *Women, Work, and Family*, pp. 126–29; Cohen, "From Workshop to Office,"

pp. 110–23; Pleck, ' 'A Mother's Wages," pp. 499–500; Hareven, *Family Time and Industrial Time*, chap . 8, esp. pp. 208–17; Bodnar, Simon and Weber, *Lives of Their Own*, pp. 99–100; Olivier Zunz, *The Changing Face of Inequality: Urbanization, Industrial Development, and Immigrants in Detroit, 1880–1920* (Chicago: University of Chicago Press, 1982), pp. 233. See also Claudia Goldin, "Family Strategies and the Family Economy in the Late 19th Century: The Role of the Secondary Worker," in *Philadelphia: Work, Space, Family, and Group Experience in the Nineteenth Century*, ed. Theodore Hershberg (New York: Oxford University Press, 1981), pp. 277–310.

82 M. family interview, 1975, Providence. See also N. family interview, 1976, Providence.

83 See George Huganir, "The Hoisery Looper in the Twentieth Century: A Study of Family Occupational Processes and Adaptation to Factory and Community Change, 1900–1950," Ph.D. dissertation, University of Pennsylvania, 1958; McLaughlin, "Patterns of Work and Family Organization," pp. 299–324; Yans-McLaughlin, "A Flexible Tradition," pp. 429–45; idem, *Family and Community*, chaps. 1, 6, 7; Hareven, "Family Time and Industrial Time," pp. 365–89; idem, "The Laborers of Manchester," pp. 249–65; idem, "The Dynamics of Kin in Industrial Communities," pp. S151–82; idem, *Family Time and Industrial Time* chap. 5; John Bodnar, "Immigration and Modernization: The Case of Slavic Peasants in Industrial America," *Journal of Social History* 10 (1976), pp. 44–67; Bodnar, Simon, and Weber, "Migration, Kinship, and Urban Adjustment," pp. 548–65; idem, *Lives of Their Own*, chap. 3.

84 Mr. C. Guerra, Bridgeport, interviewed by Vincent Frazzetta in 1940, WPA-Conn, box 23. Interviewee born in 1885 in Italy; moved to Pittsburgh in 1915. Mr. Merlo, Bridgeport, WPA-Conn, box 23; Mr. DiMartino, Bridgeport, WPA-Conn, box 23; Wolfe Baron, New Haven, WPA-Conn, box 58.

85 See Alfred DuPont Chandler, "The Beginnings of 'Big Business' in American Industry," in *New Perspectives in the American Past 1877– Present*, ed. Stanley Katz and Stanley Kutler (Boston: Little Brown, 1969), pp. 3–31; idem, *Strategy and Structure* (Cambridge: MIT Press, 1962), pp. 19–51; Harry Braverman, *Labor and Monopoly Capital* (New York: Monthly Review Press, 1974). Olivier Zunz has also argued that the modernization of the economy in the twentieth century contributed to a structural mobility too often confused with real individual gains. In his interpretation, structural factors determined that the children of immigrants would work at white-collar occupations more often than their fathers (Zunz, *The Changing Face of Inequality*, p. 8).

86 Frederick Winslow Taylor's most prominent disciple of scientific management, Frank Gilbreth, came to Providence to supervise the introduction of time-motion studies and scientific management techniques at New England Butt Company. Gilbreth was in Provi-

dence from 1910 to 1913. See "Moving Pictures on the Job," *Providence Journal*, 22 December 1912, sec. 5, p. 3; and Gilbreth's obituary in the *Providence Journal*, 15 June 1924, p. 11. For evidence of scientific management's effect on the labor process in Providence see *Labor Advocate* (Providence), 30 November 1913, 22 March 1914, 13, 20 and 27 February 1915; *Labor World* (Woonsocket, R.I.), 4 December 1915. See also Editha Hadcock, " Labor Problems in Rhode Island Cotton Mills, 1790–1940," Ph.D. dissertation, Brown University, 1945, pp. 193–253.

87   See also Perlmann, "Education and the Social Structure of an American City," tables, pp. 205, 250, 475. To compare Providence findings with Boston, see Thernstrom, *The Other Bostonians*, pp. 145–75, 250–56. For New York patterns of Italian and Jewish fathers and children, see Kessner, *Golden Door*, pp. 102–26, 181–84. For New York Italian mothers and daughters, see Cohen, "From Workshop to Office," chaps. 3, 6. For Cleveland patterns of Italian fathers and sons, see Barton, *Peasants and Strangers*, chaps. 5, 6, esp. pp. 118–20, 121, 124–25, table p. 178. For Pittsburgh Italian fathers and sons, see Bodnar, Simon, and Weber, *Lives of Their Own*, chap. 9. In communities dominated by one industry, immigrants moved earlier into the factories and mills and children followed their fathers into the same work into the 1930s and 1940s. See Jeremy Brecher, Jerry Lombardi, and Jan Stackhouse, ed., *Brass Valley: The Story of Working People's Lives and Struggles in an American Industrial Region* (Philadelphia: Temple University Press, 1982); Bodnar, Weber, and Simon, *Lives of Their Own*, chap. 9.

88   Miccarelli and Calire families, neighborhood data; Silverman, Kessler, and Ruberto families, neighborhood data; Berarducci and Dwares families, neighborhood data.

89   Perlmann makes a similar argument in "Education and the Social Structure of an American City," p. 230. His analysis of the importance of ethnicity, class, and educational attainment in the achievement of social mobility led him to state that "it was Jews' involvement in commercial pursuits, not unusual levels of schooling, not a commitment to learning, that must account for Jewish upward mobililty in the early part of the twentieth century."

90   Mr. DiMartino, Bridgeport, WPA-Conn, Box 23; Mr. Amore, Bridgeport, WPA-Conn, box 23; Wolfe Baron, New Haven, WPA-Conn, box 58; and Mr. Merlo, Bridgeport, WPA-Conn, box 23.

91   Mr. J. R., Bridgeport, interviewed by Vincent Frazzetta in 1940, WPA-Conn, box 23. Interviewee born in 1889 in Italy; moved to New Jersey in 1907. Mr. C., Bridgeport, WPA-Conn, box 23; Mr. DiMartino, Bridgeport, WPA-Conn, box 23; Mr. C., Bridgeport, WPA-Conn, box 23; Mr. DiMartino, Bridgeport, WPA-Conn, box 23; Mr. Amore, Bridgeport, WPA-Conn, box 23. The historical transformation of the work ethic has been analyzed by Daniel

Rodgers in *The Work Ethic in Industrial America, 1870–1920* (New York: Oxford University Press, 1978). Skilled workers describe similar changes in the attitudes of younger workers in Robert S. and Helen Lynd, *Middletown* (New York: Harcourt Brace Jovanovich, 1929), pp. 73–83. A more complex and dynamic relationship between the movies and ethnic culture is described in Sharon Hartman Strom, "Italian-American Women and Their Daughters in Rhode Island: The Adolescence of Two Generations, 1900–1950," in *The Italian Immigrant Woman in North America*, ed. Betty Boyd Caroli, Robert F. Harney, and Lydio F. Tomasi (Toronto: Multicultural History Society of Ontario, 1978), pp. 191–204, esp. pp. 196, 199; Elizabeth Ewen, "City Lights: Immigrant Women and the Rise of the Movies," *Signs* 5 (Spring 1980), pp. S45–S65; Roy Rosenzweig, *Eight Hours for What We Will: Workers and Leisure in an Industrial City, 1870–1920* (Cambridge and New York: Cambridge University Press, 1983), chap. 8.

92 For the decline of neighborhood markets in relation to super-markets, see *Providence Journal Almanac*, 1935, pp. 74–75. See Judith E. Smith, "Remaking Their Lives: Italian and Jewish Immigrant Family, Work, and Community in Providence, Rhode Island from 1900 to 1940," Ph.D. dissertation, Brown University, 1980, pp. 87–89, 99–101, for tables measuring unemployment of neighborood immigrants, working sons, and working daughters as reported in the 1915 and 1935 state censuses. For a discussion of the issue of secure employment in the labor movement in the 1930s, see David Montgomery, "Comments on Panel on Transfer and Change in the Formation of Working-Class Culture," Social Science History Association, October 1977. See also idem, "Immigrant Workers and Managerial Reform," in *Workers' Control in America: Studies in the History of Work, Technology, and Labor Struggles* (New York: Cambridge University Press, 1979), pp. 40–44; idem, "American Workers and the New Deal Formula," in *Workers' Control in America*, pp. 161–68. Daniel Rodgers has argued that over time immigrants in factories learned to be more confident and stubborn in making demands about their conditions of employment. See Rodgers, "Tradition, Modernity, and the American Industrial Worker: Reflections and Critique," *Journal of Interdisciplinary History* 7 (1977), pp. 655–81.

93 RIWB no. 13, Providence, interviewed by a family member in 1974; interviewee born in 1924. RIWB no. 228, 1975, Providence. For a discussion of education for white-collar workers as an aspect of family strategy, see Cohen, "From Workshop to Office," chap. 5; idem., "Changing Educational Strategies among Immigrant Generations," pp. 452–460. See also Miriam Cohen, "Italian-American Women in New York City, 1900–1950: Work and School," in *Class, Sex, and the Woman Worker*, ed. Milton Cantor and Bruch Laurie (Westport, Conn.: Greenwood Press, 1977), pp. 120–43.

94 Flora Wolfe Bromberg, interviewed by Francis C. Sadler in 1972, Long Coll., folder 7, box 175; interviewee born in Baltimore in 1901. Anna Frucht, 1978, Providence, RIJHSL.

95 New management policies that moved control of hiring from individual foremen and women to personnel offices did not necessarily diminish the opportunity for informal recruitment and employment of kin. In her study of French-Canadian textile workers in Manchester, New Hampshire, Tamara Hareven found that from 1910 to 1924, new personnel policies did not impede the development of kin networks since textile workers were able to ignore the personnel office and continued to be hired by foremen. See Hareven, "Family Time and Industrial Time," p. 374; idem, "The Laborers of Manchester," pp. 252, 256–57; idem, *Family Time and Industrial Time*, p. 89. In her study of department-store workers, Susan Porter Benson has found that at Filene's department store in Boston, the adoption of the most advanced personnel policies did not require cessation of family and friend-influenced hiring. See Benson, *'The Great Theater': Managers, Saleswomen, and Customers in American Department Stores, 1890–1940* (Urbana: University of Illinois Press, forthcoming). In 1920, Macy's department store in New York advertised that it would pay its employees a $10 bonus if they recruited new employees who remained at Macy's at least six months. This notice appeared in *Sparks*, the internal employees' newsletter at Macy's, June 1920, p. 6. See Sarah S. Malino, "Faces Across the Counter: A Social History of Female Department Store Employees, 1870–1920," Ph.D. dissertation, Columbia University, 1982.

96 Patalano family, neighborhood data; see, for example, Maiorano family, neighborhood data.

97 Del Nero family, neighborhood data. See also Russillio family, neighborhood dta.

98 RIWB no. 13; M. family interview, 1975, Providence.

99 Homework has persisted in Rhode Island despite state and federal legislation intended to eliminate it. See Benson, "Women, Work, and the Family Economy," p. 1. Homework was prohibited by the National Recovery Administration codes in 1933, flourished after the NRA was declared unconstitutional in 1934, and then was prohibited again through further federal legislation—the Fair Labor Standards Act—in 1938. See Rhode Island Department of Labor, *Annual Report for 1935* (Providence, 1935), p. 115.

100 M. family interview, 1975, Providence; RIWB no. 228.

101 U.S. Department of Labor, Women's Bureau, Home Visits of Rhode Island Working Women Folder, 1920, National Archives, Industrial and Social Division, Record Group 86, box 181.

102 Bertha Brill, 1978, Providence, interviewed by Sonya Michel, RIJHSL. Interviewee born in Austria in the 1890s; moved to Brooklyn in the 1890s.

103   RIWB no. 228, 1975, Providence; RRC and JCD family interview, 1976, Providence.

104   For a discussion of the interaction between American bourgeois ideals of domesticity and Jewish and Italian ethnic culture, see Charlotte Baum, Paula Hyman, and Sonya Michel, *Jewish Women in America* (New York: Dial Press, 1976), pp. 120, 187–233; Elizabeth Ewen, "city Lights," pp. 545–65. See also, idem, *Immigrant Women in the Land of Dollars* (New York: Pantheon, forthcoming.) In her study of French-Canadian textile workers, Tamara Harven found that married immigrant women were more than two times as likely to work than second-generation or native-born women, and she argued that for the second generation of native-born women, American values of domesticity had become dominant over the desire for maximum employment. See Hareven, *Family Time and Industrial Time*, p. 202. In this study, the difference between immigrant mothers and their daughters does not show an absolute decrease or increase in employment but rather suggests that the shift in location of employment made it difficult to compare the economic contribution of the two generations exactly.

105   *Providence Journal Almanac*, 1935, p. 81; Dorothy Meyers, *One Family in Five: A Study of Families Receiving Assistance* (Providence: Providence Council of Social Agencies, 1939), pp. 4–9; Norma LaSalle Daoust, "Providence at the Grass Roots: Neighborhood Change and Continuity During the Great Depression," paper presented at the Organization of American Historians, April 1983. Mark Gelfand made Daoust's paper available to me.

106   For women's work patterns in the depression, see Ruth Milkman, "Women's Work and the Economic Crisis: Some Lessons from the Great Depression," in *A Heritage of Her Own*, ed. Nancy F. Cott and Elizabeth H. Pleck (New York: Simon and Schuster, 1979), pp. 507–41. Milkman calls special attention to the economic importance of women's unpaid domestic work; see pp. 520–28. See also Lois Scharf, *To Work and To Wed: Female Employment, Feminism, and the Great Depression* (Westport, Conn: Greenwood Press, 1980). Joseph Lazarro, Bridgeport, interviewed by Vincent Frazzetta in 1939; WPA-Conn, box 23. Interviewee born in Naro, Argiento, Italy in 1866; moved to Bridgeport in 1920. Jane, Malden, Mass in *The Rosie Papers: Oral Histories of Twentieth Century Women*, ed. Laurie Crumpacker and Marie Benfatto (Boston: Simmons College, 1979), p. 36. Interviewee born 5 April 1928.

CHAPTER THREE   THE BONDS OF KINSHIP

1   Josef Barton, "Eastern and Southern Europeans," in *Ethnic Leadership in America*, ed. John Higham (Baltimore: Johns Hopkins University

Press, 1978), pp. 151–54; Irving Howe, *The World of Our Fathers* (New York: Harcourt Brace Jovanovich, 1976), pp. 15–24. See also Barton, *Peasants and Strangers: Italians, Roumanians, and Slovaks in an American City, 1890–1950* (Cambridge: Harvard University Press, 1975), pp. 27–47.

2   For southern Italy, see Sydel Silverman, "Agricultural Organization, Social Structures, and Values in Italy: Amoral Familism Reconsidered," *American Anthropologist* 70 (1968), pp. 1–20; William Douglass, "The South Italian Family: A Critique," *Journal of Family History* 5 (Winter 1980), pp. 338–59; Rudolph M. Bell, *Fate and Honor, Family and Village: Demographic and Cultural Change in Rural Italy since 1800* (Chicago: University of Chicago Press, 1979), chaps. 5, 7; Leonard Covello, *The Social Background of the Italo-American School-Child* (1944: reprint, Leiden: E. J. Brill, 1967), chaps. 6, 7, esp. p. 151. For Sicily, see Charlotte G. Chapman, *Milocca: A Sicilian Village* (1935; reprint, Cambridge: Schenkman, 1971), chaps. 2, 4, 5, esp. pp. 72–73, 129; Constance Cronin, *The Sting of Change: Sicilians in Sicily and in Australia* (Chicago: University of Chicago Press, 1970), chaps. 4–6, esp. pp. 43, 66; Jane Schneider and Peter Schneider, *Culture and Political Economy in Western Sicily* (New York: Academic Press, 1976), chaps. 4, 5; Donna R. Gabaccia, "Sicilians in Space: Environmental Change and Family Geography," *Journal of Social History* 16 (Winter 1982), pp. 53–66; idem, *From Sicily to Elizabeth Street: Housing and Social Change Among Italian Immigrants, 1880–1930* (Albany: State University of New York Press, 1983), chaps. 1–3. For eastern Europe, see Mark Zborowski and Elizabeth Herzog, *Life Is with People: The Culture of the Shtetl* (1952; reprint, New York: Schocken, 1969), pp. 291–307; Ruth Rubin, *Voices of a People: Yiddish Folk Song* (New York: Thomas Yoseloff, 1963), p. 81.

3   Silverman, "Agricultural Organization," p. 14; Douglass, "South Italian Family," pp. 348–49; Cronin, *Sting of Change*, pp. 62, 118; Phyllis Williams, *South Italian Folkways in Europe and America* (1938; reprint, New York: Russell and Russell, 1969), p. 75; Covello, *Social Background*, pp. 169–70; Chapman, *Milocca*, p. 82; Walter Goldschmidt and Evalyn J. Kunkel, "The Structure of the Peasant Family," *American Anthropologist* 73 (1971), p. 1069; Evalyn J. Michaelson and Walter Goldschmidt, "Female Roles and Male Dominance Among Peasants," *Southwestern Journal of Anthropology* 27 (1971), p. 345; Bell, *Fate and Honor, Family and Village*, pp. 75–76.

4   Chapman, *Milocca*, pp. 70–71, 105–6; Cronin, *Sting of Change*, pp. 114–15; Covello, *Social Brackground*, pp. 196.

5   Cronin, *Sting of Change*, pp. 115. Anecdotes cited by Covello, *Social Background*, pp. 218–19, 193.

6   Chapman, *Milocca*, pp. 105–6; Cronin, *Sting of Change*, pp. 115–16; Massimo Livi-Bacci, *A History of Italian Fertility During the Last Two Centuries* (Princeton: Princeton University Press, 1977), pp. 100, 107;

Miriam Cohen, "From Workshop to Office: Italian Women and Family Strategies in New York City, 1900–1950," Ph.D. dissertation, University of Michigan, 1978, p. 41. Interviews cited by Covello, *Social Background*, pp. 201–2.

7 Chapman, *Milocca*, pp. 74, 79; Cronin, *Sting of Change*, p. 116, Williams, *South Italian Folkways*, pp. 78, 185; Covello, *Social Background*, pp. 195; Chapman, *Milocca*, pp. 112.

8 Covello, *Social Background*, pp. 192–96; Cronin, *Sting of Change*, pp. 80; Chapman, *Milocca*, pp. 82–83, 112; Covello, *Social Background*, pp. 217

9 Chapman, *Milocca*, pp. 81–82; Cronin, *Sting of Change*, pp. 62, 117–18.

10 Chapman, *Milocca*, pp. 68–69; Covello, *Social Background*, pp. 149–52; Williams, *Southern Italian Folkways*, p. 73.

11 Chapman, *Milocca*, pp. 68–70; Cronin, *Sting of Change*, pp. 50, 58–59, 63–64. Anecdote cited by Cronin, *Sting of Change*, pp. 65.

12 Chapman, *Milocca*, pp. 69–70, 122–25; Cronin, *Sting of Change*, pp. 61; Covello, *Social Background*, pp. 179; Williams, *South Italian Folkways*, pp. 185. See also Gabaccia, "Sicilians in Space," pp. 55–56.

13 In general, eastern European Jewish family arrangements have been less widely observed and documented than those in southern Italy. For evidence on eastern European Jewish extended family relationships, see Zborowski and Herzog, *Life Is with People*, pp. 130, 272, 299; Rubin, *Voices of a People*, pp. 117–78; Rose Cohen, *Out of the Shadow* (New York: G. H. Doran, 1918), pp. 29, 47; Sydelle Kramer and Jenny Masur, eds., *Jewish Grandmothers* (Boston: Beacon Press, 1976), pp. 39. KG, New Haven, interviewed by Rahel Mittelstein in 1939, WPA-Conn, box 58. Interviewee born in Orlov, near Pobelov, White Russia in 1891; moved to New Haven in 1921. Charles Reznikoff, *Family Chronicle* (1929, 1936; reprint, New York: Universe Books, 1971), pp. 12–13, 23. Anecdote cited by Mary Antin, *The Promised Land* (1912; reprint, Boston: Houghton Mifflin, 1969), pp. 4, 67; folksong cited by Rubin, *Voice of a People*, pp. 117–18.

14 Zborowski and Herzog, *Life Is with People*, pp. 124, 291–99. Childrearing described by Morris Shapiro, Hartford, interviewed by Morris Tonken in 1938, WPA-Conn, box 61. Interviewee born in Uman, Kiev, Russia, ca. 1903; moved to Hartford in 1923. Proverb collected in Hanan J. Ayalti, *Yiddish Proverbs* (1949; reprint, New York: Schocken, 1963), p. 34; Zborowski and Herzog, *Life Is with People*, p. 298.

15 Zborowski and Herzog, *Life is with People*, pp. 272–77; Morris Shapiro, Hartford, WPA-Conn, box 61; see also Morris Kavitsky, Hartford, interviewed by Morton Tonken in 1938, WPA-Conn, box 61. Interviewee born in Kachinovitch, Grodno, Russia ca. 1873; moved to New York City in 1914.

16   Ayalti, *Yiddish Proverbs*, pp. 90–91. Zborowski and Herzog, *Life Is with People*, pp. 270–73; Rubin, *Voice of a People*, pp. 72–74, 81. See also Morris Shapiro, Hartford, WPA-Conn, box 61; Morris Kavitsky, Hartford, WPA-Conn, box 61; Mary Antin, *Promised Land*, p. 35.

17   Zborowski and Herzog, *Life Is with People*, pp. 304, 270, 276–77. Marriage negotiations described by Antin, *Promised Land*, pp. 57–58. Kin social life described in the family interview, Newton, Mass., interviewed by Judith Smith on 15 December 1979. Father born in Husiatyn, Galicia, Austria in 1899; moved to Providence in 1911. Zborowski and Herzog, *Life Is with People*, p. 284.

18   Zborowski and Herzog, *Life Is with People*, pp. 304–6; Ayalti, *Yiddish Proverbs*, pp. 102–3.

19   Zborowski and Herzog, *Life Is with People*, pp. 229, 306; Fannie Savage Schindler, interviewed by Jill Grossberg in 1972, Long Coll., tape. Interviewee born in Bialystok, Russia in 1889; moved to New York City in 1900.

20   Josef Barton, quoted by David Montgomery, Comments on Panel on Transfer and Change in the Formation of American Working-Class Culture, presented to the Social Science History Association, October 1977. Barton has argued that this process was at work in areas of emigration in southern and eastern Europe; see Barton, "Southern and Eastern Europeans," pp. 152–54; idem, "Religion and Cultural Change in Czech Immigrant Communities, 1850–1920," in *Immigrants and Religion in Urban America*, ed. Randall M. Miller and Thomas D. Marzik (Philadelphia: Temple University Press, 1977), pp. 3–24, esp. pp. 6–9. The Schneiders make the related point that cultural codes expressing norms for family honor were instruments of adaptation to secular forces and not simply a residue of a "traditional" preindustrial past. See Schneider and Schneider, *Culture and Political Economy in Western Sicily*, chaps. 4, 5. E. N. Goody's research suggested how increased incidence of godparenthood might link together kin through their common bonds with children, in "Forms of Pro-Parenthood: The Sharing and Substitution of Parental Roles," in *Kinship: Selected Readings*, ed. Jack Goody (Baltimore: Penguin, 1971), p. 337. See also Sidney Mintz and Eric Wolfe, "An Analysis of Ritual Coparenthood (compadrazgo)," *Southwestern Journal of Anthropology 6* (1950).

21   J. Davis, "An Account of Rules for the Transmission of Property in Pisticci, 1814–1961," in *Mediterranean Family Structures*, ed. Jean G. Peristiany (New York: Cambridge University Press, 1976), pp. 287–303, esp. p. 301. A parallel situation can be observed in Mediterranean Europe in the Middle Ages where the preference for cash dowries had the effect of disinheriting daughters. See Diane Owen Hughes, "From Brideprice to Dowry in Mediterranean Europe," *Journal of Family History 3* (Fall 1978), pp. 262–96, esp. p. 281.

22   Mario Puzo, *The Fortunate Pilgrim* (1964; reprint, New York: Lancer

Books, 1973), p. 13; idem, "Choosing a Dream: Italians in Hell's Kitchen," in *The Immigrant Experience*, ed. Thomas Wheeler (Baltimore: Penguin, 1973), p. 45; Livi-Bacci, *A History of Italian Fertility*, pp. 81–85, 98–107. The figures on endogamous and exogamous marriage are from Barton, *Peasants and Strangers*, p. 42. Barton's figures are roughly supported by Bell's figures on exogamous marriage in three towns in southern Italy and Sicily which show small but substantial and increasing amounts of exogamy per village in the years preceding emigration. See Bell, *Fate and Honor, Family and Village*, tables on pp. 163, 165, 174. Kevin O'Neill has made a related argument based on his research on nineteenth-century Irish emigration. In pre-Famine Ireland, emigrants were likely to be those young people whose chances to marry had become sharply limited by the pauperization resulting from the impact of British economic expansion on the Irish countryside. See O'Neill, "Migrant-Sending Families: Some Observations on Pre-Famine Ireland," paper presented at the Social Science History Association, October 1983; idem, *Killashandra: A Local Study of Pre-Famine Irish Agricultural and Demographic Change* (Madison: University of Wisconsin Press, 1984), chaps. 4, 5.

23   Cohen, *Out of the Shadow*, pp. 29–33, 149, 192–93; Kramer and Masur, *Jewish Grandmothers*, p. 6; Caroline Manning, *The Immigrant Woman And Her Job*, U.S. Department of Labor, Women's Bureau, bulletin 74 (1930; reprint, New York: Arno Press, 1970), p. 22

24   See Bell, *Fate and Honor, Family and Village*, chap. 5, esp. pp. 90–94; see also Cohen, "From Workshop to Office," pp. 44–46.

25   Giovanni Verga, *The House by the Medlar Tree* (New York: Harper and Brothers, 1890), p. 129; Sholom Aleichem [Sholom Rabinowitz], *The Tevye Stories and Others*, trans. Julius and Frances Butwin (New York: Pocketbooks, 1965); idem, *Tevye's Daughters*, trans. Frances Butwin (New York: Crown Publishers, 1949). See also Sol Gittelman, *From Shtetl to Suburbia: The Family in Jewish Literary Imagination* (Boston: Beacon Press, 1978), chap. 4.

26   See J. S. MacDonald, "Agricultural Organization, Migration, and Labor Militancy in Rural Italy," *Economic History Review* 16 (1963), p. 70; Barton, *Peasants and Strangers*, chapter 2.

27   See John S. MacDonald and Leatrice D. MacDonald, "Chain Migration, Ethnic Neighborhood Formation, and Social Networks," *Milbank Memorial Fund Quarterly* 42 (1964), pp. 82–97, esp. 89–91; idem, "Urbanization, Ethnic Groups, and Social Segmentation," *Social Research* 29 (1962), pp. 433–48, esp. 439–40, 445–46; Barton, *Peasants and Strangers*, pp. 34–36, 38–40, 47; John Briggs, *An Italian Passage: Immigrants to Three American Cities, 1890–1930* (New Haven: Yale University Press, 1978), pp. 75–86; Virginia Yans-McLaughlin, *Family and Community: Italian Immigrants in Buffalo, 1880–1930* (Ithaca: Cornell University Press, 1978), pp. 57–60. Max Horowitz, New

Haven, interviewed by Rahel Mittelstein (?) in 1939, WPA-Conn, box 58. Interviewee born near Vilna, Russia in 1868; moved to New York City in 1891. Samuel Postol, Bridgeport, interviewed by Edward Reich in 1938., WPA-Conn, box 62. Inteviewee born near Odessa, Russia in 1875; moved to Bridgeport in 1905. Joseph Lazarro, Bridgeport, interviewed by Vincent Frazzetta in 1939, WPA-Conn, box 23. Interviewee born in Naro, Argiento, Italy in 1866; moved to Bridgeport in 1920.

28   Elizabeth G. Stern, *My Mother and I* (New York: Macmillan, 1922), p. 75; U.S. Congress, Senate, *Report of the Immigration Commission: Statistical Review of Immigration, 1819–1910—Distribution of Immigrants, 1850–1900*, 61st Cong., 3d sess., Senate document 756 (Washington, D.C.: Government Printing Office, 1911), tables 38–39, pp. 360–61.

29   Kramer and Masur, *Jewish Grandmothers*, pp. 7–9; Sixty-eight-year-old Italian housewife, Bridgeport, interviewed by Vincent Frazzetta between 1938 and 1940, WPA-Conn, box 22. Interviewee born in Italy ca. 1870; moved to Bridgeport ca. 1890.

30   Puzo, "Choosing a Dream," p. 47. For a discussion of the values of *campanilismo*, see Bell, *Fate and Honor, Family and village*, chap. 7.

31   Morris Kavitsky, Hartford, WPA-Conn, box 61. For a description of families forced to move frequently, see MH, New Haven, interviewed by Rahel Mittelstein in 1939, WPA-Conn, box 58. Interviewee born near Kiev, Russia ca. 1895; moved to Baltimore in 1914. Reznikoff, *Family Chronicle*, pp. 7–31.

32   Chapman, *Milocca*, p. 108. Marie Zambiello, Bridgeport, interviewed by Emil Napolitano in 1939, WPA-Conn, box 23. Interviewee born in Airola, Benevento, Italy ca. 1867; moved to Bridgeport ca. 1903. See also Antonio Mangaro, "The Effects of Immigration upon Italy," *Charities* (4 April 1908) reprinted in *A Documentary History of The Italian Americans*, ed. Wayne Moquin with Charles Van Doren (New York: Praeger, 1974), p. 79.

33   LR, New Haven, interviewed by Rahel Mittelstein in 1939, WPA-Conn, box 58. Interviewee born in Spinowka near Kiev, Russia ca. 1899; moved to New York City in 1924. MP, Bridgeport, interviewed by Emil Napolitano, WPA-Conn, box 23. Interviewee born in Italy ca. 1900; moved to Providence in 1920. AT, Bridgeport, interviewed by William J. Burke in 1940; WPA-Conn, box 23. Interviewee born in Italy in 1903; moved to Bridgeport in 1923.

34   KG, New Haven, WPA-Conn, box 58; Stern, *My Mother and I*, pp. 155–56.

35   Both Rudolph Bell and William Douglas have argued that joint living arrangements appeared in some southern Italian towns when they appeared useful and were demographically possible. See Bell, *Fate and Honor, Family and Village*, pp. 67–77, 108–12; Douglass, *South Italian Family*, pp. 342–53, 354–56. Virginia Yans-McLaughlin has described

how immigrants expanded kin networks into residence in *Family and Community*, chap. 2, esp. pp. 63–70. Donna Gabaccia has argued that "Sicilians in New York City turned their kin into neighbors, reversing the Sicilian process that made neighbors the "real kin." See Gabaccia, "Sicilians in Space," p. 60; idem, *From Sicily to Elizabeth Street*, pp. 24–34, 78–85.

36 The methods used to assess kinship probably underestimated the actual number of immigrants with kin in Providence (see Appendix).

37 Anna Frucht, 1978, Providence, interviewed by Sonya Michel, RIJHSL. Interviewee born in Odessa, Russia in 1902; moved to Central Falls, Rhode Island in 1905. See Sonya Michel, "Family and Community Networks Among Rhode Island Jews: A Study Based on Oral Histories," *Rhode Island Jewish Historical Notes* 7 (1978), pp. 513–35.

38 Kanopky family, neighborhood data.

39 Cassarini, Saulino, and Lanzieri families, neighborhood data. The birth of the first child often seemed to have been the stimulus for a married couple to move to a separate household. See Howard P. Chudacoff and Tamara Hareven, "Newly-Weds and Family Extension: The First State of the Family Cycle in Providence, R.I., 1864–65, 1879–80," in *Family and Population in Nineteenth-Century America*, ed. Tamara Hareven and Maris Vinovskis (Princeton: Princeton University Press, 1978), pp. 179–205.

40 Virginia Yans-McLaughlin described joint residence as reciprocal assistance in the Italian neighborhood in Buffalo in *Family and Community*, pp. 64–67. John Bodnar, Roger Simon, and Michael Weber have argued that home ownership gave families increased ability to control their immediate environment and to provide housing for other family members. See Bodnar, Simon, and Weber, *Lives of Their Own: Blacks, Italians, and Poles in Pittsburgh, 1900–1960* (Urbana: University of Illinois Press, 1982), p. 154. Various historians have argued recently that the meaning of home ownership for working-class families was related to family concerns for stability rather than social mobility and a rise in status. See Daniel Luria, "Wealth, Capital and Power: The Social Meaning of Home Ownership," *Journal of Interdisciplinary History* 7 (Autumn 1976), pp. 261–82; Bodnar, Simon, and Weber, *Lives of Their Own*, pp. 153–83; Olivier Zunz, *The Changing Face of Inequality: Urbanization, Industrial Development, and Immigrants in Detroit, 1880–1920* (Chicago: University of Chicago Press, 1982), pp. 152–76.

41 Anna Frucht, 1978, Providence, RIJHSL. Iola Lombardi Ansuini, interviewed by Lola Marot in 1972, Long Coll., folder 4, box 175; interviewee born in Providence in 1904.

42 RIWB no. 231, interviewed by a family member in 1976. Interviewee born in Lucca, Italy, in 1897; moved to Providence in 1899. RIWB no.

400, interviewed by a family member in 1976. Interviewee born in Tova, Piccilli Province, Italy in 1894; moved to Providence in 1907. Gabaccia, "Sicilians in Space," p. 59.

43   RIWB no. 288, interviewed by a family member in 1976; interviewee born in Providence in 1905. RIWB no. 172, interviewed by a family member in 1973; interviewee born in Providence in 1905. RIWB no. 101, interviewed by a family member in 1973; interviewee born in Providence in 1908. Coleen L. Johnson has made a similar argument about the function of a sibling orientation in Italian-American families. See Johnson, "Sibling Solidarity: Its Origins and Functioning in Italian-American Families," *Journal of Marriage and the Family* 44 (February 1982), pp. 155–67. Elizabeth Pleck called this research to my attention. In addition to the role played by extra aunts and uncles, Robert Pascoe has argued that single male anarchist laborers livng amidst kin and *paesani* in crowded tenements in Boston's North End played a particular role in these families, providing an important "contervailing model" of an alternative analysis of American society to the young children growing up in the tenements. See Pascoe, "The Fear of the Radical Alien," paper presented at the Charles Warren Center, April 1983, pp. 17–18, to be part of Pascoe's forthcoming book, *Italian Labor, American Capital: The Italian Ambiente Within Urban America.*

44   In migration chains to Utica and Rochester, New York, and Kansas City, Missouri, John Briggs also found the majority of immigrants to be part of family- rather than village-based migration chains; see Briggs, *An Italian Passage,* p.75. See also Briggs's discussion of *campanilismo,* ibid., pp. 85–86, 90.

45   K. family interview, 15 December 1979, Newton, Mass. N. family interview, 2 September 1976, Providence, interviewed by Judith Smith; interviewee born in Providence in 1901. Carmela Maffei Mastronardi, interviewed by Janet Anthony Mastronardi in Cranston, Rhode Island, 17 April 1981, quoted in Janet Anthony Mastronardi, "Southern Italians in Federal Hill, Providence, Rhode Island: A Study in Cultural Persistence," Harvard University honors thesis, 1982, p. 48; N. family interview, 2 September 1976, Providence; Iola Lombardi Ansuini, 1972, Long. Coll. For other discussions of a female bias in kinship networks, see Cronin, *Sting of Change,* p. 80; Michael Young and Peter Wilmott, *Family and Kinship in East London* (1957; reprint, Middlesex, England: Penguin, 1968), chap. 3. See also Elizabeth Bott, *Family and Social Network* (1957; reprint, New York: Free Press, 1971); Carol Stack, *All Our Kin: Strategies for Survival in a Black Community* (New York: Harper and Row, 1974); S. Yanagisako, "Women-Centered Kin Networks in Urban Bilateral Kinship," *American Ethnologist* 5 (1977), pp. 207–25.

46   Italian Immigrant Woman—1920, interviewed by a family member in 1972, Long Coll., folder 7, box 175. Interviewee born in southern

Italy in 1896; moved to Providence ca. 1920. Filomena Daniello Villella, interviewed by Margaret M . Watkinson in 1972, Long Coll., folder 6, box 175. Interviewee born in Scafati, Naples, Italy in 1901; moved to Providence in 1902.

47   Liberato Dattolo, Bridgeport, interviewed by Vincent Frazzetta in 1939, WPA-Conn, box 23. Interviewee born in Monte Castel, Villina Province, 1899; moved to Bridgeport in 1914. CS, New Haven, interviewed in 1940, WPA-Conn, box 58. Interviewee born in Tauroggen, Lithuania in 1880; moved to New York City in 1900.

48   Filomena Daniello Villella, Long. Coll., folder 6, box 175; Fannie Savage Schindler, Long. Coll., tape. For more precise information on boarders' age and family status, see Judith E. Smith, "Remaking Their Lives: Italian and Jewish Immigrant Family, Work, and Community in Providence Rhode Island, 1900–1940," Ph.D. dissertation, Brown University, 1980, p. 155.

49   RIWB no. 1, interviewed by a family member in 1976. Interviewee born in Acri, Italy in 1899; moved to Westerly, R.I. in 1918. See also RIWB no. 232.

50   RIWB no. 101; Italian Immigrant Woman—1920, Long. Coll., folder 7, box 175. See also Ellen Ross, "Survival Networks: Women's Neighborhood Sharing in London Before World War I," *History Workshop* 15 (Spring 1983), pp. 4–27, esp. p. 5.

51   To compare the living situation of aging Providence immigrants with other populations of older Americans see Howard P. Chudacoff and Tamara K. Hareven, "From the Empty Nest to Family Dissolution: Life Course Transitions into Old Age," *Journal of Family History* 4 (Spring 1970), pp. 69–83; Daniel Scott Smith, "Life Course, Norms, and the Family Systems of Older Americans in 1900," *Journal of Family History* 4 (Fall 1979), pp. 285–98.

52   Cassarini, Saulino, Lanzieri, and Kanopky families, neighborhood data. For additional information on the proximity in 1940 of brothers and sisters who had at some point lived within two blocks of each other, see Smith, "Remaking Their Lives," p. 157.

53   John Briggs observed this same tendency in the Italian community in Monroe County, New York, which he explained as characteristic of an aging and increasingly stable community (Briggs, *An Italian Passage*, p. 112).

54   Sidney Goldstein and Kurt Mayer, *Metropolitanization and Population Change in Rhode Island*, Rhode Island Development Council Publication No. 3 (Providence: Planning Division, Rhode Island Council, State Planning Section, 1961), pp. 8–10, 34–52; Cohen, *Out of the Shadow*, p. 186.

55   In addition, nearly one-fourth of Italian and Jewish families seem to have left Providence altogether. These migrants were not individual transients; many of these people left Providence as they had arrived, as family groups. For these people, Providence seems to have been a

stopping point on their way to a place of more permanent settlement, a continuation of the migration process.

56　Kushner and Silverman families, neighborhood data; Chase family, neighborhood data; Costantino family; neighborhood data.

57　K. family interview, 1979, Newton, Mass. Elizabeth Bott has discussed the difference between the perception of neighbors in working-class and upwardly mobile middle-class areas. In working-class neighborhoods, families considered their neighbors to be similar to themselves; in upwardly mobile middle-class neighborhoods, families tended to view their neighbors as not particularly sharing common interests or experiences. See Bott, *Family and Social Network*, pp. 103–4.

58　There appears to be little research that has examined this phenomenon of single immigrant sons and daughters. One study by Patricia White has analyzed the data on single women in Boston. White used aggregate census data to show that in Boston in 1920, one-third of the American-born daughters of immigrants between the ages of thirty-five and forty-five were single. See White, "Family and Work Alternatives for Single Women: Boston, 1890–1930," paper presented at the Social Science History Association, October 1981, pp. 1–2. Hal Benenson brought this research to my attention. White's finding is supported by Niles Carpenter's 1927 observation in his census monograph that there existed higher rates of singleness among American-born sons and daughters of foreign-born parents than among native-born children of native-born parents, foreign-born children, and Afro-American children. See Carpenter, *Immigrants and Their Children, 1920* (Washington, D.C.: Government Printing Office, 1927), pp. 214, 216.

59　For a general discussion of this issue, see J. Hajnal, "European Marriage Patterns in Perspective," in *Population in History: Essays in Historical Demography*, ed. D. V. Glass and D. E. C. Eversley (Chicago: Aldine Publishing, 1965), pp. 101–37. See also the discussion of age of marriage in nineteenth- and twentieth-century southern Italy in Bell, *Fate and Honor, Family and Village*, pp. 78–108; Livi-Bacci, *A History of Italian Fertility*, particularly pp. 52–134.

60　Covello, *Social Backgrounds*, p. 201. RIWB no. 13, interviewed by a family member in 1974; interviewee born in Providence in 1924.

61　U.S. Census Bureau, *Historical Statistics of the United States* (Washington, D.C.: Government Printing Office, 1976), pp. 20–21; Ruth Milkman, "Women's Work and the Economic Crisis: Some Lessons from the Great Depression," in *A Heritage of Her Own*, ed. Nancy F. Cott and Elizabeth H. Pleck (New York: Simon and Schuster, 1979), p. 523.

62　Mrs. Q., Bridgeport, interviewed by P. K. Russo in 1939–40, WPA-Conn. Interviewee born in Hungary ca. 1880; moved to Bridgeport in 1904.

63   Rita, in *The Rosie Papers: Oral Histories of Twentieth Century Women*, ed. Laurie Crumpacker and Ann Marie Benfatto (Boston: Simmons College, 1979), p. 24. Interviewee born in the Boston area in 1909.
64   Anna Frucht, Providence, RIJHSL.
65   See the discussion of courtship and marriage in Sharon H. Strom, "Italian-American Women and Their Daughters in Rhode Island: The Adolescence of Two Generations," in *The Italian American Woman in North America*, ed. Betty B. Caroli, Robert F. Harney, and Lydio F. Tomasi (Toronto: Multicultural History Society of Ontario, 1978), pp. 194–95, 200–201. See also Cohen, *Out of the Shadow*, pp. 200–207, 224–27; Anzia Yezierska, *Bread Givers* (1925; reprint, New York: Braziller, 1975), pp. 37–110; Anna Frucht, Providence, RIJHSL. Jack Lapin, 1978, Providence, interviewed by Sonya Michel, RIJHSL. Interviewee born in 1898; moved to New Jersey in 1918. S. family interview, Cambridge, Mass., interviewed by Judith Smith, 9 September 1976; son born in Providence in 1939. S. family interview, Providence, interviewed by Judith Smith, 5 April 1977. Father born in Toronto in 1907; moved to Providence in 1908. R. family interview, Providence, interviewed by Judith Smith, 13 December 1977; mother born in Providence in 1892. M. family interview, Providence, interviewed by Judith Smith, 1 December 1975. Father born near Caserta, Italy in 1904; moved to Providence in 1913. K. family interview 1979, Newton, Mass.; Iola Lombardi Ansuini, Long. Coll., folder 4, box 175; RIWB no. 228, interviewed by a family member in 1975. Interviewee born in Pietra,Italy in1907; moved to Providence in 1911. RIWB no. 306, interviewed by a family member in 1978; interviewee born in Providence in 1918. To compare these courtships with courtships and marriage in middle-class white Anglo-Saxon Protestant families with a much greater orientation toward individual choice, see Ellen K. Rothman, *Hands and Hearts: A History of Courtship in America* (New York: Basic Books, 1984). For an analysis of the prescriptive literature on courtship and marriage, see Christina Simmons, "It's Okay When You're in Love: Sexuality in American Courtship, 1914–1941," paper presented at the Canadian Historical Association, 1977; idem, "Marriage in the Modern Manner: Sexual Radicalism and Reform, 1914–1941," Ph.D. dissertation, Brown University, 1982, pp. 105–49. Elizabeth Pleck has also analyzed the decline of parental authority for the American-born generation in the context of her discussion of family violence in "Challenges to Traditional Authority in Immigrant Families," in *The American Family in Social-Historical Perspective*, 3d ed., ed. Michael Gordon (New York: St. Martin's Press, 1983).
66   Bertha Brill, Providence, interviewed by Sonya Michel in 1978, RIJHSL. Interviewee born in Austria ca. 1890; moved to Brooklyn in the 1890s.

67   For a discussion of the tensions engendered by networks of domestic exchange, see Ross, "Survival Networks," pp. 15–18; Stack, *All Our Kin*, pp. 105–7, 113–17.

68   Cronin, *Sting of Change*, p. 115. See also Young and Wilmott, *Family and Kinship*, chap. 3.

69   The conflict between the American cultural ideal of independence and the ethnic culture's practice of mutual dependence on kin is described by Richard Sennett and Jonathan Cobb in *The Hidden Injuries of Class* (New York: Random House, 1973), pp.105–11. For a discussion of the resolution of this conflict by relegating the work of sustaining kin connections to women, see Yanagisako, "Women-Centered Kin Networks," pp. 207–25.

70   S. family interview, 1976, Cambridge, Mass.; S. family interview, 1977, Providence; Iola Lombardi Ansuini, Long Coll., folder 4, box 175.

CHAPTER FOUR   CIRCLES OF ASSISTANCE:
RECIPROCITY AND ASSOCIATIONAL LIFE

1   On reciprocity, see Marcel Mauss, *The Gift: Forms and Functions of Exchange in Archaic Societies* (1954; reprint, New York: W. W. Norton, 1967); Alvin Gouldner, *For Sociology: Renewal and Critique in Sociology Today* (London: Penguin, 1973), pp. 242–47; Carol Stack, *All Our Kin: Strategies for Survival in a Black Community* (New York: Harper and Row, 1974), chaps. 3, 6. See also James D. Smith, "Whatever Else You Might Need: A Study of Reciprocity in the Social Networks of a Community in Somerville, Massachusetts," B.A. honors thesis, Harvard University, 1979, pp. 9–13. Josef Barton has pointed out the connection between the expansion of kinship and the creation of mutual-benefit associations as parallel responses to newly created vulnerability in a market economy in late-nineteenth-century southern and eastern Europe; see Barton, "Eastern and Southern Europeans," in *Ethnic Leadership in America*, ed. John Higham (Baltimore: Johns Hopkins University Press, 1978), pp. 150–75, esp. pp. 154–60; idem, "Religion and Cultural Change in Czech Immigrant Communities, 1850–1920," in *Immigrants and Religion in Urban America*, ed. Randall M. Miller and Thomas D. Marzik (Philadelphia: Temple University Press, 1977), pp. 3–24, esp. pp. 9–12. Recent works on women's neighborhood sharing include Stack, *All Our Kin*; Ellen Ross, "Survival Networks: Women's Neighborhood Sharing in London Before World War I," *History Workshop* 15 (Spring 1983), pp. 4–27; Donna R. Gabaccia, *From Sicily to Elizabeth Street: Housing and Social Change Among Italian Immigrants, 1880–1930* (Albany: State University of New York Press, 1983), chaps. 3, 6. A separate women's culture has been described historically for middle-class women in the nineteenth century. See Carroll Smith-Rosenberg, "The Female

World of Love and Ritual: Relations Between Women in Nineteenth-Century America," *Signs* 1 (Autumn 1975), pp. 1–29; Nancy F. Cott, *The Bonds of Womanhood: Women's Sphere in New England, 1780–1835* (New Haven: Yale University Press, 1977); Mary F. Ryan, *Cradle of the Middle Class: The Family in Oneida County, New York, 1780–1865* (New York: Cambridge University Press, 1981); Ellen DuBois, Mari Jo Buhle, Temma Kaplan, Gerda Lerner, and Carroll Smith-Rosenberg, "Politics and Culture in Women's History: A Symposium," *Feminist Studies* 6 (Spring 1980), pp. 24–64. Recent attempts to apply the concept of women's culture to the historical situation of working-class women include: Temma Kaplan, "Female Consciousness and Collective Action: The Case of Barcelona, 1910–1918," *Signs* 7 (Spring 1982), pp. 545–66; Ardis Cameron, "Bread and Roses Revisited: Women's Culture and Working-Class Activism in the Lawrence Strike, 1912," in *Women in Twentieth-Century Labor History*, ed. Ruth Milkman (London: Routledge and Kegan Paul, forthcoming).

2   Differing interpretations of the meaning of mutual-benefit associations in Europe and in American cities are offered by Humbert S. Nelli, *The Italians in Chicago, 1880–1930: A Study in Ethnic Mobility* (New York: Oxford University Press, 1970), pp. 156–200; idem, "European Immigrants and Urban America," in *The Urban Experience*, ed. Raymond Mohl and James Richardson (Belmont, Calif.: Wadsworth Publishing Co., 1973), pp. 61–78, esp. 64–65, 67; Josef Barton, *Peasants and Strangers: Italians, Roumanians, and Slovaks in an American City, 1880–1950* (Cambridge: Harvard University Press, 1975), chaps. 4, 7; John Briggs, *An Italian Passage: Immigrants to Three American Cities, 1890–1930* (New Haven: Yale University Press, 1978), chaps. 2, 7.

3   On popular religious fraternities, see John Bossy, "The Counter-Reformation and the People of Catholic Europe," *Past and Present* 47 (May 1970), pp. 58–60. On the *maestranze*, see Briggs, *An Italian Passage*, p. 285 no. 4. For the numbers of mutual-benefit associations in Italy in the late-ninteenth century, see Edwin Fenton, "Immigrants and Unions, A Case Study: Italians and American Labor, 1870–1920," Ph.D. dissertation, Harvard University, 1957, p. 15; Donald Bell, "Worker Culture and Worker Politics: The Experience of an Italian Town, 1880–1915," *Social History* 3 (January 1978), p. 7; Samuel J. Surace, *Ideology, Economic Change, and the Working Classes: The Case of Italy* (Berkeley and Los Angeles: University of California Press, 1966), pp. 98, 125. Figures for the spread of mutual-benefit associations in the southern regions come from Briggs, *An Italian Passage*, pp. 17–19. See also Barton, *Peasants and Strangers*, pp. 64–65; Phyllis Williams, *South Italian Folkways in Europe and America* (1938; reprint, New York: Russell and Russell, 1969), pp. 187–88. An alternative analysis of the functions of mutual-benefit associations has been made by anthropologists and sociologists studying Sicily, who have argued that mutual-benefit associations were important personal alliances or factions linking persons of differing status into flexible

groups competing for political power, "respect," and control of
economic resources. See Anton Blok, *The Mafia of a Sicilian Village,
1860–1960* (New York: Harper and Row, 1974), and Jane Schneider
and Peter Schneider, *Culture and Political Economy in Western Sicily* (New
York: Academic Press 1976). This argument and these references were
cited by Donna Gabaccia, "Review of *An Italian Passage* by John
Briggs," *International Labor and Working-Class History* 16 (1979), pp. 98–
99.

4   Barton, *Peasants and Strangers*, pp. 66–67; Briggs, *An Italian Passage*,
pp. 18–20, 30–31; Dennish Mack Smith, *A History of Sicily: Modern
Sicily After 1713* (New York: Viking, 1968), p. 485; Surace, *Ideology,
Economic Change, and the Working Classes*, pp. 107–9.

5   *Statuto delle societa degli operai di Villarose* (Castrogiovanni, 1888),
quoted in Briggs, *An Italian Passage*, p. 22. Mary Ann Clawson has
argued that fraternal associations were linked historically with the
assertion of kinship as a significant social bond. See Clawson,
"Brotherhood, Class, and Patriarchy: Fraternalism in Europe and
America," Ph.D. dissertation, SUNY Stoneybrook, 1980, chap. 1;
idem, "Early Modern Fraternalism and the Patriarchal Family,"
Feminist Studies 6 (Summer 1980), pp. 368–91. For membership of
mutual-benefit societies, see Briggs, *An Italian Passage*, pp. 18, 20;
Surace, *Idealogy, Economic Change, and the Working Classes*, pp. 107,
113.

6   Briggs, *An Italian Passage*, p. 20; Barton, *Peasants and Strangers*, p. 68;
idem, "Eastern and Southern Europeans," pp. 154–55.

7   Leonard Covello, *The Social Background of the Italo-American Schoolchild*
(1944; reprint, Leiden: E. J. Brill, 1967), pp. 133–34; Charlotte
Chapman, *Milocca: A Sicilian Village* (1935; reprint, Cambridge, Mass.:
Schenkman, 1971), p. 146; Barton, *Peasants and Strangers*, p. 69;
Fenton, "Immigrants and Unions," p. 28; John Briggs, personal
correspondance with author, 27 November 1983; Surace, *Ideology,
Economic Change, and the Working Classes*, pp. 100–101, 107–8.

8   I. M. Rubinow, "Economic Conditions of the Jews in Russia," in U.S.
Congress, Senate, *Report of the Immigration Commission: Emigration
Conditions in Europe*, 61st Cong., 3d sess., Senate document 748
(Washington, D.C.: Government Printing Office, 1911), pp. 309–10;
Ezra Mendelsohn, *Class Struggle in the Pale: The Formative Years of the
Jewish Workers' Movement in Tsarist Russia* (Cambridge: Cambridge
University Press, 1970), pp. 7–8.

9   Mendelsohn, *Class Struggle in the Pale*, p. 42; Rubinow, "Economic
Conditions," pp. 309–10.

10   Mark Zborowski and Elizabeth Herzog, *Life Is with People: The Culture
of the Shtetl* (1952; reprint, New York: Schocken, 1962), pp. 202–10.
See also Rubinow, "Economic Conditions," pp. 333–36; Rose
Cohen, *Out of the Shadow* (New York: G. H. Doran, 1918), pp. 192–
93.

11   I. B. Singer, "The Satin Coat," in *A Day of Pleasure: Stories of a Boy Growing Up in Warsaw* (New York: Farrar, Straus, and Giroux, 1969), p. 147. One Jewish immigrant whose father was a blacksmith recalled that the male-only parties arranged by her father's burial society were a central component of his social life; see KG, New Haven, interviewed in 1939 by Rahel Mittelstein, WPA-Conn, box 61. Interviewee born in Orlov, near Pobelov, Russia, in 1891; moved to New Haven in 1921.

12   Irving Howe, *The World of Our Fathers* (New York: Harcourt Brace Jovanovich, 1976), pp. 15–24; Mendelsohn, *Class Struggle in the Pale*, pp. 41–44.

13   Mendelsohn, *Class Struggle in the Pale*, pp. 63–68, 82–115; Rubinow, "Economic Conditions" pp. 322–24; Mendelsohn, *Class Struggle in the Pale*, pp. 109–10.

14   On early Italian mutual-benefit societies in Cleveland, see Barton, *Peasants and Strangers, pp. 70–71*, 73–75; for early mutual-benefit societies in Rochester and Utica, New York, see Briggs, *An Italian Passage*, pp. 141–51. On Providence, see Ubaldo Pesaturo, *Italo-Americans of Rhode Island* (Providence: Visitor Publishing Co., 1936), p. 25; "Active Fraternal Life in Little Italy," *Providence Journal*, 21 December 1919, sec. 5, p. 5. The Bridgeport immigrant quoted was Pasquale Cruci, Bridgeport, interviewed in 1938 by Vincent Frazzetta, WPA-Conn, box 23. Interviewee born in Sassano, Coligilina Province, Salerno, in 1859; moved to New York in 1882. For an argument concerning the timing of the organization of mutual-benefit associatios, see Briggs, *An Italian Passage*, p. 142.

15   William MacDonald, "Population," in *A Modern City: Providence, Rhode Island and Its Activities*, ed. William Kirk (Chicago: University of Chicago Press, 1909), pp. 47–48; Pesaturo, *Italo-Americans*, p. 15–34; "Active Fraternal Life in Little Italy," p. 5; "Provincial Societies on the Wane But Still Active," *Evening Bulletin*, 4 March 1936, p. 19; "Italian Provincial Groups Give Way to Nationalism," *Evening Bulletin*, 16 March 1936, p. 15.

16   "Mutual Benefit Prime Aim Organizations," *Evening Bulletin*, 6 March 1936, p. 19; "In Honor of the Madonna," *Providence Journal*, 20 September 1909, p. 12; "Italians Cross Town Line to get Permit," *Providence Journal*, 2 October 1909, p. 8; "Italians Celebrate: Federal Hill Alight," *Providence Journal*, 16 July 1911, p. 2; "St. Rocco's Feast Attracts Crowds," *Providence Journal*, 21 August 1911, p. 7; "Società Arcese Typical," *Evening Bulletin*, 11 March 1936, p. 16.

17   Bessie Bloom, "Jewish Life in Providence," (1910), reprinted in *Rhode Island Jewish Historical Notes* 5 (1970), pp. 390–91; Rhode Island Historical Preservation Commission, *South Providence: Statewide Historical Preservation Report P-P-2* (1978), pp. 38–39; Rhode Island Historical Preservation Commission, *Smith Hill, Providence: Statewide Historical Preservation Report P-P-4* (1980), p. 11; personal corre-

spondence from Beryl Segal, 8 December 1977; Beryl Segal, "Congregation Sons of Zion of Providence, Rhode Island—The Orms Street Synagogue," *Rhode Island Jewish Historical Notes* 4 (1965), p. 239, 248–49, 251; "Chartered Organizations," *Rhode Island Jewish Historical Notes* 2 (1956), pp. 23 –24, 28, 21–65. Associational life in Providence in the early years appears to have differed from that described in Portland, Oregon by William Toll and in Columbus, Ohio by Marc Lee Raphael. In Portland, Oregon, the German origins of the Jewish community and the mercantile orientation of Jewish residents led to an associational life with different kinds of concerns and a different history. For example, there were not enough Jews from individual towns and provinces to form *landsmenshaften*. See William Toll, *The Making of an Ethnic Middle Class: Portland Jewry Over Four Generations* (Albany: State University of New York Press, 1982); Marc Lee Raphael, *Jews and Judaism in a Midwestern Community: Columbus, Ohio, 1840–1975* (Columbus: Ohio Historical Society, 1979). Both of these studies combine a fuller institutional history of their respective Jewish communities with an analysis of occupational and social mobility of Jewish residents.

18   "Scriptures Moved to New Structure," *Providence Journal*, 13 July 1893, as quoted in Beryl Segal, "Congregation Sons of Zion," pp. 246–47; "Sons of Jacob Move," *Providence Journal*, 17 September 1906, p. 5.

19   "Chartered Organizations," pp. 21–78; Manya Kleinburd Baghdadi, "Community and the Providence Jews," *Rhode Island Jewish Historical Notes* 6 (1971), pp. 56–75, esp. p. 58. On the Workmen's Circle, see Melech Epstein, *Jewish Labor in the U.S.A.: An Industrial, Political, and Cultural History of the Jewish Labor Movement, 1882–1914* (1950; reprint, New York: Ktav Publishing House, 1979), pp. 298–317; Judah Shapiro, *The Friendly Society: A History of the Workmen's Circle* (New York: Media Judaica, 1970). On the Workmen's Circle in Providence, see "Local Chapters of National Jewish Organizations, 1898–1965," *Rhode Island Jewish Historical Notes* 4 (1966), p. 490; Baghdadi, "Community and the Providence Jews," p. 58; interview with Beryl Segal by Paul Buhle, Providence, 1977.

20   See Clawson, "Brotherhood, Class, and Patriarchy," chap. 1; idem, "Early Modern Fraternalism and the Patriarchal Family," pp. 368–91. For the argument that family chains were at the base of village chains, see John S. MacDonald and Leatrice MacDonald, "Urbanization, Ethnic Groups, and Social Segmentation," *Social Research* 29 (1962), pp. 335–46; idem, "Chain Migration, Ethnic Neighborhood Formation, and Social Networks," *Milbank Memorial Fund Quarterly* 42 (1964), pp. 82, 88–91; Virginia Yans-McLaughlin, *Family and Community: Italian Immigrants in Buffalo, 1880–1930* (Ithaca: Cornell University Press, 1978), pp. 57–60; Briggs, *An Italian Passage*, pp. 72–75; Gabaccia, *From Sicily to Elizabeth Street*, pp. 57–59. For anecdotal

material on the relationship between mutual-benefit associations and kinship, see JM, Somerville, Mass., interviewed by James D. Smith, August 1978; CS, New Haven, interviewed by Rahel Mittelstein in 1940, WPA-Conn, box 58. Interviewee born in Tauroggen, Lithuania, in 1880; moved to New York in 1900. Wolfe Baron, New Haven, interviewed by Rahel Mittelstein in 1939, WPA-Conn, box 58. Interviewee born in Leipāja, Lettwija (Lithuania) in 1879; moved to Connecticut in 1899. Anthropologists have also argued that friendship may have functioned as an escape from the obligations of kinship. See Eric Wolfe, "Kinship, Friendship, and Patron-Client Relationships in Complex Societies," in *The Social Anthropology of Complex Societies*, ed. M. Banton (New York: Praeger, 1966), pp. 1–21; Stanley H. Brandes,"Social Structure and Interpersonal Relations in Navanogal (Spain)," *American Anthropologist* 75 (1973), pp. 750–65.

21 M. family interview, 1 December 1975, Providence, interviewed by Judith E. Smith. A. born near Caserta, Italy, in 1904, moved to Providence in 1913; M. born in Italy in 1907, moved to Providence in 1909; V. born in Providence ca. 1910. Cohen, *Out of the Shadow*, pp. 196–97.

22 Wolfe Baron, WPA-Conn, box 58. For evidence of southern Italian women's associations in Providence, see women's mutual-benefit associations affiliated with the Catholic church, mentioned by Peter Bardaglio, "The Religious and Family Life of Italians in Providence, 1890–1930: A Study in Cultural Persistence," undergraduate honors thesis, Brown University, 1975; lists of Italian women's associations in Pesaturo, *Italo-Americans of Rhode Island*, editions published in 1936 and 1940, Rosa Marie Levis papers, Schlesinger Library. For Providence Jewish women's organizations, see "Chartered Organizations," pp. 21–78; "Local Chapters of National Jewish Organizations," pp. 490–93; Sidney Goldstein and Calvin Goldscheider, *Jewish-Americans: Three Generations in a Jewish Community* (Englewood Cliffs, N.J.: Prentice-Hall, 1968), pp. 208–211. For anecdotal material on conflict between men and women who outnumber them in a Sicilian mutual-benefit society loosely affiliated with the church, see Joseph Caruso, *The Priest* (1956; reprint, New York: Arno Press, 1978), pp. 55–60, 127–34, 149. For a discussion of German and eastern European Jewish women's activities in benevolent and Jewish women's civic associations in Portland, see Toll, *Making of an Ethnic Middle Class*, chap. 2; idem, "The Female Life Cycle and the Measure of Jewish Social Change: Portland, Oregon, 1880–1930," *American Jewish History* 72 (March 1983), pp. 309–32. For eastern European Jewish women's activities in Columbus, Ohio in this period, see Raphael, *Jews and Judaism*, pp. 211–15.

23 "Chartered Organizations," pp. 21–78. For the description of the Holy Rosary Society in Bridgeport, see Marie Zambiello, Bridgeport, interviewed by Emil Napolitano in 1939, WPA-Conn, box 23.

Interviewee born in Airola, Benevento, ca. 1867; moved to Bridgeport in 1903. For other Italian women's mutual-benefit associations in Bridgeport, see Maria Frazzetta, Bridgeport, interviewed by Vincent Frazzetta in 1939, WPA-Conn, box 23. Interviewee born in Ragousa, Catania, Sicily, in 1875; moved to Bridgeport in 1907. See also sixty-eight-year-old Italian housewife, Bridgeport, interviewed by Vincent Frazzetta, 1938–40, WPA-Conn, box 22; Housewife No. 2, interviewed by Vincent Frazzetta, 1938–40, WPA-Conn, box 22.

24	For arguments that nineteenth-century American women's activities in voluntary associations broadened their self-definition, see Cott, *Bonds of Womanhood*, chap. 4; Carroll Smith-Rosenberg, "Beauty, the Beast, and the Militant Woman: A Case Study in Sex Roles and Social Stress in Jacksonian America," *American Quarterly* (1971), pp. 562–84; Mary P. Ryan, "The Power of Women's Networks: A Case Study of Female Moral Reform in Antebellum America," *Feminist Studies* 4 (Spring 1979), pp. 66–86; Susan Porter Benson, "Business Head and Sympathizing Hearts: The Women of the Providence Employment Society, 1837–1858," *Journal of Social History* 12 (Winter 1978), pp. 302–12. For an argument that participation in Jewish women's organizations changed Jewish women's relationship to home and family, see Riva Krut, "The Women of the Johannesburg Jewish Ladies Communal League," typescript, University of London, 1984. For anecdotal material on the tensions between organizational demands and family responsibility, see Sonya Michel, "Family, Community, and Institutions: The Jewish Orphanage of Rhode Island, 1909–1942," *Rhode Island Jewish Historical Notes* 7 (1977), pp. 385–400; Eleanor Horowitz, "Old Bottles, Rags, Junk: The Story of the Jews of South Providence," *Rhode Island Jewish Historical Notes* 7 (1976), pp. 189–257; Fannie Savage Schindler, interviewed by Jill Grossberg in 1972, Long Coll., tape. Interviewee born in Bialystok, Russia in 1889; moved to New York in 1900. See also Charlotte Baum, Paula Hyman, and Sonya Michel, *The Jewish Woman in America* (New York: Dial, 1976), chaps. 6, 7, esp. pp. 211–14.

25	RIWB no. 231, interviewed by a family member in 1976. Interviewee born in Lucca, Italy, in 1877; moved to Providence in 1899.

26	Rhode Island Historical Preservation Commission, *South Providence*, pp. 38–39; Rhode Island Historical Preservation Commission, *Smith Hill*, p. 11; "Chartered Organizations," pp. 21–65.

27	"Divorce Laws and Jewish Religion," *Providence Journal*, 24 April 1906, p. 14.

28	On southern Italian Catholicism in southern Italy and the United States, see Rudolph Vecoli, "Prelates and Peasants: Italian Immigrants and the Catholic Church," *Journal of Social History* 2 (1969), pp. 217–68; idem, "Cult and Occult in Italian-American Culture: The Persistence of a Religious Heritage," in *Immigrants and Religion in Urban America*, ed. Randall M. Miller and Thomas D. Marzik (Philadelphia:

Temple University Press, 1977), pp. 25–47; Williams, *South Italian Folkways*, pp. 135–45.

29 Historically the relationship between fraternities and the church had been one of conflict. Asserting the continuing authority of kin relations and organizationally independent from the church, early modern fraternities were attacked by the post-Tridentine church. See Clawson, "Brotherhood, Class, and Patriarchy," chap. 1; Bossy, "Counter-Reformation," pp. 58–60. Charles Borromeo, archbishop of Milan from 1564 to 1584, was particularly concerned with bringing Milanese fraternities under a regime of episcopal authorization and supervision. See Bossy,' 'Counter-Reformation," pp. 59–60, 62, 65. My analysis of conflict between southern Italian parishioners and northern Italian priests in Providence owes a great debt to Peter Bardaglio's 1975 Brown University undergraduate honors thesis, "The Religious and Family Life of Italians in Providence, 1890–1930: A Study in Cultural Persistence." In developing my own analysis of mutual-benefit associations as the organizational form of this protest, I have used some of the archival materials Bardaglio found and translated. Victor Greene has discussed similar conflicts within Slavic parishes in *For God and Country: The Rise of Polish and Lithuanian Ethnic Consciousness in America, 1860–1910* (Madison: State Historical Society of Wisconsin, 1975). Providence southern Italian immigrants did not participate actively in church rituals. For figures on minimal participation in Holy Communion at Easter and weak financial support of the parish, see Bardaglio, "Religious and Family Life of Italians in Providence," pp. 44–46, 49–58.

30 Letter dated 23 September 1906, Società di Mutuo Soccorso Maria SS Del Carmine to Bishop Harkins, Holy Ghost Church, Providence, Correspondence/Documents, 1896–1911, Providence Diocesan Archives, quoted in Bardaglio, "Religious and Family Life of Italians in Providence," pp. 85–86; Harkins diary, 24 September and 10 October 1906, Providence Diocesan Archives, quoted in Bardaglio, ibid., p. 86.

31 "North End Italians Rise Against Priest,"*Providence Journal*, 26 August 1907, p. 1.

32 "Christianizing of Flags Witnessed by Many," *Providence Journal*, 18 April 1910, p. 2.

33 "Italians Bless Flag Despite Bishop's Ban," *Providence Journal*, 25 April 1910, p. 1.

34 Reverend John F. Sullivan, "A Retrospect and an Appreciation of the Silver Jubilee of Monsignor Bove," in *A Historical Sketch of St. Ann's Italian Parish, Providence, Rhode Island*, by Reverend Vincent F. Kienberger (Providence, 1925), pp. 6–8, quoted by Peter Bardaglio, "Italian Immigrants and the Catholic Church in Providence, 1890–1930," *Rhode Island History* 34 (1975) pp. 47–57; "Italians Aroused by Priest's Attack," *Providence Journal*, 4 December 1918, p. 5; "Catholic

Church Antagonism Denied," *Providence Journal*, 8 December 1918, p. 5; "Father Bove Explains His Attitude Towards Sons of Italy Order," *Providence Journal*, 10 December 1918, p. 3; "Dante Alighieri to Join Order Sons of Italy," *Providence Journal*, 10 December 1918, p. 3; "Sons of Italy Initiate Three Italian Societies," *Providence Journal*, 30 December 1918, p. 12.

35   Letter dated 18 June 1920, Harry Bellinfante to Bishop Harkins, Holy Ghost Church, Providence, Correspondence/Documents, 1918–21, Providence Diocesan Archives; letter dated 11 July 1920, Anonymous to Bishop Hickey, Rev. Domenico Belliotti files, Providence Diocesan Archives; undated petition to remove Belliotti with 1,175 women's signatures, Holy Ghost Church, Providence, Correspondence/ Documents, 1918–21, Providence Diocesan Archives; undated letter, Irene Battista et al. to Bishop Hickey, Holy Ghost Church, Providence, Correspondence/Documents, 1918–21, Providence Diocesan Archives; undated letter, Enrico Monti et al. to Bishop Hickey, Correspondence/Documents, 1887, folder 5, Providence Diocesan Archives; letter dated 24 July 1920, Antonio Ciavaglia, secretary of the Holy Name Society and the Grand Committee to Bishop Hickey, Holy Ghost Church, Providence, Correspondence/Documents, 1918– 21, Providence Diocesan Archives. All of the above sources quoted in Bardaglio, "Religious and Family Life of Italians in Providence," pp. 87–91. See also ibid., pp. 91–93.

36   "Priest's Removal Believed Sought," *Providence Journal*, 14 October 1920, p. 4; "Police Make Seven Arrests at Church," *Providence Journal*, 8 November 1920, p. 3; letter dated 14 January 1921, Mauro M. Corona, Salvatore del Prete, and Domenico A. Ionata with 626 additional signatures from the Federal Hill area to Bishop Hickey, Holy Ghost Church, Providence, Correspondence/Documents, 1918– 21, Providence Diocesan Archives; letter dated 8 Februrary 1921, Mauro M. Corona, Salvatore del Prete, and Domenico A. Ionata to Rev. P. A. Foley, chancellor of the Providence diocese, Holy Ghost Church, Providence, Correspondence/Documents, 1918–21, Providence Diocesan Archives; letter dated 24 February 1921, Daniele Ionata, to Bishop Hickey, Holy Ghost Church, Providence, Correspondence/Documents, 1918–21, Providence Diocesan Archives, letters dated 19 September 1921, Daniele Ionata, president of the Holy Name of Jesus Society, et al. to Cardinal Donata Sbarretti, prefect of the Congregation of the Council, Rev. Vincenzo Vicari File, folder 2, Providence Diocesan Archives. All of the above sources quoted in Bardaglio, "Religious and Family Life of Italians in Providence," pp. 97–103.

37   Bardaglio, "Religious and Family Life of Italians in Providence," pp. 106–7. For an official church history of these events, see Reverend Flaminio Parenti's account of these years in "Parish of the Holy Ghost, Providence, Rhode Island," in *Italo-Americans in Rhode Island*,

by Ubaldo Pesaturo (Providence: Visitor Publishing Co., 1936), pp. 37–41, and Reverend Charles Sasso's biography of Father Antonio Bove, ibid., pp. 42–43. For a modest rise in church participation of the children's generation, see Bardaglio, "Religious and Family Life of Italians in Providence," pp. 43–62.

38 Stanley Aronowitz, *False Promises: The Shaping of Working-Class Consciousness* (New York: McGraw-Hill, 1973), pp. 151–52.

39 For preemigration occupations of Italian immigrants, see Robert Foerster, *The Italian Emigration of Our Times* (Cambridge: Harvard University Press, 1919), p. 531; for the preemigration occupations of Jewish immigrants, see Simon Kuznets, "Immigration of Russian Jews to the United States: Background and Structure," *Perspectives in American History* 9 (1975), pp. 72–77, 100–112. For occupations of Italian and Jewish immigrants in Providence in 1905, see Rhode Island Bureau of Industrial Statistics, *Twenty-Second Annual Report, 1908* (Providence: E. L. Freeman Co., 1909), pp. 220–21, 224–25.

40 Lester Burrell Shippee, "Some Aspects of the Population of Providence," in *Report of the Commissioner of Labor to the General Assembly for the Years 1916–1919* (Providence: E. L. Freeman, 1920), pp. 227–28, 278; personal correspondence from Beryl Segal, 8 December 1977. On Italian socialists in Providence see Fenton, "Immigrants and Unions," pp. 158–63; Paul Buhle, "Italian-American Radicals and Labor in Rhode Island, 1905–1930, *Radical History Review* 17 (Spring 1978), pp. 121–51. Various activities of Jewish socialists are recorded in the Providence Socialist newspaper, *Labor Advocate*, published between 1913 and 1915; see also interview with Beryl Segal by Paul Buhle, Providence, 1977.

41 "Directory of Trade Unions," in *Rhode Island Bureau of Industrial Statistics, Reports*, vols. for the years 1905 through 1917. For the relationship of Italian immigrants to the Rhode Island labor movement, see Buhle, "Italian American Radicals," pp. 121–51; for general overview, see Fenton, "Immigrants and Unions."

42 "1600 Building Laborers in Providence Quit: Ask More Pay," *Providence Journal*, 1 May 1910, p. 1; "First May Day Celebration a Success," *Providence Journal*, 2 May 1910, p. 1. For a more explicit reference to Providence Italian anticlericalism, see "Italian Paper Insults Church," *Providence Journal*, 10 April 1909, p. 2, in which Father Belliotti admitted that he wasn't able to persuade many shopkeepers to stop selling the paper, which attacked the Catholic church, the pope, and leading prelates, because "it sells well among the socialists and anti-Catholics." In one industrial town in northern Italy in this period, anticlericalism was the basis of an alliance between skilled workers and factory workers in the process of developing class-conscious politics. See Bell, "Worker Culture and Worker Politics."

43 "Striking Laborers Fight With the Police," *Providence Journal*, 5 May 1910, p. 2; "United Carpenters Will Join Strikers," *Providence Journal*,

7 May 1910, p. 5; "Strikers Victorious; Agreement is Made," *Providence Journal*, 8 May 1910, p. 3; "Labor Men Jubilant: Agreement is Signed," *Providence Journal*, 9 May 1910, p. 3. On the 1902 streetcar strike, see Scott Molloy, "Rhode Island Communities and the Carmen's Strike," *Radical History Review* 17 (Spring 1978), pp. 75–98. For a general discussion of the struggle for unionization among unskilled Italian building laborers, see Fenton, "Immigrants and Unions," pp. 198–258, esp. pp. 219–57.

44 On the tailors strike in 1913, see "IWW Holds Up Local Merchants," *Providence Journal*, 30 March 1913, p. 3; "IWW Persists in Coercive Move," *Providence Journal*, 31 March 1913, p. 5; "IWW Strike Move Weak," *Providence Journal*, 1 April 1913, p. 1; "Merchants Laugh at IWW Demands," *Providence Journal*, 2 April 1913, p. 1; "Permit to Parade Refused IWW," *Providence Journal*, 3 April 1913, p. 1; "Union Leaders Here Assist Tailors," *Providence Journal*, 4 April 1913, p. 1; "200 Strikers Back to Benches," *Providence Journal*, 5 April 1913, p. 6; "CFU, AFL Critical of IWW Methods," *Providence Journal*, 7 April 1913, pp. 1, 11; and more sympathetic coverage of the strike in the socialist paper, the *Labor Advocate*, 9 and 30 March 1913, 6 and 13 April 1913; Buhle, "Italian-American Radicals," pp. 133–36. On the jewelry workers' 1917 strike, see "Union Jewelers at Ostby and Barton to Strike," *Providence Journal*, 22 May 1917, p. 14; "Jewelry Strike Meeting Results in Five Arrests," *Providence Journal*, 26 May 1917, p. 12; "Help to Win the Strike in Ostby and Barton's Shop, Providence, Rhode Island," *Jewelry Workers International Bulletin*, May 1917; "Providence, Rhode Island and Attleboro, Mass.: An Attraction for the Wandering Jew-elry Maker," *Jewelry Workers International Bulletin*, May 1917; "Report on the Ostby and Barton Strike," *Jewelry Workers International Bulletin*, November–December 1917; "Providence—The Black Hole of Calcutta," *Jewelry Workers International Bulletin*, October 1918; "Address of Frank Morris," *Jewelry Workers International Bulletin*, December 1921; interview with the Jewelry Workers International Union organizers who had been in Providence in 1917, National Archives, Industrial and Social Division, Correspondence folder, Record Group 102, box 979; Buhle, "Italian-American Radicals," p. 141. Paul Buhle provided me with these references to the *Jewelry Workers International Bulletin*. In contrast to the experience in Providence, workers in Waterbury, Connecticut were able to work together in two massive general strikes in that city in 1919 and 1920. Cooperation between ethnic groups may have been facilitated by the existence in that city of a tight-knit local industrial elite, with a few families controlling all industry and employment. See Jeremy Brecher, Jerry Lombardi, and Jan Stackhouse, ed., *Brass Valley: The Story of Working People's Lives and Stuggles in an American Industrial Region* (Philadelphia: Temple University Press, 1982), pp. 78–89.

45 "Paraders Fly Red Flag; Fight Police," *Providence Journal*, 16 Septem-

ber 1912, p. 1. Samuel Baily has attempted to analyze the factors that encouraged a movement of mutual-benefit associations to support working-class organization. He has argued that in Buenos Aires, Argentina, the high percentage of skilled workers among the immigrating population and the impact these workers had on the less-well-developed Argentinian economy allowed them to influence the mutualist movement in the direction of support for trade unionism. See Samuel Baily, "The Adjustment of Italian Immigrants in Buenos Aires and New York City, 1870–1914," *American Historical Review* 88 (April 1983), pp. 281–305; idem, "The Italians and the Development of Organized Labor in Argentina, Brazil, and the United States, 1880–1914," *Journal of Social History* 3 (Winter 1969), pp. 123–34.

46 For discussions of the Jewish food riots in New York City in 1902, see Herbert Gutman, "Work, Culture, and Society in Industrializing America, 1815–1919," in *Work, Culture, and Society in Industrializing America: Essays in American Working-Class and Social History* (New York: Vintage, 1977), pp. 61–63; Howe, *World of Our Fathers*, pp 124–25; Paula Hyman, "Immigrant Women and Consumer Protest: New York City Kosher Women's Meat Boycott of 1902," *American Jewish History* 70 (1980), pp. 91–105. Elizabeth Ewen discusses Jewish food riots in New York City in 1902 and 1917 in *Immigrant Women and the Land of Dollars, 1890–1930* (New York: Pantheon, forthcoming). For an interpretation of food riots in eighteenth-century England, see E. P. Thompson, "The Moral Economy of the English Crowd in Eighteenth Century England," *Past and Present* 50 (1971), pp. 76–136. For a discussion of women's special relationship to bread riots, see Sheila Rowbotham, *Women, Resistence, and Revolution: A History of Women and Revolution in the Modern World* (New York: Pantheon, 1972), pp. 102–4; Louise A. Tilly and Joan W. Scott, *Women, Work, and Family* (New York: Holt, Rinehart, and Winston, 1978), pp. 55–56; Olwen Hufton, "Women in Revolution, 1789–1796," *Past and Present* 53 (1971), pp. 94–95.

47 "Jewish Women Put Ban on Kosher Meat," *Providence Journal*, 22 June 1910, p. 1; "Jewish Women Here Picket Kosher Shops," *Providence Journal*, 23 June 1910, p. 1; "Jewish Women Push Kosher Butcher War," *Providence Journal*, 24 June 1910, p. 3; personal correspondence from Beryl Segal, 8 December 1977. For demands of Dvinsk domestic servants and Kishinev shop workers, see I. M. Rubinow, "Economic Conditions of the Jews in Russia," Department of Commerce and Labor, *Bulletin of the Bureau of Labor* 72 (1907), pp. 562–66.

48 "Italians Protest High Food Prices," *Providence Journal*, 23 August 1914, p. 5; "Federal Hill Mob Wrecks Four Stores," *Providence Journal*, 30 August 1914, p. 1; "Eighteen Hurt in Food Riot On Federal Hill," *Providence Journal*, 31 August 1914, p. 1; "Conference Halts Food Price War," Providence Journal, 1 September 1914, p. 1;

"La Revolta," *L'Ecco*, 5 September 1914 (Paul Buhle translated this editorial). See also "Twenty-three Arrests Mark Federal Hill Riot," *Providence Journal*, 8 September 1914, p. 1; "Alledged Rioter Gets Jail Term," *Providence Journal*, 12 September 1914, sec. 2, p. 9; articles on the Federal Hill riot in the *Labor Advocate*, 5 and 12 September 1914.

49   On age segregation, see Howard P. Chudacoff, "The Life Course of Women: Age and Age Consciousness, 1865–1915," *Journal of Family History* 5 (Fall 1980), pp. 274–92; idem, "Age Consciousness and Age Grading in American Society," paper presented at the Social Science History Association, 1982. On the Catholic church's appeal to the children of immigrants, see Bardaglio, "Religious and Family Life of Italians in Providence," pp. 43–62; see also Barton, *Peasants and Strangers*, pp. 163–69, 173. On the transformation of the synagogue, see Goldstein and Goldscheider, *Jewish-Americans*, pp. 175–78. See also Deborah Dash Moore, *At Home in America: Second Generation New York Jews* (New York: Columbia University Press, 1981), pp. 123–147; Jeffrey S. Gurock, *When Harlem Was Jewish, 1870–1930* (New York: Columbia University Press, 1979), pp. 114–36. Gurock also discusses the emergence of new Jewish organizations to meet the needs of the children's generation; see pp. 86–113, esp. pp. 92–93.

50   The tensions between an orientation toward mutual benefit and a commitment to Americanization and/or philanthropy within the middle-class order B'nai Brith are described by Deborah Dash Moore, *B'nai Brith and the Challenge of Ethnic Leadership* (Albany: State University of New York Press, 1981), especially chap. 3. The connections between the emergence of an American-born middle-class ethnic leadership and an emphasis on Americanization within ethnic organizations are discussed by Roy Rosenzweig, *Eight Hours For What We Will: Workers and Leisure in an Industrial City, 1870–1920* (Cambridge and New York: Cambridge University Press, 1983), pp. 163–68. On ethnicity as a variable, socially constructed phenomenon, see William L. Yancey, Eugene P. Ericksen, and Richard Juliani, "Emergent Ethnicity: A Review and Reformulation," *American Sociological Review* 41 (June 1976), pp. 391–403; Kathleen Neils Conzen, "Immigrants, Immigrant Neighborhods, and Ethnic Identity: Historical Issues," *Journal of American History* 66 (December 1979), pp. 603–15; James D. Smith, "Ethnic Consciousness and Class Hegemony: Tension and Contradiction in the Ideology of Ethnicity," M.Sc. dissertation, London School of Economics, 1980. Sometimes an immigrant group's ethnic identity was formed in response to pressures from American society. This was the case with recent Haitian immigrants in New York City, whose community was divided by lines of class, education, color, culture, politics, territory, and immigration status. Working together as a group came not as a result of a common culture or a need to be with their own kind, but rather from a shared interest in establishing a

stake in the American political system. See Nina Glick-Schiller, "Ethnic Groups Are Made Not Born: The Haitian Immigrant and American Politics," in *Ethnic Encounters: Identities and Contexts,* ed. George Hicks and Philip Leis (N. Scituate, Mass.: Duxbury Press, 1977), pp. 23–35.

51 "Provincial Societies on the Wane But Still Active," *Evening Bulletin,* 4 March 1936, p. 15; "Italian Societies Broaden Membership," *Evening Bulletin,* 18 March 1936, p. 21; 'Italian Provincial Groups Give Way to Nationalism," *Evening Bulletin,* 16 March 1936, p. 15. On suburbanization in Providence, see Sidney Goldstein and Kurt B. Mayer, *Metropolitanization and Population Change in Rhode Island,* Rhode Island Development Council Publication Number 3, Planning Division (Rhode Island Development Council, 1961), pp. 8–10, 34–52. On metropolitanization in general, see Joseph Interrante,"The Road to Autopia: The Automobile and the Spatial Transformation of American Culture" *Michigan Quarterly Review* 15–16 (Fall 1980–Winter 1981), pp. 502–17; idem, "You Can't Go to Town in a Bathtub: Automobile Movement and the Reorganization of Rural American Space, 1900–1930," *Radical History Review* 21 (Fall 1979), pp. 151–68; idem, "A Moveable Feast: The Automobile and the Spatial Transformation of American Culture, 1890–1940", Ph.D. dissertation, Harvard University, 1983. On the relationship between the ethnic community and commercial amusements, see Rosenzweig, *Eight Hours for What We Will,* chaps. 7, 8; see also Elizabeth Ewen, "City Lights: Immigrant Women and the Rise of the Movies," *Signs* 5 (Spring 1980), pp. S45–S65; idem, *Immigrant Women in the Land of Dollars* (New York: Pantheon, forthcoming). Extra-curricular activities in public high schools may have provided an arena where students grouped themselves into ethnic enclaves although the schools themselves provided a general context for ethnic mixing. Paula S. Fass's research has shown that members of different ethnic groups consistently chose certain extra-curricular activities and not others. See Fass, "New Sources on Ethnic Culture: New York High Schools in the 1930s and 1940s," paper presented at the Annual Meeting of the Organization of American Historians, April, 1984.

52 See James Weinstein, *The Corporate Ideal in the Liberal State, 1900–1918* (Boston: Beacon Press, 1968), pp. 40–61 for an analysis of the impact of company insurance and pension plans on the labor movement. See Gerald Suttles and David Street, "Aid to the Poor and Social Exchange," in *The Logic of Social Hierarchy,* ed. Edwin O. Laumann, Paul M. Siegel, and Robert W. Hodge (Chicago: Markham Publishing Co., 1970), pp. 744–55, esp. pp. 744–48, for the argument that welfare systems administered by the state have the effect of making the poor relate as individuals to the state rather than turning to one another for help and thus establishing ties of mutuality. Mary Ann Clawson provided me with this reference. On the Workmen's Circle,

see Beryl Segal, Providence, interviewed by Paul Buhle in 1977; Epstein, *Jewish Labor in the U.S.A.*, pp. 261–82. The Italian woman interviewed in Bridgeport was Housewife No. 2, Bridgeport, WPA-Conn, box 22.

53   "Active Fraternal Life in Little Italy," *Providence Journal*, 21 December 1919, sec. 5, p. 5; Dr. T. G. Granata, "I Remember Federal Hill," *Providence Journal*, 7 December 1947, sec. 6, p. 1; "Chartered Organizations," pp. 21–78. For an example of a parallel movement away from economic benefits, a study of Jewish family clubs organized in New York City demonstrated the historical progression from economic to social concerns. Eighty-one percent of the clubs founded between 1908 and 1918 gave equal emphasis to goals of family solidarity and economic aid, but only 53 percent of the clubs founded between 1928 and 1938 gave equal emphasis to economic aid. Almost 40 percent of the clubs founded in the earlier period provided burial benefits for members, but this decreased to only 14 percent of the clubs founded in the 1920s and only 3 percent of the clubs founded in the 1930s. See William E. Mitchell, *Mishpokhe: A Study of New York City Jewish Family Clubs* (The Hague: Mouton Publishers, 1978), pp. 41–47. See also I. E. Rontch, ed., *Jewish Families and Family Circles of New York* (New York: Yiddish Writers Union, 1939). In Waterbury, Connecticut, the children of immigrants left mutual-benefit societies for mixed ethnic organizations like the Knights of Columbus or middle-class-oriented service clubs, rather than moving into the reoriented citywide ethnic organizations; see Brecher, Lombardi, and Stackhouse, *Brass Valley*, pp. 33–34, 110–11.

54   On the Sons of Italy in Providence, see "Sons of Italy Adds 600 New Members," *Providence Journal*, 14 January 1918, p. 12; "Italian Societies Merge and Discuss War Stamps," *Providence Journal*, 8 February 1918, p. 5; "Italians Aroused by Priest's Attack," *Providence Journal*, 4 December 1918, p. 5; "Catholic Church Antagonism Denied," *Providence Journal*, 8 December 1918, p. 5; "Sons of Italy Initiate Three Italian Societies," *Providence Journal*, 30 December 1918, p. 12; "Sons of Italy Becomes Thriving Organization," *Providence Journal*, 25 December 1921, sec. 5, p. 5; "Mussolini and Fascism Lauded at Sons of Italy Dinner in Providence at Biltmore," *Providence Journal*, 30 October 1923, p. 1; "Radical Delegates Fight Expulsion," *Providence Journal*, 30 October 1923, p. 1. The argument that the emergence of the Sons of Italy was connected to a reorientation of Italian community life has also been made by Barton in relationship to the Italian community in Cleveland, *Peasants and Strangers*, pp. 83–85, 157–58; and by Briggs with regard to the Italian community in Utica, New York, *An Italian Passage*, pp. 151–53. In Cleveland, all the village and regional societies formed between 1900 and 1912 had joined the Sons of Italy by 1920 (Barton, *Peasants and Strangers*, p. 85). Annecdotal information on the goals of the women's auxiliaries to the

Sons of Italy comes from RIWB no 230, Providence, 1974, interviewed by a family member; interviewee born in Providence in 1915. Pesaturo, *Italo-Americans of Rhode Island*, (1940), pp. 180–81, 184–85. See also Marie Frazzetta, Bridgeport, WPA-Conn, box 23.

55 Goldstein and Goldscheider, *Jewish-Americans*, pp. 25–27; "Chartered Organizations," pp. 21–78; Seebert J. Goldowsky, "Jews in Medicine in Rhode Island,' *Rhode Island Jewish Historical Notes* 2 (1957), pp. 151–91, esp. 173–83; idem, "The Jewish Home for the Aged," *Rhode Island Jewish Historical Notes* 2 (1958), pp. 241–53; idem, "The Jewish Orphanage of Rhode Island," *Rhode Island Jewish Historical Notes* 3 (1959), pp. 88–105; Sonya Michel, "Family, Community, and Institutions: The Jewish Orphanage of Rhode Island, 1909–1942," *Rhode Island Jewish Historical Notes* 7 (1977), pp. 385–400; Rhode Island Historic Preservation Commission," *South Providence*, p. 39; David C. Adelman, "The Providence Jewish Community Unites," *Rhode Island Jewish Historical Notes*, 3 (1960), pp. 160–191.

56 "Italian Orphanage Fund Data Sought," *Providence Journal*, 25 August 1932, p. 3; "Italian Orphanage Fund," *Providence Journal*, 26 August 1932, p. 22.

CONCLUSION

1 This discussion of the meaning of ethnicity as historically constructed draws particularly on arguments presented in two recent essays: William L. Yancey, Eugene Ericksen, and Richard Juliani, "Emergent Ethnicity: A Review and a Reformulation," *American Sociological Review* 41 (June 1976), pp. 391–403; Kathleen Neils Conzen, "Immigrants, Immigrant Neighborhoods, and Ethnic Identity: Historical Issues," *Journal of American History* 66 (December 1979), pp. 603–15. In describing the immigrant definition of ethnicity as supportive of an alternative culture, I am using the term as Raymond Williams does, to suggest that immigrant culture was separate and distinct from the dominant culture but not a direct challenge to it. See Williams, "Base and Superstructure in Marxist Cultural Theory," *New Left Review* 82 (November–December 1973), pp. 3–16, esp. pp. 10–11.

2 Some recent historical studies that discuss the relationship between these institutions and a diminishing of ethnic consciousness include Olivier Zunz, *The Changing Face of Inequality: Urbanization, Industrial Development, and Immigrants in Detroit, 1880–1920* (Chicago: University of Chicago Press, 1982); Gary Gerstle, "The Rise of Industrial Unionism: Class, Ethnicity, and Labor Organization in Woonsocket, Rhode Island, 1931–1941", Ph.D. dissertation, Harvard University 1982; Roy Rosenzweig, *Eight Hours For What We Will: Workers and Leisure in an Industrial City, 1870–1920* (Cambridge and New York:

Cambridge University Press, 1983); Francis Couvares, "The Remaking of Urban Culture in Late Nineteenth and Early Twentieth Century America," paper presented at the Conference on Lowell Industrial History, April 1983.

Index